James Luther Garner

The Physics of the Natural Philosophers

PEARSON

Custom
Publishing

Printed in the United States of America

ISBN 0-536-50180-7

2007460077

KC/JM

Please visit our web site at *www.pearsoncustom.com*

PEARSON CUSTOM PUBLISHING
501 Boylston Street, Suite 900, Boston, MA
A Pearson Education Company

CONTENTS

Preface vii

Acknowledgments xi

SECTION I.

FOUNDATIONS.

A. The Experimental Method, Inductive and Deductive Reasoning 2

B. Systems of Units and Conversion of Units 8

C. How to Solve Physics Problems Exactly and Inexactly by Making
    Estimates 9

D. Mathematical Review 11

SECTION II.

CLASSICAL MOTION.

CHAPTER I.   **Ancient Greek Ideas on Motion** **24**

    A. Ancient Greek Views of the Universe at Large 24

    B. Aristotle's Views of Motion on Earth and the Heavens 27

Chapter II.   **Motion in One Dimension** **34**

    A. Galileo 34

    B. Describing and Graphing Motion in One Dimension 37

    C. Special Motion: Free Fall 45

    D. Curved Graphs, Tangent Lines, and Instantaneous Quantities 47

Chapter III.   **Motion in Two Dimensions** **61**

    A. Vector Addition and Subtraction 61

    B. Special Motion: Projectile Motion 65

C. Application: Projectiles 66
D. Special Motion: Uniform Circular Motion 70

Chapter IV. Newton's Views on Motion **82**
A. Isaac Newton 82
B. Newton's Laws of Motion 84
C. Examples of Some Important Forces 87
D. Applications: Newton's Laws 89

Chapter V. Rotational Motion and Gravitation **107**
A. Fundamental Force: Newton's Universal Force of Gravitation 107
B. The Gravitational Field: A Field Theory 110
C. Torque on and Angular Momentum of a Simple System 112
D. Applications: Gravitation 116

Chapter VI. Things That Don't Change in Motion **131**
A. Descartes, Huygens, and Leibniz 131
B. Impulse and Momentum 137
C. Constancy of Momentum 140
D. Work, Kinetic, and Gravitational Potential Energy 143
E. Constancy of Energy 147
F. Applications: Constancy of Momentum and Energy 150
G. Power 151

Chapter VII. Wave Motion and Light **174**
A. Special Motion: Vibrations 174
B. Special Motion: Traveling and Standing Waves 176
C. Reflection and Refraction of Light 180
D. Other Properties of Light: Diffraction, Interference, Dispersion,
and Polarization 184

SECTION III.

ELECTRICITY.

Chapter VIII. Stationary Charges **203**
A. Charles Augustin Coulomb 204
B. Electric Charges at Rest 205

C. Fundamental Force: Coulomb's Electric Force 207

D. The Electric Field: A Field Theory 209

E. Electric Potential Energy and Electric Potential (Voltage) 211

F. Applications: Static Charges 219

Chapter IX. Moving Charges **233**

A. Electric Current and Ohm's Law 233

B. DC Circuits 236

C. Ohm's Law and Electric Power 240

SECTION IV.

MAGNETISM.

Chapter X. Magnetic Forces on Moving Charges **257**

A. Magnets in Antiquity 257

B. The Magnetic Field: A Field Theory 258

C. Fundamental Force: Magnetic Force on a Moving Charge 260

D. Fundamental Force: Magnetic Force on a Current-Carrying Wire 264

E. Application: Magnetic Forces and Electric Motors 265

SECTION V.

ELECTROMAGNETISM.

Chapter XI. Accelerated Charges and Electromagnetic Fields **279**

A. Michael Faraday 280

B. Magnetic Flux 281

C. Faraday's Law of Electromagnetic Induction 284

D. Applications: Generators and Transformers 287

E. James Clerk Maxwell 291

F. Maxwell's Equations for the Electromagnetic Field 293

G. Application: The Anatomy, Spectrum, and Creation of Light 297

SECTION VI.

HEAT.

Chapter XII. Internal Random Motions in Complex Systems **315**

    A. What Are Temperature, Heat, and Internal Energy? 317

    B. The Ideal Gas-Piston System 320

    C. James Joule 322

    D. First Law of Thermodynamics 324

    E. Ludwig Boltzmann 326

    F. Entropy 327

    G. Second Law of Thermodynamics and the End of It All 330

    H. Two Mysteries 332

    Glossary 350

    Index 356

PREFACE

"And we should call every truth false which was not accompanied by at least one laugh."

—Nietzsche

The field of physics is a tremendously exciting ongoing activity partly due to a rich array of unusual and fascinating topics. For example, many people are often attracted to the more **bizarre** topics in physics, such as, black holes, string theory and superconductivity. Students are not immune to the all too human attraction toward the unusual and should not be dissuaded from pursuing these fascinating topics. But before one can gain a truly deep understanding of *current* physics research it is helpful to first gain some initial understanding of the *foundations* of physics that form what is known as classical physics. Classical physics has its own fascination provided it is presented in a fresh, imaginative, and enthusiastic manner. Wasn't it Einstein who said, "Imagination is more important than knowledge"?

Historically, a student enters the "on ramp" of formal physics coursework via one of three routes: calculus-based physics, algebra-based physics, or conceptual physics. Alas, for many students this adventure is more like entering through the gates of hell above which Dante placed his sign reading, "Abandon hope all ye who enter here." It is my desire for this book to provide more hope while at the same time remembering, in physics you learn the meaning of work.

The first two ramps mentioned above must necessarily place an almost exclusive emphasis on a rather technical, narrow, problem-solving presentation of the subject. After all, most students in these courses "need physics" to advance toward the promised land of medical school, engineering studies or eventual commencement to graduate physics departments to do cutting edge research. Many students who plan to enter these more technical courses are in need of a stronger grounding in physics, however. In view of this need and others, the purpose of this book is three-fold: first, to help students learn the concepts of physics by applying them to the solution of physics problems. Second, to present some of the history of physics and biographical sketches of a few leading physicists. Third, to provide some examples and problems that really captivate the interests of students (there is more on this feature below). The latter two points are not strongly emphasized by the more technical presentations of the subject.

The conceptual physics "on ramp" often attempts to go to the opposite extreme to the algebra- and calculus-based physics courses by offering a glimpse of physics without much mathematics or homework problems. Various conceptual physics approaches have been tried and with varying degrees of success. One presents physics by emphasizing the implications of physics for society, such as energy and environmental policies. Another approach brings in physics via the backdoor by stressing how physics underlies the operation of everyday devices like microwave ovens, automobiles, etc. or how physics underlies fields like sports or weaponry. The primary strength of these various modes of presentation is their relevance to everyday life. The above list is not exhaustive, indeed some have presented physics from an historical perspective that introduces the history of physics and biographical material about famous physicists. All of these approaches have their strengths and weaknesses. However, I am inclined to think that each of these modes are most useful if they are used in moderation. To use an analogy, creating a physics textbook is similar to creating a delicious dish for a banquet. As all great chefs know, spice is important but it must be used in moderation.

Therefore, this textbook is an attempt to provide an imaginative and fresh approach to physics that lies in between the conceptual physics and the algebra physics routes. The focus is on classical physics and a concerted effort is made to resist the temptation of trying to cover far too many topics than is possible in a single-semester course. The central theme that serves to connect the various topics is *motion* or in the Latin, *locomotion*. By choosing motion as our central theme we are, in fact, returning to the ancient Greek roots of physics since the contemplation of change is where physics began over two millennia ago. I try to connect each chapter with motion. There is motion in one and two dimensions, circular motion, Newton's laws of motion, constants of motion (energy and momentum), vibratory and wave motion, electric forces on stationary and moving charges, forces on moving charges in magnetic fields, the electromagnetic emanations that originate with the acceleration of charges, and finally, the random motions of internal energy and heat. Motivating these topics and forming an essential subtext is the presentation of physics within its philosophical and historical framework. Biographical sketches of some of the most famous classical physicists is an integral part of the history. In this text, the history and philosophical roots of physics are not some peripheral material in a gray box off to the side that is rarely read but here these topics are weaved into the main thread of discussion.

Lastly, our presentation strikes a middle ground by offering both conceptual questions for class discussion in addition to a moderate number of non-trivial homework problems. I have found that most students need additional practice with algebra in the context of solving physics problems. These skills only come via practice and consequently, this book gives students an opportunity to strengthen such skills before they are totally immersed in physics problems in their future, more technical and fast paced physics courses. Students are aided also by a better grounding in the concepts and thus the end of chapter questions often are more conceptually oriented which basically means they may be solved without a calculator or without extensive algebraic manipulations. Numerous worked out examples are contained within the chapters. It is my hope that the students will actually want to read the textbook and so a virtual buffet of eclectic (and in some cases perhaps, eccentric) examples and problems are drawn from various avenues of life including: crime stories, world records, mythology, sports, amusement park rides, films, warfare, automobile accidents, everyday devices, etc. These examples are a means of making the text interesting, engaging, and sometimes amusing— I think. Hopefully the "spice" is not overdone. Finally, occasionally the examples and problems might even be—**bizarre**.

To students, I recommend the following:

For this course you should purchase the *least* expensive *solar*-powered *scientific* calculator. It is not uncommon for introductory level physics students to purchase sophisticated calculators that are difficult to operate. Frequently, this leads to mistakes that have little to do with physics misunderstandings.

Now, a word for our sponsors. Many individuals contributed to this book including all my previous teachers in schools and universities but I would like to especially thank my (Vermilion, Ohio) high school physics and chemistry teachers, Mr. McMullen and Dr. Decker, respectively. One of the most serious flaws of society in the United States is the general lack of appreciation of teachers. I'm afraid it will be our undoing if things are not changed.

Books make a big difference, too. I have especially benefited from the following books:

The Project Physics Course, Rutherford, Holton, and Watson (Holt, Rhinehart and Winston, 1970). This was the textbook I used as a student in high school physics. *Project Physics* provides an excellent historical introduction to physics.

Physics, the Human Adventure, Holton and Brush (Rutgers University Press, 2001). This long-lasting book is unsurpassed as a sophisticated historical introduction to physics and scientific methodology. My textbook does not pretend to give the same depth of history and philosophy as Holton and Brush achieved. I encourage students who have deeper historical and philosophical interests to explore Holton and Brush.

A Guide to Introductory Physics Teaching, Arons (Wiley, 1990). Arons draws attention to many of the most common pitfalls students encounter in learning basic physics. Prospective science teachers are especially encouraged to consult this book.

Peer Instruction, Mazur (Prentice Hall, 1997). Mazur introduces a method of physics teaching based on "clickers." In addition, many student misconceptions are reviewed. I especially recommend Mazur's book to prospective science teachers as a no nonsense method of active learning in the classroom. The book also contains a number of conceptual exercises.

I would also like to express my appreciation to Dr. Nirmal Patel for his enthusiasm and support for this project, although the errors that remain in the book are my fault. My 13-year-old daughter, Katherine, used a preliminary version of the text and my experience with her was quite illuminating and helped to make numerous modifications. Seasoned physicists can easily forget the hurdles new students must mount to be successful in physics. In advance I thank the many students who will help to further improve the text. Finally, I was most fortunate to receive a teaching grant from the University of North Florida as a means of supporting the development of the textbook while teaching the class one summer. Who said universities no longer care about undergraduate teaching!

One last word—I promise. Students might be thrown off by the words "natural philosophy" in the title of this book. But I should point out, the original title of Newton's Principia when translated from Latin reads, "Mathematical Principles of **Natural Philosophy.**" Even in the days of Maxwell in the mid- to late-nineteenth century it was routine to refer to what we now call physics as natural philosophy. Therefore, the subject of this book is natural philosophy and profiles of some of the leading natural philosophers who developed this field of study during the three-hundred-year-long period from roughly 1600 to 1900.

"Life is what happens to you when you are busy making other plans."

—John Lennon

"It is the glory of God to conceal things, but the glory of kings is to search things out."

—Proverbs 25:2

ACKNOWLEDGMENTS

Many heartfelt thanks to

my wonderfully energetic wife,

Dr. Carol Murphey Garner

(vectors are good)

and my endlessly entertaining daughters,

Katherine Murphey Garner and *Anne Randolph Garner*

ℛSECTION I.

FOUNDATIONS.

Courtesy of Foto Marburg/Art Resource, NY.

"MELANCHOLIA"

Notice the numerous mechanical toys, and mathematical and scientific instruments in the above copper engraving by Albrecht Dürer (1471–1528). Science begins with observations but it must progress to experimentation on to theories. "Melancholia" in Dürer's time was synonymous with thought.

Abstract.

This chapter presents an overview of material that is needed before beginning a study of physics. The topics include the nature of experimental science, a carefully chosen selection of topics in mathematics that are most relevant to this course, a quick review of systems of units, scientific notation, and how to convert from one set of units to another set, and some general remarks on how to solve physics problems.

Definitions. epistemology, scientism, reductionism, deductive and inductive reasoning, falsifiable, conversion factor, Fermi problem, scientific notation, significant figures, and unit conversions

Principles. law of inertia, law of parsimony

Fundamental Equations. none

A. The Experimental Method, Inductive and Deductive Reasoning.

How do you know something is true? This is the basic question of an area of philosophy known as ***epistemology***. Various answers have been offered over the centuries. One position is to believe the views expressed by a renowned expert in the field. Sometimes the source of the expertise is a person, while other times the expertise may be found in a book. For example, the average person might believe the earth is experiencing global warming because many famous scientists have expressed this opinion. Believing something because you read it in a book or heard it from someone you trust is belief based on ***authority***. This kind of belief is commonplace—in fact, in practice, we could not live without authority since no one has the time and expertise to "check everything out." Authority was preeminent in Europe during the middle ages when people accepted the Bible and writings of Aristotle on the grounds of authority.

A moments thought leads us to conclude authority *is* an important source of knowledge. Unfortunately, authority also has its limitations. For example, experts can and very often disagree with one another. This is not such a terrible situation, after all the world would be rather boring if everyone agreed on the answers to all the important questions. Another strike against authority is, once you accept something on authority it is hard to make changes based on further evidence. Authoritative sources usually do not allow for changes in our state of knowledge—authority based knowledge is called closed-ended.

Although some fields of human experience, such as, politics, history, philosophy, and religion, may be largely based on authority—especially the latter, ultimately science is not dependent on authority. Indeed, one hallmark of science is scientists *encourage* their students to doubt and challenge authorities. Scientific work is ongoing and never finished—science based knowledge is open-ended.

With the impressive success of science over the past four centuries some scientists have come to the conclusion that essentially the only form of truth is scientific truth, a belief known as **scientism**. Scientism is often accused of oversimplifying the world because it engages in reductionism. On page 7 of the book by Barbour, which is cited in the references to this section, a succinct definition of reductionism appears, "Briefly put, reductionism is taken to imply that religion is just psychology, psychology is basically biology, biology is the chemistry of large molecules, whose atoms obey the laws of physics, which will ultimately account for everything!" Many scientists today, however, understand that science also has its limits and is not the only reliable truth. Some scientists would argue that science is not even the most reliable source of knowledge since, in their view, deductive logic and mathematics are fields where one can know things for sure.

This leads to another way of knowing, logic or *reason*. The prime example of a field where reason reigns is mathematics. Physicists admire mathematics and use it to such an extent that it is common for people to think physics is only a branch of mathematics. This is understandable since physicists so frequently use mathematics as a tool for expressing physical concepts. However, physics transcends mathematics. That is to say, physics is partly based on mathematics but also relies on experience via experimentation. Let us further consider the nature of physics.

Physics has a two-fold nature which consists of both **deductive** and **inductive** reasoning. The aspect that is inductive is the experimental side of physics where one makes relevant observations, create hypotheses and test predictions that follow from the hypotheses. We quote Rule 4 from Isaac Newton's book, *Principia*, wherein he sets forth four " Rules of Reasoning in Philosophy":

"Rule 4. In experimental philosophy, propositions gathered from phenomena by induction should be considered exactly or very nearly true notwithstanding any contrary hypotheses, until yet other phenomena make such propositions either more exact or liable to exceptions."

Ultimately, all physical theories are grounded on laboratory experimentation. Indeed, fundamental ideas in physics are tested repeatedly against what can be measured in careful experiments. Experiments normally go beyond simple observations, however. Experiments are designed to ask a question of nature. For example, from ancient times people have asked the question, why do things move? According to Aristotle, one form of motion is violent motion where objects remain at rest unless they experience a *force* (a push or pull). This seems to be in accord with common sense: a chair doesn't move across the floor unless someone pushes it. It wasn't until the time of Galileo and Newton that this viewpoint was overthrown and replaced with the **law of inertia**: an object moves with constant speed in a straight line unless it experiences a net force. Only experimentation was able to determine whether Aristotle or Newton was right. No amount of mathematics and arm-chair reasoning could decide the issue—someone had to enter the laboratory to conduct detailed measurements. Clearly, although crucial to physics, reason and mathematics alone are not enough to comprehend the physical world.

Let us further explore the characteristics of inductive arguments. It is often said inductive reasoning goes from the specific to the general. For example, a man enters a long hallway with a set of twelve identical doors. He opens the first door and notices a party taking place. He opens the second door and observes the same. On opening nine more doors he always finds a party taking place. He reasons that there is likely a party taking place behind door twelve. This is inductive reasoning. Science is inductive because all experiments pertain to only one time and place. By induction we assume the results are valid for all time and space. Because of its inductive nature experiment alone is incomplete. Another way of understanding inductive reasoning is to note, in an inductive argument, if the premises of the argument are true then the conclusion of the argument is *probable*. Historically, the inductive nature of experimental science led some individuals to be critical of science. Among the harshest critics was the eighteenth century Scottish philosopher, David Hume. Hume was such an extreme critic of induction that he accused science of being irrational and only a source of uncertain knowledge.

Science also has aspects that are deductive since it often goes from a general set of statements (e.g. premises or hypotheses) and from these inferences (conclusions) are drawn. In deduction, if the premises are true then the conclusion is true without a doubt. One of the major goals of physics is to make predictions (conclusions) based on premises (hypotheses). Mathematics is replete with examples of deductive systems such as Euclidean geometry. In so far as physics uses mathematics, physics also is deductive. But no matter how logically consistent a physical theory is one cannot believe the theory solely based on its mathematical correctness. In the end, all theories in physics must face the experimental challenge to be confirmed, i.e., to be made probable.

In view of the above discussion, suppose two theories are devised to explain some set of observations, and that these two theories do equally well by all of the criteria we have set forth, namely, the theories agree equally with all observations and are logically consistent and mathematically correct. Some have argued that historically the Ptolemaic and Copernican models of the planetary system are examples of such rival theories. How do we decide between the two? There is a prejudice in physics for simplicity and for this reason the theory that is simplest or most economical usually becomes dominant. For example, one of the theories might require making more assumptions than the other, in which case the theory needing the fewest assumptions is often preferred. This prejudice for simplicity is given a name, the **law of parsimony**. Once again quoting Newton from the same source as above we read,

"Rule 1. No more causes of natural things should be admitted than are both true and sufficient to explain their phenomena."

Returning to our planetary system example we find this law comes to the fore since during the time of the ancient Greeks and also during the middle ages, people were divided about whether the universe is heliocentric (sun centered) or geocentric (earth centered). Copernicus and Galileo eventually won this argument primarily because the heliocentric view was a much simpler system since one did not have to invent elaborate schemes to account for all of the astronomical data. The Ptolemaic (geocentric) model was more complex than the heliocentric theory.

Even if at some future date physical theories are in accord with experiments and are mathematically correct, scientific knowledge at that time would still be incomplete. Why is this? The reason is, our understanding of physics has evolved over millennia and it will likely continue to evolve without an end. Due to this open-endedness of physics it is not possible for physics to arrive at final and absolute truth. This should be a humbling thought.

We have only scratched the surface of the nature of science. To progress further, consider a word that people rarely associate with science, **imagination**. This is understandable since on the surface it looks like scientists simply collect data and from the data it is easy to suggest a theory. After all, scientists do not make the laws of nature but only uncover them. But there is a place for imagination in science. On the experimental physics side, one must often be very creative in order to design an effective experiment with the associated equipment. Theoretical physicists must also use their imaginations. To site just a few examples, consider Galileo. In his studies of free fall and his law of inertia, he imagined a world without friction. Sometimes knowing what to ignore, in this case friction, is half the battle in developing physical ideas. In other instances, one must be willing to shift the focus in a problem. In the case of the motion of a pendulum, according to the ancient Greeks, the key to the motion is the pendulum eventually stops moving and settles to its lowest point. But for Galileo the key was to ignore friction and under those conditions the pendulum sways back and forth forever. Thus, Galileo shifted the focus from the Aristotelian fixation on the stationary pendulum to a consideration of the state of motion of the pendulum. In fact, quite generally the Greeks asked the teleological question of *why* things move while Galileo shifted the discussion to *how* things move. By an act of imagination Galileo and subsequent physicists invented the language of physics. Nothing short of creativity led Isaac Newton to postulate his law of gravitation. Newton had to take the intellectual leap of assuming somehow the earth could attract the moon even though the two are far apart. Imagination and creativity are essential to the design of experiments, in the choice of what to ignore and what to focus on, in the development of new language, and concepts. Clearly, creative risk taking is at the heart of the development of new theories in physics. Indeed, one of the benefits of studying the history of physics is to learn how long it has taken to develop physics and to see the many blind alleys and discarded theories that appear along the way.

Another question about the foundations of science is, what makes a theory scientific? The theory of evolution is a prominent example of a theory that has been considered by a few as being non-scientific. We have mentioned mathematical correctness and simplicity as requirements that must be met by a valid scientific theory. Another requirement is the theory must be able to make predictions. And yet many discarded theories from the history of science meet these conditions. One of the most important twentieth century philosophers of science, Karl Popper, has suggested an additional requirement: a scientific theory must be ***falsifiable***. By this Popper means, the predictions of the theory must be such that experiments may be performed that can, at least in principle, disprove the theory. For example, suppose I take a philosophical position known as solipsism. A solipsist believes he is the only thing that exists in the world—the rest of the world exists only within his mind. Such a stance is not scientific since it is impossible to design an experiment that could disprove the theory. To take another example, there is a belief that aliens are living among us. Once again this is non-scientific according to Popper's criterion. It should be pointed out, just because a belief is non-scientific by this criterion does not mean it cannot be true. Failing the Popper criterion only means an assertion is beyond the bounds of what can be tested scientifically. Not surprisingly, some current philosophers of science are critical of Popper's ideas and consequently the nature of science debate continues.

It is apparent the above statements about the nature of science fall short of completely elucidating the topic. In modern times the foundations have become even more murky. For example, this text focuses only on classical physics where historically the world was viewed as fully objective. This viewpoint is known as scientific *realism* in which it is assumed all observers perceive the same thing. But there are some theories in modern physics (e.g. quantum mechanics) which suggest the world cannot be fully described without taking into account the person who performs the observations. Furthermore, in recent years it has been pointed out that a person's perceptions can be influenced by their particular set of scientific assumptions. From these considerations we can only conclude, the nature of science itself remains an open-ended field of study.

Admittedly, the above discussion on the nature of science is incomplete. Often a more complete understanding of science is gained by knowing how science differs from other avenues of truth. In the example below we contrast science and history.

Example One.—*History and science.*

Today the word science has been so broadened in meaning that even librarians are called library scientists. This is not meant to disparage the librarians but rather is indicative of how highly modern society values (worships?) science. To arrive at a more narrow and accurate picture of what science is—at least how we are defining the word, discuss how science and history are similar and how they differ.

Solution.

History is based on eyewitness accounts of everyday events. The events are recorded by journalists in newspaper and magazine articles. The job of the historian is to sift the events and provide some broader interpretation of their meaning. In a few cases the events are recorded by cameras. All but the most extreme skeptics accept the truths revealed by historians. Although there are different renditions of history, e.g. the Japanese history of World War II is not the same as that told by Western historians, nevertheless there is substantial agreement. Here in the US, most people agree that George Washington existed. There is such a thing as historical truth.

Experimental physics is also based on eyewitness accounts and the events are recorded in journal articles. However, it is not necessary to use a camera to record a scientific experiment because one of the hallmarks of science is the *reproducibility* of experiments. An experiment that can not be reproduced is not a scientific experiment. Science is reproducible but history is not. Truth is broader than science, though. The life of George Washington is not reproducible but we still believe he lived because of our knowledge of history. Another difference of science from history is, in science one performs *controlled* experiments. Scientists in general do not simply observe natural events as historians observe historical happenings. Rather, scientists use equipment to ask a question of nature in order to tease out the truth. Therefore, although history and science have some similar features, they differ in that science must involve reproducible and controlled experiments.

A final point to be made is to say the raw data of history and physics is collected by journalists and experimental physicists, respectively. The work of the historian is more like that of the theoretical physicist— both try to uncover a deeper meaning to the raw data of history and experiments. Both physics and history are worthwhile endeavors that lead to truth but along different pathways. Perhaps we can say the degree of certainty of the truth uncovered differs in the two fields? Which is more reliable, physics or history? Different people will answer this question differently. For further reading on this topic see pp. 194–202 of Barbour's book cited in the reference below.

In summary of this section, physics is a triumph of both reason and experience. We have said little about the practicality of science since this seems most obvious given our modern electrical and mechanical society that has advanced by discoveries in physics. In addition, scientific theories must be simple, mathematically correct, rich in predictions, in agreement with all known experiments (therefore, falsifiable), and open-ended. Finally, the scientific imagination cannot answer all of life's questions, such as, why am I here on Earth? But physics can make life much more livable and interesting!

"Reason and experiment have been indulged, and error has fled before them. It is error alone which needs the support of government. Truth can stand by itself."—Thomas Jefferson.

References.

Thinking Through Philosophy, Chris Horner and Emrys Westacott, (Cambridge University Press, 2000).

Introduction to Logic, Irving M. Copi, 7th Edition (Macmillan, 1986).

Issues in Science and Religion, Ian G. Barbour (Harper, 1966). This book addresses the various ways of knowing in addition to the fundamental nature of humanity and, if there is a God, how does such a being interact with a law-abiding physical world. A good overview is presented of enlightenment science and a short review is given of the romantic movement which was a reaction to the enlightenment. Speaking of God, there are two relatively recent books written by scientists that address the question of God's existence. For the theistic position see the following, which was written by a physicist who is also a theologian, *Belief in God in an Age of Science*, John Polkinghorne (Yale UP, 1998) and for the atheistic position see the following, written by a biologist, *The God Delusion*, Richard Dawkins (Houghton Mifflin, 2006). Most scientists lean toward the agnostic to atheistic side of this debate. Then again, many would agree that such a question is outside the field of expertise of scientists and therefore, scientific opinion is likely to be no better than the opinion of other intellectuals who have no particular expertise in philosophy and religion. *Physics, the Human Adventure*, Gerald Holton and Stephen G. Brush (Rutgers University Press, 2001).

B. Systems of Units and Conversion of Units.

The most popular system of units is the metric system which is used throughout the world except in everyday life in the United States. In this book we will primarily employ the metric system but occasionally it will be helpful to know how to convert quantities into British units. However, even if we only used the metric system we would still need to be able to change from one set of metric quantities to another.

In the metric system fundamental quantities are based on standards for length (Meter), mass (Kilogram), time (Second), and there are others primarily related to electric quantities. The metric system is therefore called the *MKS* system of units. It is important to know some of the most popular prefixes. These prefixes are expressed in **scientific notation** below where numbers are stated in terms of powers of ten. The table below may serve as a short review of basic scientific notation:

$$1 \text{ km} = 1000 \text{ m} \qquad = 10^3 \text{ m}$$
$$1 \text{ cm} = 0.01 \text{ m} \qquad = 10^{-2} \text{ m}$$
$$1 \text{ mm} = 0.001 \text{ m} \qquad = 10^{-3} \text{ m}$$
$$1 \text{ } \mu\text{m} = 0.000001 \text{ m} \quad = 10^{-6} \text{ m}$$
$$1 \text{ nm} = 0.000000001 \text{ m} = 10^{-9} \text{ m}$$

See the flyleaf of this text for a complete set of prefixes.

In working physics problems in this book we will always work in the MKS system. In a given problem one must convert all quantities in a non-MKS system of units to the MKS system. This allows one to avoid "mixing" units. For example, in the same equation one can not have some quantities expressed in meters while other are expressed in feet. But how do you change feet to meters? This is a process called converting units and is detailed below.

Let us look in detail how to change the units for a quantity. The way this is done is to treat the units as fractions and use **conversion factors**, which is an equality of a quantity expressed in two different units (e.g. 1 mile = 1610 m). Multiplying a quantity by a conversion factor is like multiplying by one. A number of conversion factors may be found on the flyleaf of this book. The examples below illustrate the process of converting units.

Example Two.—*How may seconds are there in a year?*

Solution.

To answer this question we use the following familiar conversion factors:

1 year = 365 days, 1 day = 24 hours, 1 hour = 60 minutes, and 1 minute = 60 seconds

No. seconds in a year = 1 year $\times$ (365 day/year) $\times$ (24 hr/day) $\times$ (60 min/hr) $\times$ (60 s/min)

$$= \underline{31{,}536{,}000 \text{ s} = 3.1536 \times 10^7 \text{ s}}$$

Notice how the units cancel like fractions, leaving the final quantity in the desired units.

Example Three.—*Converting miles per hour to meters per second.*
Convert 60 mph to m/s.

Solution.

To do this, we need only recall the conversion factor 1,610 m = 1 mile.

60 mile/hour $\times$ 1,610 m/mile $\times$ 1 hour/3600 s = $\underline{26.8 \text{ m/s}}$

Knowing the proper units and how to convert between systems of units is important. Another significant thing is knowing how many *significant figures* to keep in an answer. For example, the numbers 1, 2.3 and 3.89, have one, two, and three significant figures. There are detailed rules on how many significant figures to include in an answer when performing computations with input numbers. However, for this elementary text, we only ask you to not egregiously violate significant figures by including the entire output of your calculator! Just to be clear on this, if you are multiplying the following numbers, each of which has three significant figures: 3.45 $\times$ 5.89, your calculator will return the answer: 20.3205, which has 6 significant figures. You should round this answer down to a more reasonable number like, 20.3, which also has three significant figures. By including an overly large number of significant figures in an answer one makes the error of suggesting a greater accuracy and precision than is warranted. On the other hand, we do not want to overemphasize this topic since our goal is for you to learn physics fundamentals not accounting.

C. How to Solve Physics Problems Exactly and Inexactly by Making Estimates.

The necessity of working physics problems in order to learn physics can hardly be overemphasized. The importance was very well stated by a veteran of physics,

"To use mathematics effectively in [physics] applications, you need not just knowledge but *skill*. Skill can be obtained only through practice. You can obtain a certain superficial *knowledge* of mathematics [and physics] by listening to lectures, but you cannot obtain *skill* this way.

How many students have I heard say "It looks so easy when you do it," or "I understand it but I can't do the problems!" Such statements show lack of practice and consequent lack of skill. The *only* way to develop the skill necessary to use this material in your later courses is to practice by solving many problems. ... this means practice, practice, practice! The *only* way to learn to solve problems is to solve problems."

—From the section "To the Student," *Mathematical Methods in the Physical Sciences*, 3rd Edition, Mary L. Boas (JWiley, 2006).

Often times a student can be convinced of the importance of working problems to learn physics but has difficulty getting started. Solving problems is a bit of an art form and like any art or sport activity, excellence is only acquired by practice, as the above quote states. Although it is not possible to give a person a magic recipe that will work for all physics problems, there are some general guidelines that are pertinent to how to solve different kinds of physics problems. The following remarks are relevant to nearly all problems in physics but again, practice makes perfect, as is expressed by the following tagline for Mattel's classic board game *Othello*, which reads:

"A minute to learn, a lifetime to master."

On Problem Solving.
- Make a diagram for the problem.
- Decide what the *system* is in the problem.
- List the values of and symbols for the quantities that are given and use a symbol to represent the quantity one is looking for.
- After a careful reading of the problem, decide what basic physics principles will be needed to obtain the solution. This is usually the most challenging part of a physics problem. This step will conclude with a mathematical set of equations. The answer to the problem will then be found by "doing the math." *Always wait until the end of the problem before putting in numbers, i.e., work in terms of symbols.* If you follow this practice it will be easier to find mistakes and recall your work at a later date.
- Once you have solved the mathematics for the unknown, make sure your final answer has the proper units and seems reasonable by considering some extreme values for the input variables.
- Some people prefer to work alone but others do better as part of a team. If you prefer a team, I suggest not having more than a total of three people in your problem solving team. Too many people can be counterproductive,

    "The crowd is untruth."—Soren Kierkegaard

Sometimes one may not be interested in finding an exact answer to a problem but only an approximate solution is called for. Physicists call this kind of a solution a "back of the envelope" calculation. For example, there is a class of problems called **Fermi problems** in which only a ballpark figure for the answer is sought. Enrico Fermi was an Italian-American physicist who was famous for considering this kind of a question. Perhaps the most famous Fermi-type problem is one that he is reported to have asked a physics graduate student during the student's Ph.D. oral examination at the University of Chicago: "How many piano tuners are there in Chicago?" Although the question has little to do directly with physics, the nature of the solution gives one an idea of how to reason through Fermi questions. For Fermi questions all that is expected is to arrive at an answer by using only common knowledge. No recourse to books and references is needed.

Let us now solve the piano tuner question. Begin by estimating the current population of Chicago, say about 8 million people. Then assume there are on average 3 people per family and therefore, $8 \times 10^6 / 3$ equals 2.7×10^6 families in Chicago. Assume there is 1 piano for every 100 families, so there would be $2.7 \times 10^4 \approx 27,000$ pianos in Chicago. How many of these pianos need tuning once every year? Say about 1/4, giving $27,000/4 \approx 7000$ tunings occuring in a year. Using this gives $7000/250$ days ≈ 28 family pianos tuned each day. If a piano tuner takes about two hours to tune a piano then each piano tuner would tune four pianos a day, giving us the final answer, $28/4 = 7$ *piano tuners in Chicago*. One can certainly quibble with many of these estimates but remember the idea is to only get a ballpark answer based solely on some reasonable assumptions. The answer might be off by a factor of 5 or 10 but even so, the power of this line of reasoning is evident.

D. Mathematical Review.

"In real life, I assure you, there is no such thing as algebra."—Fran Lebowitz

The above quote notwithstanding, this textbook assumes a knowledge of elementary algebra and basic trigonometry. The flyleaf of the text provides some geometric formulas, such as the area and circumference of a circle. These formulae may arise in the course of our study. In this section, some examples are presented to help you review the mathematics that is relevant to the material of future chapters.

Example Four.—*One equation with one unknown.*

Given $7x + 4 = 13$ find the value of x.

Solution.

We desire to isolate x.

Subtract 4 from both sides, $7x = 13 - 4$

$7x = 9$

Divide both sides by 7, $x = \underline{9/7 = 1.29}$

Example Five.—*Using the quadratic formula.*

Given the equation, $9x^2 - 12x + 4 = 0$, find the value(s) of x that satisfies the equation.

Solution.

Method One.

Notice this equation may be re-written as $(3x - 2)^2 = 0$ and this leads immediately to the solution <u>$x = 2/3$</u>.

Method Two.

Recall, if $ax^2 + bx + c = 0$ then $x = [-b \pm \sqrt{(b^2 - 4ac)}\,]/(2a)$. The latter is the *quadratic formula* from elementary algebra. Making the identifications, $a = 9$, $b = -12$, $c = 4$, we find,

$$x = [--12 \pm \sqrt{(144 - 4*9*4)}\,]/(2*9) = [12 \pm \sqrt{0}\,]/(18) = \underline{2/3}.$$

For a quadratic equation usually there are two roots, one from choosing the $+$ and the other from choosing the $-$ in the quadratic formula. Sometimes the two roots are the same and we say there is a *double root*, here the double root was, 2/3, 2/3.

Example Six.—*Finding an angle.*

Given $\tan \theta = 0.3$, find the value of the angle θ.

Solution.

Take the inverse tangent using your calculator, $\theta = \tan^{-1}(0.3) = 16.7°$.

Comment: $\tan^{-1}$ uses the TAN^{-1} button on your calculator, not the 1/X button. Also, you must set your calculator to degree mode to get the angle in degrees not radians.

Refer to the flyleaf of this textbook for the definitions of the sine, cosine and tangent functions.

Example Seven.—*Two equations–two unknowns.*

Given $6x + 8y = 12$ and $12x + 4y = 10$, find the values for the unknowns, x and y.

Solution.

Solve the first equation for y by subtracting $6x$ from both sides, $8y = 12 - 6x$

Divide both sides by 8, $y = 12/8 - 6x/8$

Use this result in the second equation for y, $12x + 4(12/8 - 6x/8) = 10$

Multiply (   ) by 4, $12x + 48/8 - 24x/8 = 10$

$12x + 6 - 3x = 10$

$9x + 6 = 10$

Subtract 6 from both sides, $9x = 10 - 6$

$9x = 4$

Divide by 9,   <u>$x = 4/9 = 0.444$</u>

Use this for x in the first equation,

$$6(4/9) + 8y = 12$$
$$2.66 + 8y = 12$$

Subtract 2.66 from both sides,

$$8y = 12 - 2.66$$
$$8y = 9.33$$

Divide both sides by 8,

$$y = \underline{1.166}$$

As a check, make sure the second equation is also solved by these values for x and y,

$$12x + 4y = 10$$
$$12(0.444) + 4(1.1666) = 5.333 + 4.666 = 10$$

Example Eight.—*Two equations–two unknowns.*

In a problem in electricity the following two equations are given,

$$F = kQq/r^2 \quad \text{and} \quad V = kQ/r$$

Assume F, k, q and V are known quantities and solve these equations for the two unknowns, Q and r, in terms of the known quantities.

Solution.

Solve the second equation for r,
$$r = kQ/V$$

Place this into the first equation,
$$F = kQq/(kQ/V)^2$$

Simplifying this gives,
$$F = qV^2/kQ$$

Solving this for Q,
$$Q = qV^2/kF$$

Place this for Q into the above result for r,
$$r = k(qV^2/kF)/V$$
$$r = \underline{qV/F}$$

Summary.

The way of knowing in science is through experiment (induction) and mathematical logic (deduction). Simplicity is highly valued and a theory must be falsifiable to be scientific. On a more mundane level, it is impossible to overestimate the importance of units. Often times changing from one set of units to another is needed and conversion factors are used for this operation. Physics problem solving is an art and science. There are rules of thumb that can provide assistance but in the end the only way to excel in physics is to practice problem solving. Finally, elementary algebra and basic trigonometry are crucial for this course. Solving simultaneous equations is especially important since this procedure arises quite often in physics problems.

QUESTIONS.

1. Which of the following are scientific statements?

(a) Neglecting air friction, an object at rest near the surface of the earth falls a distance of about 20 m during a time interval of 2 seconds.

(b) The Mona Lisa is a beautiful painting.

(c) The current president is a lousy leader.

(d) Gravitational forces decrease like one over distances squared.

(e) The first president of the United States was George Washington.

(f) There is only one God in the universe.

(g) Like electrical charges repel each other but unlike charges attract.

2. Can science determine what is scientific?

3. Classify which of these arguments is inductive and which is deductive.

(a) All men have hair.
    Charlie is a man.
    Charlie has hair.

(b) I measured the acceleration due to gravity in our physics lab.
    My measurement gave a value of 10 m/s^2.
    The acceleration due to gravity on earth is 10 m/s^2.

(c) God created everything.
    I exist.
    God created me.

(d) I measured the speed of light in our physics hallway.
    My measurement gave a value for the speed of light of 3×10^8 m/s.
    The speed of light in the universe is 3×10^8 m/s.

(e) For the last ten years my neighbor gave a party on Halloween.
    This year my neighbor had a Halloween party.
    Next year my neighbor will have a Halloween party.

4. Are Fermi questions answered scientifically?

5. Is it possible to learn physics without using mathematics?

6. In the chapter we compared science to history, pointing out the similarities and differences. Do the same for science and religion.

Recommendation:

For this course you should purchase the *least* expensive *solar*-powered *scientific* calculator. It is not uncommon for introductory level physics students to purchase sophisticated calculators that are difficult to operate. This often leads to mistakes that have little to do with physics misunderstandings.

PROBLEMS.

The data in Exercises 1 through 12 are from the *2007 Guinness World Records*.

1. Xi Shun of China is the world's tallest man, standing at a height of 2.361 m. Convert his height into feet.

2. The Barringer Meteorite Crater in Arizona is a hole in the ground approximately 1,200 m wide and 173 m deep. Convert the first number into miles and the second number into feet.

3. The deepest depression on dry land is the Bentley Trench in Antarctica with a depth below sea level of 2,538 m. Convert this to feet. Express your answer in scientific notation.

4. The Mariana Trench in the Pacific Ocean is the deepest point in an ocean at a depth of 10,911 m. Convert this to feet and miles. Express your answer in scientific notation.

5. The deepest snowfall in a single day was 1,930 mm at Silver Lake, Colorado. What is this depth in inches?

6. Under the heading of gross. The longest human parasite is the fish tapeworm that has been known to reach a length of 15.24 m. What is that in feet?

7. The longest jump by a kangaroo occurred in Australia (surprise!) and was 12.8 m. Convert this to feet.

8. One of the seven wonders of the ancient world was the great pyramid in Egypt. It was 146.6 m tall. Find its height in feet.

9. The fastest rocket was the X-15A-2 fired over California in 1967 and it reached a speed of 7,274 km/h. Convert this to mph. A test pilot was onboard this thing. Express your answer in scientific notation.

10. Among the seven wonders of the modern world is the tunnel under the English Channel that connects England to France. The tunnel is 50 km long. What is that in miles?

11. The fastest combat jet is the Russian Mig-25, clocking in at a speed of Mach 3.2 (Mach 1 is the speed of sound, so this is 3.2 times the speed of sound.) What is its speed in mph?

12. The fastest speed achieved in a quarter mile drag race was 540.98 km/h in Hebron, Ohio in 2005. Convert this into mph.

13. In a certain physics problem you are given an equation: $v = v_0 + a\,t$. (a) Solve this equation for t and (b) given $v = 30$ m/s, $v_0 = 12$ m/s, and $a = 6$ m/s^2 find the value of t.

14. Suppose we know $x = x_0 + v_0 t + \frac{1}{2} a t^2$. (a) Solve this equation for t (Hint: consult the quadratic formula) and (b) given $x = 2$ m, $x_0 = 0$, $v_0 = 2$ m/s and $a = \frac{1}{2}$ m/s^2, find the value of t.

15. In a problem we find $\tan \theta = A_y / A_x$. Solve this for (a) θ and (b) given $A_y = 2$ and $A_x = 4$, determine the value of θ in degrees.

16. Suppose $F_x = F\cos\theta$. Solve this for (a) θ and (b) given $F = 200$ and $F_x = 100$ find the value of θ in radians.

17. Given the following two simultaneous equations, solve for the unknowns, x and y.

$$2x + 4y = 8 \text{ and } x + y = 12$$

18. In a certain physics problem we find: $6F + 8F' = ma$ and $12F - 4F' = ma$. Solve for F and F' in terms of ma.

19. Suppose $x = \frac{1}{2} a t^2$ and $v = a t$

Solve the second equation for t, and place your result into the first equation. Simplify your result.

20. Solve for x and y, $2x + 22y = 4$ and $-5x + 10y = 12$

Hints and answers to problems.

1) 7 ft 8.95 inches   2) 0.7 mile and 570 feet   3) 8.326×10^3 ft   4) 3.5797×10^4 ft and 6.8 miles   5) 76 inches   6) 50 ft   7) 42 ft   8) 481 ft   9) 4.520×10^3 mph   10) 31 miles 11) 2,370 mph   12) 336.15 mph   13) (a) $t = (v - v_0)/a$ (b) $t = 3$ s 14) (a) $t = [-v_0 \pm \sqrt{\{v_0^2 - 2a(x_0 - x)\}}]/a$ (b) $t = 0.899$ s or -8.899 s   15) (a) $\theta = \tan^{-1}(A_y/A_x)$ (b) $\theta = 26.6°$ 16) (a) $\theta = \cos^{-1}(F_x/F)$ (b) $\theta = 1.047$ rad   17) $x = 20$ and $y = -8$ 18) $F = ma/10$ and $F' = ma/20$.   19) $x = v^2/2a$ 20) $x = -1.723$ and $y = 0.339$

Section II.

CLASSICAL MOTION.

CHAPTER I.
ANCIENT GREEK IDEAS ON MOTION.

Abstract.

The fascinating ancient Greek views on cosmology are well worth studying even today. This ancient mythology forms a point of view that is in marked contrast to the later scientific theories of motion developed by Galileo and Newton. Here we explore three fundamental questions to which the Greeks gave an answer: how is the world structured? of what is the world made? how does the world function or move? The first two questions have major implications for the Greek answer to the third question, which is the central question to be addressed by this textbook.

Definitions. Cosmology, hades, geocentric and heliocentric models, shades, elysian fields, tartarus, terrestrial and celestial realms, prime mover, natural place, natural motion, violent motion, ether

Principles. Aristotle's categories of motion

Fundamental Equations. Aristotle's "equations of motion"

"There is nothing new—only the history you haven't read."—Larry Swedroe

A. Ancient Greek Views of the Universe at Large.

We begin with the Greek's answer to the first question of this chapter, how is the world structured?

To answer this question we return to the late 300s BCE in Greek history. This is a period known as the Greek classical period or golden age. The period was a time of tremendous intellectual fervor. It is not an exaggeration to say our modern western civilization is founded largely on the thoughts set forth by the ancient Greeks and the Hebrews. When it comes to physics, the Greeks are our intellectual ancestors. The ancient Hebrews primarily contributed in non-scientific areas of learning. Even the subsequent Roman civilization borrowed heavily from the Greeks. Although the Romans made significant contributions (e.g. an excellent system of roads), we will focus on the Greeks as the pioneers of physics and philosophy.

In this short chapter, we will not be able to examine all of the contributions to science made by the Greeks but rather we will recall some of their views in three broad areas: cosmology, the elements, and motion. By *cosmology* is meant the study of the physical universe at large. This is the big picture of the universe. Of course, the Greeks were aware of the stars and planets, the latter they termed wandering stars. They assumed the earth to be the center of the universe which is a viewpoint referred to as the **geocentric** model (geo is Greek for earth). The *geocentric* model is an *ego*centric viewpoint since it places the earth at the center with all things revolving around the fixed earth. (This is in contrast to the **heliocentric** model where the Sun is at the center.) In addition, the earth was believed to be spherical. This may be surprising to you since there is a common modern misconception that the ancients uniformly thought the earth to be flat. The Greeks new better.

Let us begin a magnificent journey through the mythological world of the ancient Greeks. Our odyssey will touch on Greek thinking about the structure of the universe and will begin inside the earth and proceed all the way out to the stars and beyond. The region inside the earth was the dwelling place of the dead, a region the Greeks called **hades**. You may recall from your reading of the *Odyssey* and *Iliad* by Homer the frequent references to this afterlife where people are called **shades** and wander around in this shadowy existence only half awake. In Greek mythology it was believed the dead drank from the river of forgetfulness and therefore experienced only the present with little hope for the future. Hades consisted of several compartments. Most people endured a largely lifeless existence with little joy or pain. However, those who had lived an especially virtuous and heroic life while on earth settled in a utopian area of hades known as the **elysian fields** (later known as heaven) while extremely evil persons spent eternity in a region called **tartarus** (later known as hell.) The elysian fields consisted of beautiful meadows with plenty of sunlight and fresh air where everyone led happy, peaceful lives. In contrast, tartarus was a dark pit occupying the lowest place of existence and where an evil person was punished forever. Foremost among the sins was pride, which was particularly offensive to the gods. Tartarus was an inferno of suffering and pain. You will note that this viewpoint is not entirely consistent. For example, Tartarus is somehow both dark and an inferno (a fire). As we examine this mythology a number of contradictions will surface.

Digging out from under the earth we come to the earth's surface where humans dwell during their short lifespan. A common belief held by many ancient peoples was the notion that humans were literally created from dirt.

Journeying above the earth we come to a spherical shell containing water (lakes and oceans). As we go further up and away from earth the next spherical shell is air (the atmosphere) and finally, the spherical shell of fire. These shells: under the earth, earth, water, air, and fire make up the **terrestrial realm** in Greek cosmology. As we venture above the fire shell, a new realm is entered, the celestial realm.

The **celestial realm** consists of the remaining spherical shells. All of the terrestrial and celestial shells are concentric, meaning they all have the same center, which is the center of the earth. The first of the celestial shells we encounter is the shell containing the moon and the planets. The Greeks believed the planets were perfect spheres that were embedded in the planet shell like raisins in a pudding.

Above the shell containing the planets is the spherical shell containing the stars. The stars also are spheres. In this view, both the planets and stars are eternal, conscious beings (gods). The role of the dozen major gods in the Greek pantheon is similar to the role that force plays in modern physics—gods(forces) make things happen. For example, today we know lightning is caused by electromagnetic forces in nature. The Greeks attributed lightning to the action of one of their gods, Zeus, who was the most powerful and important of the Greek gods.

Outside the star shell, farthest away from earth, we find a being called the ***prime mover*** or unmoved mover. This changeless primary divinity resides outside the universe and is the penultimate originator of all change. The being keeps the celestial shells rolling along by continually spinning the star shell. Friction between the star shell and the planet shell causes the planet shell to also rotate. Without the prime mover all celestial motion would cease. Celestial motion is dependent upon the continual application of force and will cease should the prime mover take a break from his or her job. Figure 1 depicts the Greek cosmos.

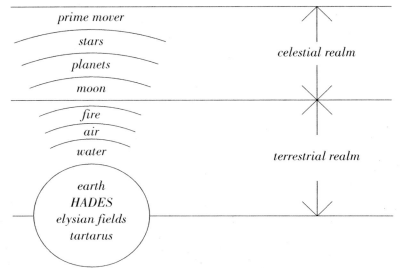

FIG. 1. THE COSMOLOGY OF THE ANCIENT GREEKS CONSISTED OF TWO REALMS: THE TERRESTRIAL AND THE CELESTIAL.

We have briefly traced the Greek views about the geometry of the cosmos. Our second question of this chapter is: of what is the world made? That is, what are the constituents of the cosmos? Today we know there are about 100 elements in the periodic table that make up all matter. The ancient Greeks had a much simpler periodic table consisting of only five elements. All objects residing in the terrestrial realm are a mixture of just four elements: earth, water, air and fire. Some terrestrial objects may be almost pure since they are made of nearly one element alone but most objects are compounds that consist of significant amounts of two or more of the four elements. The terrestrial realm is the place of impurity, finite lives, and imperfection.

The fifth element was called the quintessence—*quint* is the Greek word for five. This element was also called the ***ether***. All objects residing in the celestial realm are pure since they are made of just the ether. (Incidentally, the belief in the ether continued until about the year 1900 CE!) This realm is the place of perfection and purity. All celestial objects have a perfect shape (spherical), a perfect motion (circular motion), and a perfect composition, pure ether. You may have noted the

Greek preoccupation with circles. The reason for this thinking is: a circle has no point one could identify as the beginning or end. But, they argued, that which has no beginning or end is eternal. Only eternal beings reside in the celestial realm and they are supposed to be perfect. The gods are eternal, the rest of us never make it to the celestial realm—at best we can enjoy an afterlife on the elysian fields situated inside the earth. Once again the Greeks are inconsistent since their gods are frequently depicted in their mythological stories as being grossly imperfect and human-like.

We have examined the structure and composition of the universe according to the ancients. Next, we consider Greek thought about how the universe functions, that is, how things move. We will see that the motion of something is intimately related to where it is and its composition. Overall, we will find there are two broad ways of understanding the function or movement of the world: as a machine or as an organism. As we study physics through the ages, at certain times one of these models dominates while at other times, the other model holds sway. Clearly, many of the earliest Greeks viewed the world as an organism but later some, for example the atomists, thought of the world as a machine. One's point of view on this question has major philosophical implications in the area of free will versus determinism but such thoughts lie outside the domain of physics.

B. Aristotle's Views of Motion on Earth and the Heavens.

The final question to be addressed in this chapter is, how does the world function or move? To understand the Greek answer to this question we consider one of the foremost of Greek thinkers, Aristotle. Aristotle (384–322 BCE) is considered by many as the greatest philosopher of all time. His prodigious quantity of work spanned the entire spectrum of human understanding including a slight amount of work in the field of physics. Aristotle was held in such high esteem during the late middle ages that scholars read his works and gave them nearly the same authority as they gave to the Bible. In short, he was called *the* philosopher. One of the central themes of his thought was the idea that everything has a purpose or function. This teleological (i.e. purpose driven) philosophy crept into his physics also and it will become manifest as we now examine Aristotelian physics in further detail.

According to Aristotle the laws of physics in the sublunary regions are different from the laws at work in the celestial realm. This is not surprising given the marked difference in composition of the two realms and the belief that celestial objects are perfect and eternal while terrestrial things are impure, evil, and transitory. To describe the physics of the world let's go from celestial physics to terrestrial—opposite to the order we followed in describing the structure and composition of the world.

Celestial objects move in only one way, circular motion with constant speed, which you will recall is the perfect kind of motion. Ultimately, the motion arises because of the action of the prime mover, who imparts movement to the star shell. This causes the stars to move in a circular manner, as is confirmed by observation of the night sky. The star shell rubs against the planet shell thereby causing the planets to also move in circular motion.

There are some deviations from celestial circular motion (e.g. retrograde motion, comets, etc.) but the Greeks largely ignored such exceptions. We should not be too critical of the Greeks for ignoring aspects that did not fit neatly into their tidy conception of things. From the vantage point of centuries of scientific development it is clear in all physical theories there will arise exceptions. Frequently progress in physics is only made by ignoring the anomalies until later refinements are introduced. Physics starts simple in order to uncover the basic principles and then complications are considered that often make it necessary to revise these principles. If we must wait until the development of a perfect theory then we will never be able to make progress in physics. Neglecting the above astronomical anomalies yields a picture of an unchanging circular motion in the heavens. This is certainly in line with everyday astronomical observations. The place where things are more in a state of flux is the terrestrial realm.

In the terrestrial realm things are more complicated and we will find that exceptions to Aristotle's physics will proliferate. Aristotle divided all motion, whether celestial or terrestrial, into two categories: **natural** motion and **violent** motion. To build his classification scheme of motion Aristotle first made the assumption that all things in the world have what he termed their natural place. The **natural place** of an object is determined by its composition and the location of the object within the cosmological picture illustrated in Figure 1. For example, water has its natural place in the water shell, and a rock, being mostly earth, has its natural place on the surface of the earth. The Aristotelian universe is an extremely hierarchical place where everything has its place.

But what if something is out of place? Aristotle said objects that are out of place will, if allowed, execute natural motion thereby returning to their natural place. Therefore, a rock that is above the earth will fall down to its natural place, the earth. Of course, I can prevent this from occurring by holding the rock or placing it on a table. But if nothing is preventing the rock from falling, it will fall to the ground. Another example of natural motion comes from a container of boiling water. The bubbles inside the water are air pockets, and the bubbles naturally rise to enter the air shell, i.e. the atmosphere. In short, natural motion is generally motion in the vertical direction, either up or down, and occurs so the object can return to its natural place.

However, not all terrestrial motion is up or down but sometimes things go sideways. This other kind of motion Aristotle classified as violent motion. Violent motion arises because of the action of a force, i.e. a push or pull. For example, the reason objects in the celestial realm always move in circles is because these objects are never out of place and so they do not have to move up or down to get back "home." The circular motion of stars and planets is an example of violent motion that is caused by the prime mover and friction, respectively, pushing the bodies along their trajectory. Consider once again a rock. I can pick up a rock off the ground and move it up away from its natural place on earth. I exert a force on the rock to move it away from the ground since the rock will not naturally hop up off the ground. Or consider a chair at rest on the floor. The chair remains at rest since it is mostly made of earth and so it is in its natural place. I can exert a horizontal force on the chair and it will move across the floor executing violent motion but otherwise the chair remains at rest on the floor. From these everyday observations Aristotle concluded that objects in their natural place do not move unless a force is applied to them. Reasoning further, suppose we have two chairs, one that is light and the other that is heavy. The chairs have a different mass, m_A, where the "A" is a reminder that this is Aristotelian mass. Applying the same force to both we notice the heavy chair acquires a smaller velocity than the light chair. Aristotle was aware of these kinds of observations.

Although what follows is not strictly historical, for instructional purposes, let us quantify things and summarize the above ideas giving them the name, Aristotle's laws of motion. Later, we shall see how these laws get changed by Galileo and Newton, in short how Newton found $m_A v$ must be changed to ma. But we are getting ahead of our story. The hypothetical Aristotelian laws of motion are stated in the box below.

"Aristotle's Laws of Motion."

Aristotle's Law One (Law of Inertia).

All objects in the universe that are in their natural place remain at rest unless a force is applied.

Aristotle's Second Law.

Any object of Aristotelian mass m_A that is in its natural place will move with a speed v if a force F is

$$F = m_A v.$$

The second law implies several things. For a given value of F, if m_A is large then v is small. This is in agreement with the above example of the heavy and light chairs experiencing the same force. In addition, notice the second law contains the first law as a special case. That is, if F is zero then v must be zero and the object remains at rest. It is important for you to realize that we are playing with history here. Aristotle never wrote down these laws in the form given above. Nevertheless, the laws capture, in a mathematical framework, many of Aristotle's ideas about motion.

Although quite reasonable in many instances, Aristotle's laws of motion have some obvious flaws and inconsistencies. Perhaps the most striking flaw is they do not account for the everyday motion of projectiles. For example, a baseball pitcher winds up and violently releases a baseball from his hand. In the comic book world of Aristotelian physics, the moment he releases the ball it will no longer move horizontally since no force acts on it. But since the baseball is mostly earth, it will immediately start its natural descent straight down to the earth when the pitcher releases the ball.

In this funny world one could not play baseball or any sport. Indeed, the Aristotelian universe is a static and sluggish world. To circumvent this obvious flaw the Aristotelians appealed to their belief that it is impossible to form a vacuum which is summarized by the well-known phrase: "nature abhors a vacuum." Reasoning along these lines they said when the baseball leaves the pitcher's hand, a momentary vacuum is left behind the ball, and so the air in front of the ball rushes to fill the vacuum behind. In so doing this air is what propels the ball forward. One physics textbook author said this viewpoint is similar to propelling a bar of soap by squeezing on one end! However, on other occasions the Aristotelians argued that the friction with air is what slows a projectile down. So, at once, we have the contradictory statements that the air both propels and slows the baseball.

In conclusion, one reason for our reviewing Aristotle's outdated views on motion is that most people are Aristotelian when it comes to their uninformed views of motion. This is a deep seated conception of motion that is very difficult to overcome, primarily because Aristotle's views are based on common sense. After all, chairs don't move unless we push them. But to progress in our understanding of motion will require us to go beyond common sense in order to achieve an understanding of motion that Galileo and Newton were able to uncover. Do not underestimate the effort it will take to leave behind Aristotelian views of motion since the time from Aristotle to Galileo and Newton is measured in millennia and the intellectual distance between the theories requires even a greater leap!

References.

Mythology, Edith Hamilton (Warner Books, 1969). If you want to learn more about the Titans, The Twelve Olympian Gods, Greek Heroes, Greek and Roman myths, etc., I highly recommend you consult this very readable book. There is even a short section on Norse myths.

Greek Religion, Walter Burkert (Harvard University Press, 1985).

Thinking through Philosophy, Chris Horner and Emrys Westacott (Cambridge University Press, 2000).

Aristotle's Physics I, II translated by W. Charlton (Oxford University Press, 1970).

Aristotle's Physics III, IV translated by E. L. Hussey (Oxford University Press, 1981).

Aristotle, Jonathan Barnes (Oxford University Press, 1982).

Physics, the Human Adventure, Gerald Holton and Stephen G. Brush (Rutgers University Press, 2001).

Ed Disy and J. Garner, The Physics Teacher (**37**), 42 (1999).

Summary.

The ancient Greeks envisioned a static universe where everything had its natural place. In this framework the material world consists of four elements in the terrestrial realm and the ether in the celestial. The gods occupied the perfect heavens while mortals, after spending an impure existence on earth, spend their afterlife in hades. Terrestrial motion was one of two sorts: natural and violent. Celestial motion is of one kind: violent motion caused by the prime mover. The Greeks were especially attracted to the perfection exhibited by the heavenly circular motion. These viewpoints were held by the most famous philosopher of all time, Aristotle. The Aristotelian worldview dominated Western thought for centuries but it was finally overturned at the end of the middle ages with the arrival of modern science.

QUESTIONS.

1. What answer would the ancient Greeks give to the question, what elements make up the human body?

2. List the ways in which the terrestrial realm differs from the celestial.

3. The Greeks believed what shape to be perfect? Why did they think this shape is perfect?

4. Give some examples of natural motion.

5. Is natural motion possible in the celestial realm? Justify your answer.

6. Give some examples of violent motion.

7. How would the ancient Greeks classify the motion of a comet?

8. Aristotle believed that a single force acting on an object

   (*a*) will cause the object to have a velocity

   (*b*) will cause the object to remain at rest

   (*c*) will cause the object to have an acceleration

   (*d*) caused it to behave in a way he did not understand since he had no opinion on this

   (*e*) caused it to behave in a way he did not understand since he didn't believe in forces, only gods

9. Answer this question based on Aristotle's "second law." When the force on a mass is doubled, its velocity is

   (*a*) unchanged

   (*b*) halved

   (*c*) doubled

   (*d*) increased

   (*e*) decreased

10. How would Aristotle explain the circular motion of an object?

11. How would Aristotle explain the vibratory motion of an object?

12. Using Aristotelian dynamics, describe how the game of pool would be played.

13. How would the ancient Greeks account for the motion of a rocket?

14. In what way did Isaac Newton change Aristotle's "second law"?

15. In view of the answer to question 14, how would Aristotle's "first law" be altered by Newton?

CHAPTER II.
MOTION IN ONE DIMENSION.

Abstract.
The study of motion is called **mechanics**, which is the oldest and most fundamental area of physics. This textbook adopts motion as its central theme and unifying concept. Our modern understanding and language of motion was the major contribution of Galileo. In this chapter we consider his life as background to a discussion of the language, mathematics, and concepts he developed to mathematically describe motion along a line.

Definitions. time, position, initial position, time interval, displacement, average velocity, velocity, speed, initial velocity, average acceleration, and acceleration

Principles. The physics of motion with constant velocity and constant acceleration (e.g. free fall)

Fundamental Equations. Equations for position and velocity for an object with constant velocity and constant acceleration

In spite of the significant contributions of the ancient Greeks and various individuals who lived during the Middle Ages, progress in understanding motion was relatively slow until Galileo. In this chapter we review major milestones in the life of Galileo. After this background, we set out the fundamental language now used by physicists in their description of motion. One important special kind of motion we examine is that of an object moving with constant acceleration as in free fall.

A. Galileo (1564–1642).

"We marry the spirit of the age at the risk of widowhood."
—Chesterton

"In all affairs it's a healthy thing now and then to hang a question mark on the things you have long taken for granted."
—Bertrand Russell, famous mathematician, philosopher and atheist

Courtesy of Erich Lessing/Art Resource, NY.

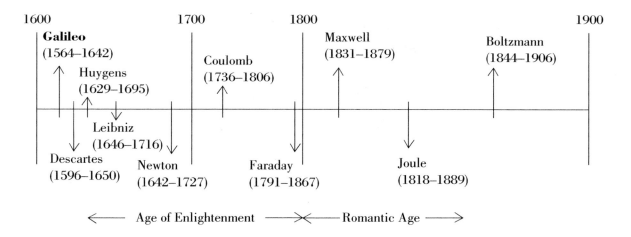

Galileo Galilei is considered by many to be the first modern scientist. Today Galileo has become almost an icon of science as it seeks to differentiate itself from other ways of perceiving reality, especially views based on religious authoritative sources. This, at the time controversial figure, was born in Pisa, Italy in 1564 shortly after a period known as the Renaissance. His birth coincided with the year of Shakespeare's birth and Michaelangelo's death. Galileo's wide interests ranged over a number of fields including physics, which at that time was called natural philosophy and was a subfield of mathematics. Galileo initially entered the university to study medicine, largely at the urging of his father. His primary interest, however, was in mathematics. The universities of his day were dominated by the philosophical viewpoints espoused by the prominent ancient Greek philosopher, Aristotle. Scholars of his day routinely read the works of Aristotle in order to understand nature since Aristotle's opinions were received nearly on the same level of authority as Biblical writings. Although Galileo was a faithful member of the church, he had a rebellious streak that led to his desire to question ancient authorities. His fiery personality and independent sharp mind eventually led to conflicts with certain dogmatic church authorities. The conflict centered on whether the Earth (geocentric model) or the Sun (heliocentric model) is the center of the solar system. Church officialdom taught the geocentric model which was the dominant model in ancient Greece and apparently the model found in the Bible (Joshua 10:13). Galileo followed the heliocentric views of Copernicus. He was not reticent about expressing his heretical opinions openly and he had the gall of writing in the vernacular (Italian) rather than the language of the scholars, Latin.

Galileo wrote several books, one of which was *The Sidereal Messenger* (published in 1610) which set forth results of his investigations of the solar system using the newly invented telescope. In 1632 Galileo published another book, *Dialogue Concerning the Two Chief World Systems*, where his Copernican views were expressed in terms of a dialogue involving three individuals: Salviati (who represented Galileo's views, an intelligent Copernican), Simplicio (the not so intelligent representative of the Aristotelian philosophers), and the impartial, intelligent, and open-minded Sagredo. In 1638 he wrote another book, *Two New Sciences*, which consisted of most of his findings in physics proper. Therein, he set forth his findings in the study of motion using the inclined plane and a water clock (the first science) while the latter part of the book dealt with the strength of materials (the second science). Even in this text the geocentric versus heliocentric debate was entered when Galileo argued for his views of why the earth moves. In particular, Galileo considered dropping an object from a tall tower and he explained why the object would hit the ground at the base of the tower even though the earth is rotating. The argument was made transparent by analogy with dropping an object from the top of the mast of a moving ship. Perhaps the most significant observation of Galileo was his argumentation for the "law of inertia." This law, which we will find later to resurface as Newton's first law of motion, states that a free object moves with constant velocity. The law of inertia is in profound violation of Aristotle's thoughts on motion since Aristotle thought a force was necessary to maintain motion. The overarching significance of Galileo's physics lies in his willingness to conduct careful, precise experiments to test hypotheses involving simple systems and his abundant use of mathematics as the most natural language for the expression of physical principles.

In 1616 the Inquisition warned Galileo to cease propagating his Copernican views. Given the seriousness of the matter, and the fact that heretics often were sentenced to capital punishments such as being burned at the stake, for awhile Galileo refrained from publicly advancing the Copernican cause. Yet, eventually the controversy reignited and as a result he was tried in Rome before the Pope. Under the threat of torture, he renounced his Copernican views but even so, he was sentenced to spend the last ten years of his life under house arrest. The authorities probably knew that Galileo really did not change his mind. The *Two New Sciences* was written after the trial and was even more damaging to the Aristotelian models than the *Two World Systems*. It was not until 1835 that his book, the *Two World Systems*, was removed from the Church's *Index of Forbidden Books*. Remarkably, it took until 1992 for the Roman Catholic church to finally admit error in sentencing Galileo. Galileo died while under house arrest in 1642, and as if the torch was passed to a new generation in a different nation, that year happened to be the year of birth of Isaac Newton in England.

References.

Dialogues Concerning Two New Sciences, Galileo Galilei (Dover, 1954).

Galileo, Stillman Drake (Hill and Wang, 1980).

Remarkable Physicists, Ioan James (Cambridge UP, 2004).

Great Physicists, William H. Cropper (Oxford UP, 2004).

Physics, the Human Adventure by Gerald Holton and Stephen Brush (Rutgers University Press, 2001).

B. Describing and Graphing Motion in One Dimension

As is so often in physics, it is best to follow Galileo's lead and start with simple situations. After we have clearly and fully understood the simple case we will add in real world complications. The situation we start with is that of a particle moving in one direction. The notion of a particle is one of the fundamental concepts used in physics. A particle is any object that can be accurately described by assuming it has no internal structure, i.e. it acts as if it is zero dimensional. (Later, we will find another fundamental concept to be useful, that of a wave.)

Imagine then a particle (say a marble) moving along a line. Let the line coincide with an x-axis as shown in Figure 1.

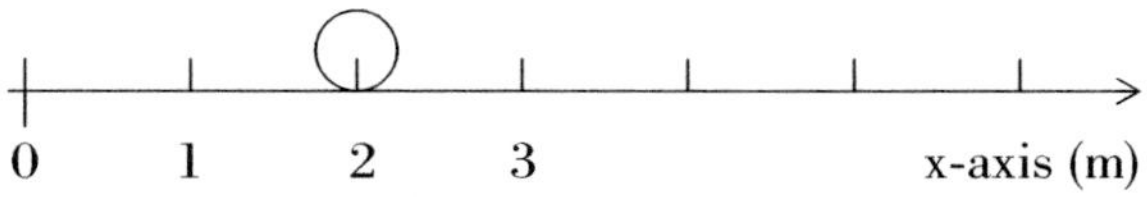

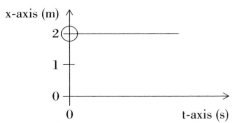

FIG. 1. MOTION OF A PARTICLE IN ONE DIMENSION ALONG THE X-AXIS.

Locations along the x-axis are marked off using a meter stick. One measures the distance from the origin of the axis over to the marble and define this distance (in meters, for example) as the **position**, x, of the marble. In Figure 1, $x = 2$ m. To fully describe motion we will also need a time measuring device, let's say a stopwatch. The reading of the stopwatch at any given moment we denote the **time**, t. The position of the marble when the stopwatch reads zero is given a special name and symbol, the initial position, $x_0 = x(t = 0) = x_i$. (We use various symbols for the same quantity since physics does not have a universal nomenclature and so different texts use different symbols—you should be aware of this bit of confusion.)

A firm grasp of motion may be obtained by considering graphs of the motion. Assuming the marble is stationary at position 2 m, a graph of its position, x, (on the vertical axis) versus the time, t, (on the horizontal axis) is shown in Figure 2.

Notice the graph is simply a horizontal straight line that crosses the x-axis at $x = 2$ m. No matter the time coordinate, t, the x-coordinate (position) of the particle remains 2 m.

FIG. 2. POSITION VERSUS TIME FOR A STATIONARY PARTICLE AT $x = 2$ M.

Things would not be very interesting if the marble never moved. When the marble moves from one position, say x_1 to a new position, x_2 this takes time to occur. We observe that when the marble is at x_1 the time on the stopwatch reads t_1 while the stopwatch reads a new time, $t_2 > t_1$, when the marble arrives at x_2. The **time interval**, Δt, is defined as the later time, t_2, minus the earlier time, t_1, or in symbols,

$$\Delta t \equiv t_2 - t_1 \quad \text{(time interval, s)} \tag{1}$$

The symbol $\equiv$ is commonly used by mathematicians to represent a definition. The symbol Δ is another common symbol that is used to represent the change in a quantity, in the case of equation (1), it is the change in the time. Time intervals are always positive since time is always increasing in value, $\Delta t > 0$. Evidently the units for time intervals are those of time, seconds.

When the marble moves, another quantity that changes is the position of the marble. The change in position is called the ***displacement***, Δx, (in meters) of the marble and in symbols we write,

$$\Delta x \equiv x_2 - x_1 \quad \text{(displacement, m)} \tag{2}$$

Time intervals and displacements are the nuts and bolts of understanding motion. However, displacements are slightly more complicated than time intervals. Why? Because displacements can be positive or negative. This is easy to see. If the marble moves to the right (in the direction of the +x-axis) then the displacement of the marble will be positive since x is increasing in value. On the other hand, if it moves to the left (in the direction of the –x-axis) then the displacement of the marble will be a negative number. Therefore, the sign of the displacement indicates the direction of the motion.

Example One.—*Displacements of a rabbit.*

(a) Find the displacement of a rabbit that starts at position of +3 m and ends in a position of 8 m.

(b) Find the displacement of a rabbit that starts at position 5 m and ends in a position of –4 m.

Solution.

(a) $\Delta x = x_f - x_i = 8 - 3 = \underline{5 \text{ m}}$.

(b) $\Delta x = x_f - x_i = -4 - 5 = \underline{-9 \text{ m}}$.

Suppose the graph of the marble is given by Figure 3, where the line is no longer horizontal but tilted upward. What kind of motion does this describe?

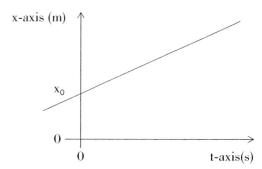

FIG. 3. POSITION VERSUS TIME OF A PARTICLE
WITH CONSTANT VELOCITY.

On the graph we see that at time 0 the marble has an ***initial position*** on the x-axis of x_0, the "y-intercept" of the graph. It is clear from the graph that the marble's position does not remain at the value x_0 but in fact increases as time goes by. Figure 3 is an example of a linear graph, which you will recall from elementary algebra has an equation of the form, $y = mx + b$, with m being the slope of the graph and b the "y-intercept." This is the situation at hand, with a slight difference. Instead of the vertical axis being called y and the horizontal axis called x we have made the substitution,

$$\text{(vertical) } y \to x \text{ and (horizontal) } x \to t$$

and so the equation for the graph in Figure 3 becomes,

$$y = \mathbf{m}x + b \rightarrow \mathrm{x} = \mathrm{m}\,t + b.$$

The b is the intercept, which we have already identified as x_0, so our equation now reads,

$$x = \mathbf{m}\,t + x_0.$$

What about the slope, m? From algebra, recall the slope of a straight line is defined as the rise divided by the run, which is

$$\mathrm{m} \equiv \mathrm{rise/run} = \Delta x/\Delta t = (x_2 - x_1)/(t_2 - t_1),$$

where 1 and 2 denote any two points on the line. The quantity represented by m, the slope, is called the ***average velocity*** of the marble during the time interval Δt,

$$\mathrm{v}_x(\text{average}) \equiv \Delta x/\Delta t \quad \text{(average velocity, m/s)} \tag{3}$$

To determine the slope one needs to find the coordinates of two points on the line in Figure 3. For a straight line, any two points chosen will give the same slope and therefore let us use $x(0)$ with $t = 0$ as our first point and an arbitrary position, x, that corresponds to an arbitrary time, t, as our second point on the line.

$$\mathrm{m} = (x - x_0)/(t - 0)$$

Since m doesn't change for a straight line this means the value of the ***velocity*** doesn't change, where velocity is a special kind of average velocity when the time interval is chosen to be very small,

$$v_x \equiv \Delta x/\Delta t \quad \text{with } \Delta t \text{ very small.} \quad \text{(velocity, m/s)} \tag{4}$$

The velocity represented in equation (4) is sometimes called the instantaneous velocity since this is the number one reads on an automobile's speedometer at any given instant. The term ***speed*** is defined as the absolute value of the velocity.

Since the velocity doesn't change, we can evaluate the slope using the ***initial velocity*** of the marble, v_{x0},

$$\mathrm{m} = v_{x0} = (x - x_0)/(t - 0)$$

This gives,

$$v_{x0} = (x - x_0)/t$$

or multiplying both sides by t and solving for x we get,

$$x = x_0 + v_{x0}\,t \quad \text{(motion with constant velocity)} \tag{5}$$

This result simply states that the position of the marble when the stopwatch reads time t, is the position at time zero plus how much the position has increased because the marble has a constant velocity. Equation (5) illustrates a general feature of equations in physics. All equations have hidden assumptions and one must always remember under what conditions the equation is valid. I have explicitly stated the assumption in (5), i.e. motion of the particle with constant velocity.

The graph of velocity versus time for the marble with constant velocity would be very simple, as shown in Figure 4.

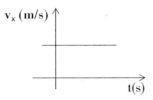

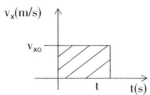

FIG. 4A. VELOCITY
VERSUS TIME FOR A
PARTICLE HAVING
CONSTANT VELOCITY.

FIG. 4B. THE
DISPLACEMENT IS THE
AREA UNDER THE
VELOCITY VERSUS TIME
GRAPH.

This graph is interesting because we can use it to find the displacement of the marble between time 0 and time t. Consider the area of the rectangle in Figure 4 b

$$\text{Area under } v_x \text{ vs } t \text{ between time 0 and time } t = v_{x0} t$$

According to equation (5) this area is also simply the displacement, $x - x_0$:

$$x - x_0 = \text{Area under } v_x \text{ vs } t \text{ between time 0 and time } t = v_{x0} t \qquad (6)$$

Example Two.—*Bank robber moving with constant velocity.*

Below is shown the graph of the position of a bank robber's car versus time.

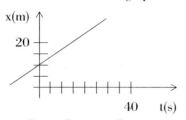

BANK ROBBER GRAPH

From this graph determine (a) the initial position of the robber, (b) the average velocity of the robber from time zero to time 30 s, and (c) the equation of the line in the figure.

Solution.

(a) $x_0 = \underline{10 \text{ m}}$

(b) $v_x(\text{avg}) = \Delta x / \Delta t = (30 - 10)/(30 - 0) = 20/30 = \underline{2/3 \text{ m/s.}}$

(c) using (5) with v_{x0} set to $v_x(\text{avg})$ since here the velocity is not changing,

$$x = x_0 + v_{x0} t = x_0 + v_x(\text{avg}) t = \underline{10 + 2/3 \, t.}$$

We have come a long way, we started with a marble that had position equal to a constant (it was at rest) and then we considered a marble with constant velocity where we found its position to be given by equation (5), a linear function of time. The graph for constant velocity is in Figure 4. Now suppose the horizontal line in Figure 4 is tilted up as in Figure 5. What kind of motion does this describe?

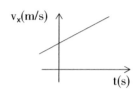

FIG. 5A. VELOCITY VERSUS TIME
FOR A PARTICLE HAVING CONSTANT
ACCELERATION.

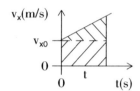

FIG. 5B. THE AREA UNDER
VELOCITY VERSUS TIME GRAPH
GIVES THE DISPLACEMENT.

Clearly, v_x is not staying the same in Figure 5 but rather increasing in a linear fashion. The equation of the straight line in the figure is

$$v_x = b + \text{slope } t$$

or

$$v_x = v_{x0} + \text{slope } t.$$

where in the last step I have made the identification, $b = v_{x0}$. The slope of this graph is known as the **average acceleration** over the time interval Δt.

$$\text{Slope of } v_x \text{ vs } t \text{ graph} = \text{rise/run} \equiv \Delta v_x/\Delta t \equiv a_x(\text{average}) \quad \text{(average acceleration, m/s}^2\text{)} \quad (7)$$

Equation (7) implies that the sign of a_x(average) is fully determined by the sign of Δv_x since $\Delta t > 0$. The units for a_x(average) are m/s divided by s, often written m/s². The slope can be found using any two points of the line, let's use the point v_{x0} with $t = 0$ and the second point v_x at an arbitrary time, t.

$$a_x(\text{average}) \text{ in Figure 5} = (v_x - v_{x0})/(t - 0)$$

or

$$a_x(\text{average}) = (v_x - v_{x0})/t$$

Since the figure is linear, the average acceleration (i.e. the slope) does not change and so it equals the **acceleration** defined by,

$$a_x \equiv \Delta v_x/\Delta t, \ \Delta t \text{ very small} \quad \text{(acceleration, m/s}^2\text{)} \quad (8)$$

So we have,

$$a_x(\text{average}) = a_x = (v_x - v_{x0})/t$$

Multiplying both sides by t and solving for v_x leads to the very important result,

$$v_x = v_{x0} + a_x t \text{ (constant acceleration)} \tag{9}$$

In words, the marble at time t has a velocity v_x given by its initial velocity plus how much the velocity increased because of the acceleration over the time interval $t - 0$.

Finally, we know at time t the marble has velocity v_x but where will the marble be at time t? The clue to this question is given in equation (6)

The displacement, $x - x_0$ equals the area under the v_x vs t graph from time 0 to t.

However, that area is no longer that of a rectangle as in Figure 4, i.e. $v_{x0}t$, but consists of the rectangle *plus* triangle in Figure 5b.

$$x - x_0 = \text{Area} = \text{rectangle} + \text{triangle} = v_{x0} t + \tfrac{1}{2} t (v_x - v_{x0}) = \tfrac{1}{2} v_{x0} t + \tfrac{1}{2} t v_x$$

or using equation (9) for v_x,

$$x - x_0 = \tfrac{1}{2} v_{x0} t + \tfrac{1}{2} t (v_{x0} + a_x t)$$

which finally gives another very important result,

$$x = x_0 + v_{x0} t + \tfrac{1}{2} a_x t^2 \quad \text{(constant acceleration)} \tag{10}$$

Any problem involving the motion of a particle in one dimension with constant acceleration can be solved using just equations (9) and (10). Even so, there are some subtleties involved in the problem-solving process that need to be explicitly stated as is done in the box below.

Advice on solving problems where v_x or a_x is constant
- draw a **picture** of the situation
- know where your **origin** of coordinates is and the direction of the +x-**axis** inside the above picture
- in view of the above two points, you may now determine values for x_0, v_{x0}, and a_x
- use equation **(5)** (if v_x is constant) or equations **(9)** and **(10)** (if a_x is constant) in order to solve the algebra for the unknowns
- watch **units** and make sure your answer seems **reasonable!**

Example Three.—*The "shortcut" equation.*

Although equations (9) and (10) are all that's needed for constant acceleration problems, sometimes it can save time using a third equation, the "shortcut equation." Show that (9) and (10) can be algebraically combined to yield the shortcut equation given by,

MOTION IN ONE DIMENSION.

$$v_x^2 = v_{x0}^2 + 2a_x[x - x_0]$$

Solution.

Starting with (9) we have,

$$v_x = v_{x0} + a_x t,$$

which on rearrangement gives,

$$t = (v_x - v_{x0})/a_x.$$

Inserting this result for t into (10) gives,

$$x = x_0 + v_{x0} t + \tfrac{1}{2} a_x t^2 = x_0 + v_{x0} (v_x - v_{x0})/a_x + \tfrac{1}{2} a_x ((v_x - v_{x0})/a_x)^2$$

$$x = x_0 + v_{x0} v_x/a_x - v_{x0}^2/a_x + \tfrac{1}{2} a_x (v_x^2/a^2_x + v_{x0}^2/a^2_x - 2 v_x v_{x0}/a^2_x)$$

$$x = x_0 + \underline{v_{x0} v_x/a_x} - v_{x0}^2/a_x + \tfrac{1}{2} v_x^2/a_x + \tfrac{1}{2} v_{x0}^2/a_x - \underline{v_x v_{x0}/a_x}.$$

Notice the underlined quantities cancel out and we can combine the other terms to get,

$$x = x_0 + \tfrac{1}{2} v_x^2/a_x - \tfrac{1}{2} v_{x0}^2/a_x = x_0 + \tfrac{1}{2} (v_x^2 - v_{x0}^2)/a_x$$

Rearranging, we arrive at the "shortcut equation,"

$$v_x^2 = v_{x0}^2 + 2 a_x (x - x_0).$$

Example Four.—*Another formula for average velocity.*

Start with the definition of average velocity given by equation (3) and use equations (10) and (9) to show that the average velocity over the time interval from time zero to time t is given by,

$$v_x(\text{avg}) = (v_x + v_{x0})/2$$

Solution.

From (3)

$$v_x(\text{average}) \equiv \Delta x/\Delta t = (x - x_0)/(t - 0)$$

$$v_x(\text{average}) = (x - x_0)/t$$

Using (10) for x in this gives,

$$v_x(\text{average}) = (v_{x0} t + \tfrac{1}{2} a_x t^2)/t = v_{x0} + \tfrac{1}{2} a_x t$$

Solving (9) for t and inserting that in the above equation gives,

$$t = (v_x - v_{x0})/a_x$$

$$v_x(\text{average}) = v_{x0} + \tfrac{1}{2} a_x ((v_x - v_{x0})/a_x) = v_{x0} + \tfrac{1}{2} v_x - \tfrac{1}{2} v_{x0}$$

which simplifies to the desired result,

$$v_x(\text{average}) = \tfrac{1}{2} (v_x + v_{x0}).$$

Example Five.—*Constant acceleration of a policeman.*

A typical car goes from zero to 60 mph in 6.7 s. Suppose a police car starts from rest with this acceleration. After 10 s find (a) the velocity of the car in m/s and the distance traveled in m. (1 mile = 1610 m and 1 h = 3600 s)

Solution.

(a) First convert v_x from 60 mph to m/s using the given conversion factors,

$$v_x = 60 \text{ miles/h } (1610 \text{ m/1 mile}) (1 \text{ h/ } 3600 \text{ s}) = 26.83 \text{ m/s}$$

Next, find the average acceleration which is also the instantaneous acceleration since the acceleration is constant,

$$a_x = \Delta v_x / \Delta t = (26.83 \text{m/s})/6.7 \text{ s} = 4 \text{ m/s}^2$$

Use this a_x in (9) with $t = 10$ s and zero initial velocity,

$$v_x = v_{x0} + a_x t = 0 + 4 (10) = \underline{40 \text{ m/s.}}$$

(b) The distance traveled is found using (10) with zero initial conditions and the acceleration we found above,

$$x = x_0 + v_{x0} t + \tfrac{1}{2} a_x t^2 = 0 + 0 + \tfrac{1}{2} 4 (10)^2$$

$$x = \underline{200 \text{ m.}}$$

Example Six.—*A policeman accelerating to catch a speeder moving with constant velocity.*

The above police car, again starting from rest, pursues a car that is moving with a constant velocity of 80 mph and is initially 300 m in front of the police car.

$$(1 \text{ mile} = 1610 \text{ m and } 1 \text{ h} = 3600 \text{ s})$$

(a) How many seconds does it take the policeman to catch up to the speeder and

(b) how fast is the police car traveling at the time in (a)?

Solution.

(a) Use the acceleration found in the previous problem, $a_x = 4$ m/s², in (10), along with the fact the police car has zero initial conditions (we place our origin at the initial location of the police car),

$$x = x_0 + v_{x0} t + \tfrac{1}{2} a_x t^2 = 0 + 0 + \tfrac{1}{2} 4 t^2 = 2 t^2. \quad \text{(police car)}$$

We need the position for the speeder. First, convert the speeder's speed from mph to m/s using the given conversion factors,

$$v_{x0} = 80 \text{ miles/h } (1610 \text{ m/1 mile}) (1 \text{ h/3600 s}) = 35.8 \text{ m/s}$$

Place this result into (5) since the speeder has a constant velocity, noting the speeder has an initial position of $x = 300$ m,

$$x = x_0 + v_{x0} t = 300 + 35.8 t \quad \text{(speeder)}$$

The police car catches the speeder when he has the same position, so equate the two positions,

$$x = 2 t^2 = 300 + 35.8 t,$$

or

$$2 t^2 - 35.8 t - 300 = 0.$$

Using the quadratic formula from elementary algebra we find the time,

$$t = \{35.8 \pm \sqrt{[(35.8)^2 - 4 (2)(-300)]}\}/(2 (2))$$

$$t = \underline{24.1 \text{ s}}$$

where we have used the positive root (the negative root leads to a negative time, which is unphysical here.)

(b) We use (9) to obtain the velocity of the police car when he catches up to the speeder, again the police car started from rest and from above has an acceleration of 4 m/s²

$$v_x = v_{x0} + a_x t = 0 + 4 (24.1s) = \underline{96.4 \text{ m/s}}.$$

This high velocity is somewhat unrealistic since normally the police car will slow down as it gets close to the speeder.

C. Special Motion: Free Fall.

One of the most common examples of motion is that of free fall, where an object near earth falls straight down to the ground along the y-axis or is thrown straight up away from earth. (It is traditional to use a y-axis rather than an x-axis when discussing free fall.) Based on laboratory tests, it is found that *all objects near earth accelerate with the same constant acceleration, g, provided we neglect air friction.* Measurements have been made and give g = 9.8 m/s².

IN THIS TEXTBOOK WE WILL OFTEN ROUND g to g = 10 m/s²

This means every second a falling object increases its speed by 10 m/s, a nice round number. Since the motion has constant acceleration we may use equations (9) and (10) to determine the position and velocity of a falling object. However, there are a couple of subtleties that must be addressed before we can solve free fall problems.

The first subtlety involves the sign of the acceleration in free fall. Do we use $a_y = g$ or $a_y = -g$? The answer to this question is infrequent in physics—it depends. Why? Because it depends on how we orient our y-axis, either pointed up or down relative to earth. Shown in Figure 6 is the geometry we are describing.

case i   a = −g = −10 m/s/s   case ii   a = +g = +10 m/s/s

FIG. 6. THE DIRECTION OF THE Y-AXIS DETERMINES THE SIGN
OF THE ACCELERATION.

Case i. Here we choose our +y-axis to point up, away from the earth. If a ball is thrown up it will have a positive velocity since it is moving in the +y direction (i.e. $\Delta y > 0$). But as it moves up it will be slowing down so that $\Delta v_y < 0$ and so its acceleration has to be a negative number, therefore $a_y = -g = -10$ m/s^2.

Consider the opposite situation where the ball is falling from a height. In this situation the ball will have a negative velocity since it is moving in the −y direction (i.e. $\Delta y < 0$). As the ball falls it is speeding up so, because the velocity is negative, we get $\Delta v_y < 0$ and $a_y = -g = -10$ m/s^2. This can be confusing, so let's put in some numbers. Say at time zero the ball has a downward velocity of −10 m/s. Because $g = 10$ m/s/s, each second it will speed up by 10 m/s. At time 1 second the ball will have a downward velocity of −20 m/s. Therefore, its (average) acceleration over the 1 s interval is

$$a_y(\text{avg}) = (-20 - -10)/1s = (-20 + 10)/1s = -10 \text{ m/s}^2.$$

Since a_y is constant, its average equals the instantaneous, $a_y = a_y(\text{avg}) = -10 \text{m/s}^2$.

We conclude, whether the ball is going up or coming down it will have a constant negative acceleration, −10 m/s^2.

Case ii. Using similar reasoning, when the +y-axis points toward the earth the value of the constant acceleration, whether the object is going up or falling, is $a_y = +g = +10$ m/s^2.

The equations that describe an object in free fall are then those we already developed for motion in one dimension with constant acceleration, namely equations (9) and (10). One only needs to draw a coordinate system, determine from the orientation of your coordinate system whether a_y is +g or −g (see above discussion), and place into the equations the initial conditions, y_0 and $v_{y,0}$. The value for y_0 will depend on where you place the origin of your coordinate system—you must know where your origin is to solve free fall problems and so it is necessary to make a diagram. The examples below will illustrate these ideas.

Example Seven.—*The movie* **Vertigo.**

In the beginning of the Alfred Hitchcock thriller film *Vertigo*, a police officer falls from a skyscraper while chasing a villain. If the officer takes 6.0 s to fall, find (a) his speed just before hitting the ground and (b) the height of the building.

Solution.

(a) Place the origin of the y-axis at the top of the building and let the positive direction point up. Then $t = 6$ s, $a_y = -10$ m/s^2 and since the police officer started from rest, v_{y0} is zero. Using these data in (9),

$$v_y = v_{y0} + a_y t = 0 - 10t = -10\,(6\text{ s}) = -60 \text{ m/s},$$

his speed at the ground is $|v_y| = $ 60 m/s. This makes sense because each second of the 6 s fall his speed increases by 10 m/s.

(b) Using zero initial conditions in (10),

$$y = y_0 + v_{y0} t + \tfrac{1}{2} a_y t^2 = 0 + 0 + \tfrac{1}{2}(-10)\,(6)^2 = -5(36) = -180 \text{ m},$$

and so the height of the building is 180 m.

Example Eight.—*Falling past a window.*

For the officer in the previous example, find the time for the officer to pass a 1.5 m tall window that has its upper side a distance of 20.0 m below the roof of the building where the officer fell from.

Solution.

Let's find the time when the officer reaches the top of the window by using (10) with zero initial conditions and $y = -20$ m,

$$y = -20 \text{ m} = y_0 + v_{y0} t + \tfrac{1}{2} a_y t^2 = 0 + 0 + \tfrac{1}{2}(-10)t^2$$

Solving this for t we get,

$$t = \sqrt{[(-20)(2)/(-10)]} = \sqrt{4} = 2 \text{ s}.$$

Do the same thing over again but this time find the time when he gets to the bottom of the window where $y = -21.5$ m.

$$y = -21.5 \text{ m} = y_0 + v_{y0} t + 1/2\, a_y t^2 = 0 + 0 + 1/2\,(-10)t^2,$$

$$t = \sqrt{[(-21.5)(2)/(-10)]} = \sqrt{4.3} = 2.07 \text{ s}.$$

Taking the difference gives the answer, $2.07 - 2 = $ 0.07 s.

D. Curved Graphs, Tangent Lines, and Instantaneous Quantities.

To recap, we started with a marble at rest and found the x vs t graph is a horizontal straight line. Next, we examined the x vs t graph of a marble's motion where the line was tilted. The corresponding v_x vs t graph was a horizontal straight line indicative of motion with constant velocity. Then

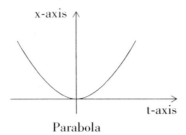

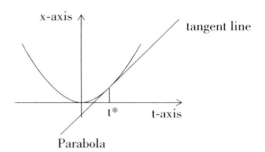

FIG. 7A. POSITION VERSUS
TIME FOR CONSTANT
ACCELERATION.

FIG. 7B. VELOCITY AT TIME T* IS THE
SLOPE OF THE TANGENT TO THE
POSITION VERSUS TIME GRAPH AT T*.

we considered a tilted straight line graph of v_x vs t and found this corresponds to motion with constant acceleration, a_x. The graph of position versus time when the acceleration is constant can be found from equation (10), which is quadratic in t since t is raised to the second power. The curve one finds is a familiar mathematical curve called a parabola which typically looks like the graph in Figure 7a.

By considering two points on the graph in Figure 7a, the average velocity may be calculated for the corresponding time interval by finding the slope of the line segment joining the two points. As these two points get closer together, the calculated average velocity gets closer to the instantaneous velocity, for then Δt gets small. The line segment connecting the two points becomes parallel to the so-called tangent line when Δt approaches zero (see Figure 7b). The tangent line just touches the curve at one time, t^*, and has an inclination matching that of the curve. The *slope of the tangent line at t^* is precisely what we mean by (instantaneous) velocity at t^*.* (For students who are familiar with calculus, the velocity is the first derivative of the position function.)

Once the velocity is found at a number of times, a graph of velocity versus time can be produced. Recall from before, *the displacement from time zero to time t is the area under the velocity versus time graph from time zero to time t.* Therefore, by finding the area under the velocity versus time graph obtained one can find the position versus time graph. (For students who are familiar with calculus, the area under the curve is the integral.)

Example Nine.—*Position versus time of a rocket.*

The graph of position versus time for a rocket is shown below. Use this graph to determine the velocity of the rocket at time $t^* = 4.0$ s.

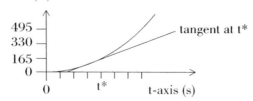

Solution.

We determine the velocity at t^* by finding the slope of the tangent line drawn on the figure at time t^*,

$$v_y = \text{rise/run} = \underline{60 \text{ m/s}} .$$

Summary.

Galileo introduced the basic building blocks for motion: position, velocity and acceleration. These are reviewed for the case of one dimensional motion. The equations describing motion with constant velocity and constant acceleration are presented. The latter is pertinent to free fall. Motion can be understood either algebraically or graphically. The tangent to a position versus time curve may be drawn and from its slope the velocity is determined. The acceleration is the slope of the tangent to the velocity versus time graph.

QUESTIONS.

1. Zeno was a pupil of the famous Pre-Socratic Greek philosopher Parmenides. Zeno lived during the 5th century BCE and is most famous for several paradoxes he created that suggest motion is impossible. This conclusion sounds preposterous but consider his first paradox (called "the dichotomy") before dismissing him as insane. Suppose you want to cross a football field. Here is Zeno's argument.

Premises:

I. To cross the field you would have to cross an infinite number of points.

II. An infinite number of points is an infinite distance.

III. To travel an infinite distance will require an infinite amount of time.

Conclusion:

Crossing the field and motion is impossible.

Criticize Zeno's argument.

2. Zeno's second paradox concerns a race between "Achilles and the Tortoise " (see previous question for information on Zeno). Achilles was a Greek soldier and hero who supposedly fought in the Trojan War. Achilles gives the tortoise a head start in the race. Achilles runs much faster than the tortoise who is up ahead but in this paradox it is argued Achilles can never catch up to the tortoise. Here is the argument.

Premises:

I. There is initially a space between Achilles and the tortoise.

II. When Achilles arrives at a point where the tortoise had been, the tortoise will have moved ahead to a new place.

III. Achilles can never catch up to the tortoise and therefore, the tortoise wins the race.

Conclusion:

The slower moves as fast as the faster and this is a contradiction. Consequently, motion is impossible.

Criticize Zeno's argument.

3. This is a Fermi problem—there is no right answer. In the Bible we find the story of the exodus of the Hebrew slaves out of Egypt and we are told the number of Hebrews was " ... about 600,000 men on foot, besides women and children." (Exodus 12:37) Estimate how long a line of people this would be in miles.

4. Estimate how much time would be required for the Hebrew escapees to pass a given point on the road (see the previous problem).

5. An ancient marathoner covered the first 20 miles of the race in 4 hours. Can you determine how fast he was running when he passed the 10-mile marker? Explain.

6. A motorcycle moves along the +x-axis and is slowing down. Which of the following is true?

(*a*) $v_x > 0$ and $a_x > 0$

(*b*) $v_x > 0$ and $a_x = 0$

(*c*) $v_x < 0$ and $a_x < 0$

(*d*) $v_x > 0$ and $a_x < 0$

(*e*) one cannot answer the question without additional information such as numbers

7. A student goes to the top of a tall building and drops two bowling balls of the same shape and size but one of the balls weighs 20 pounds while the other weighs only 2 pounds. Describe what Galileo would predict as the outcome of this experiment and what Aristotle would predict. Neglect air friction.

8. A baseball player runs from home plate to first base. Estimate his acceleration during the first phase of his motion when he is speeding up.

9. Estimate the maximum speed with which you can throw a ball straight up into the air.

10. Assume that in the same time interval the following accelerations occur:
Airplane goes from 500 to 520 mph
Automobile goes from 60 to 70 mph
Bicycle goes from 0 to 10 mph

Which, if any, of these has the largest acceleration?

The following two questions are from *Peer Instruction*, Eric Mazur (Prentice-Hall, 1997) who took the questions from: David Hestenes and Malcolm Wells, A Mechanics Baseline Test, *The Physics Teacher* **30**, March 1992, p. 159–166.

The diagram below represents a multiflash photograph of an object (represented by the small circles) moving along a horizontal surface. The positions next to the ruler are separated by equal time intervals. The first flash occurred when the object was at rest at the origin and the last flash occurred when the object just came to rest.

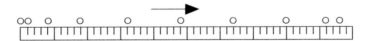

11. Select the graph below that best represents the velocity versus time for this particle.

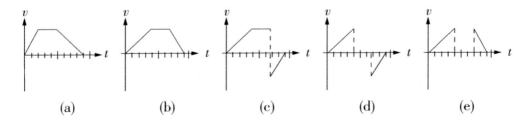

(a)   (b)   (c)   (d)   (e)

12. Select the graph below that best represents the particle's acceleration versus time.

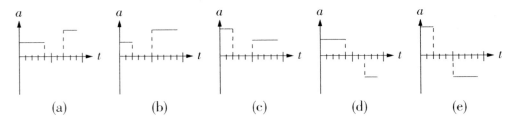

   (a)   (b)   (c)   (d)   (e)

13. A ball is thrown straight up. What is its acceleration at the top of its flight?

14. Is $\Delta v / \Delta x$ constant in free fall? Prove your answer. Historically, Galileo had to decide which is constant in free fall, $\Delta v / \Delta x$ or $\Delta v / \Delta t$.

PROBLEMS.

1. A spacecraft travels in a straight line a distance of 1200.0 m with an average velocity of 20.0 m/s. Determine the time interval for this motion.

2. An automobile moves along a straight highway at the rate of 25 km/hr for four minutes then 50 km/hr for eight minutes and lastly, 20 km/hr for two minutes. Assume the car is always traveling east. Find the total distance traveled.

3. In the previous problem, determine the average velocity of the automobile.

4. A high-speed camera takes pictures of the position of a motorcycle at a rate of 2400 pictures per minute. If the motorcycle has a speed of 100 km/hr, how far does it travel in between picture frames?

5. An average person can walk 1 kilometer in 10 minutes. Calculate the person's speed in mph.

6. How long would it take the average person in the previous problem to walk 3.5 miles?

7. A typical car driver in the US travels 25,000 miles annually. Assuming the average speed of travel while in the car is 45 mph, find the total number of hours an average driver spends in their car per year and per day.

The next two problems are from *Peer Instruction*, Eric Mazur (Prentice-Hall, 1997) who took the questions from: David Hestenes and Malcolm Wells, A Mechanics Baseline Test, *The Physics Teacher* **30**, March 1992, p. 159–166.

The graph below represents the motion of a particle along the x-axis.

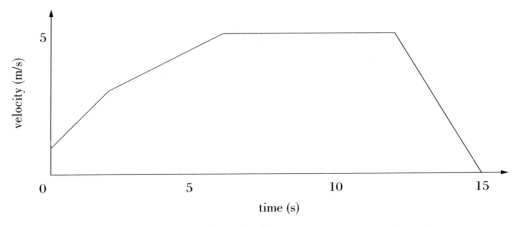

8. Determine the particle's average acceleration between time zero and $t = 6$ s.

   (a) 3.0 m/s²

   (b) 1.5 m/s²

   (c) 0.83 m/s²

   (d) 0.67 m/s²

   (e) none of the above

9. How far did the particle travel between time zero and $t = 6$ s?

   (a) 20.0 m

   (b) 8.0 m

   (c) 6.0 m

   (d) 1.5 m

   (e) none of the above

10. A young boy running with a speed of 7 m/s slides into third base. If the boy's acceleration is −4 m/s², how much time is required for the boy to stop?

11. At a drag strip automobiles travel 0.25 miles in a typical time of 6 s. Determine the average acceleration of the dragster in m/s².

12. Find the speed, in mph, of the dragster in problem 11 at the end of the drag strip assuming the acceleration is constant.

13. One of the world's tallest buildings is the Sears Tower in Chicago. The height of the tower is 443 m. Ignoring friction, how long would it take a penny to hit the ground starting from rest at the top of this building?

14. How fast would the penny in the previous problem be traveling just before it hit the ground? Express your answer also in mph.

15. A marble dropped from a bridge strikes the water in 5.0 s. Find the speed of the marble just before its strikes the water.

16. Find the height of the bridge in the previous problem.

17. A basketball player can jump 28 inches off the floor from a standing position. Calculate the player's speed when leaving the floor.

18. A rock is gently dropped into a deep well. It takes 3.16 s before you hear the splash of the rock at the bottom of the well. Assuming the speed of sound is infinite, how deep is the well?

19. The tortoise and the hare are at the starting line together. As the race begins the tortoise moves off at a constant speed of 0.2 m/s. The hare starts from rest at the starting line but waits 30 s, then has a constant acceleration of 2 m/s². At what time (after the 30 s) does the hare catch up to the tortoise?

20. A herd of bulls stampede at a constant speed of 7 m/s. A cowboy, initially at rest 20 m in front of the bulls, accelerates at the constant rate of 3 m/s². Will the herd trample the cowboy? Justify your answer.

21. Allegedly Galileo dropped two rocks from the Leaning Tower of Pisa. The tower is 55 m high, and for this problem assume the tower is vertical, i.e. not leaning. Suppose Galileo accidentally dropped one of the rocks 0.5 s before the other. How fast would he have to throw the rock that was dropped later so that both rocks reach the ground at the same time?

22. A cannon is fired vertically upward— not a smart thing to do, but this is physics. The cannon ball has an initial speed of 50 m/s. How long is the ball in the air for the total trip up and back? Neglect air friction and the length of the barrel of the cannon.

Hints and answers to problems.

1) 60.0 s   2) 9.0 km   3) 10.7 m/s   4) 0.69 m   5) Hint: 0.447 m/s = 1 mph 3.73 mph
6) 0.94 h   7) Hint: 1 year = 365 days. 556 h and 1.52 h   8) (d)   9) Hint: consider the area under the curve. (a)   10) 1.75 s   11) Hint: 1 mile = 1609 m 22.3 m/s^2 12) Hint: 0.447 m/s = 1 mph 299 mph   13) Using a = 10 m/s^2, 9.4 s   14) 0.447 m/s = 1 mph 94 m/s or 210 mph.
15) 50 m/s   16) 125 m.   17) Hint: 1 m = 39.4 in 3.8 m/s   18) 50 m   19) Hint: use the quadratic formula. 2.55 s   20) no, using the quadratic formula the time is imaginary when the bull's position equals the cowboy's   21) Hint: use the quadratic formula. 5.38 m/s   22) 10 s

CHAPTER III.
MOTION IN TWO DIMENSIONS.

Abstract.

In this chapter we begin with a discussion of how to add and subtract vectors. These ideas are then used to model the position and velocity components for a particle undergoing projectile motion. Projectile motion is a combination of motion with constant velocity and motion with constant acceleration. A number of applications of projectile motion are presented. Finally, uniform circular motion is investigated.

Definitions. scalar, vector, vector addition, negative of a vector, vector subtraction, net force, centripetal acceleration, and period of motion

Principles. adding and subtracting vectors, independence of x and y motions

Fundamental Equations. the four equations for $x(t)$, $y(t)$, $v_x(t)$, $v_y(t)$ that describe projectile motion, centripetal acceleration

A. Vector Addition and Subtraction.

In physics there are numerous quantities among which are entities called **scalars** (e.g. temperature, mass, etc.) and **vectors** (e.g. velocity, acceleration, force, electric field, etc.). Scalars are quantities that are fully described by a number and a unit (e. g. his mass is 80 kg). Scalars are familiar to everyone since they obey ordinary arithmetic, that is, we add and subtract scalars just like we add and subtract ordinary numbers.

Vector quantities, however, are not fully described by a single number but require for their complete specification two numbers called the magnitude (or length) and direction. Vectors are represented by an arrow; the magnitude of the vector is found from the length of the arrow and the direction is given by the direction of the arrow relative to a coordinate system. Vectors are, therefore, more complicated than scalars and so vectors tend to give people heartburn at first. Nevertheless, understanding how to manipulate vectors is crucial to success in physics since many objects in physics are vectors and frequently we must add or subtract them. As we progress in the study of physics it will be necessary to define vector multiplication but this topic will be delayed until needed. Let us now define vector addition.

Consider two cowboys, Hoss and Little Joe (not shown), pulling on a steer with two ropes (Figure 1). For simplicity assume the forces are parallel to the ground. In the figure we are looking down from above.

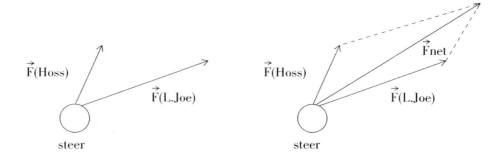

FIG. 1. VIEW FROM ABOVE OF TWO ROPES PULLING ON A STEER BY COWBOYS.
$\vec{F}$NET IS THE VECTOR SUM OF THE TWO FORCES.

The steer will undergo some kind of motion as a result of the tension in the two ropes. Suppose it is desirable to replace the two tensions with a single tension that will have the same effect as the original two ropes. This single tension is called the vector sum of the original tensions. The vector sum of the forces is a vector called the ***net force***. We write the sum as,

$$\vec{F}_{net} = \vec{F}_{Hoss} + \vec{F}_{L.Joe}.$$

There are two ways to determine the vector sum, the geometrical (or head to tail) method and the algebraic method.

Geometric or Head to Tail Method of Vector Addition.

For this technique one needs a ruler and a protractor. The first step is to establish a scale. For example, using graph paper that has a square grid on it, we could define our scale as: 1 cm = 1 Newton of force (a Newton is the unit of force). Place a Cartesian coordinate system on our graph paper with the origin coinciding with the steer. Suppose Hoss' rope makes an angle of 60° with our +x-axis (the x-axis is horizontal in Figure 1) and the angle for Little Joe's rope is 30° (this is about how we've drawn $\vec{F}_{Hoss}$ and $\vec{F}_{L.Joe}$ in Figure 1). Using your protractor draw lines from the origin that are at 30° and 60° above the +x-axis. Next, suppose the magnitude or length of the forces are $\vec{F}_{Hoss}$ = 10 N while $\vec{F}_{L.Joe}$ = 20 N. Use the ruler to mark off a distance of 10 cm along the line tilted at 60° and place an arrow on the end of that line segment, this will be the arrow that represents $\vec{F}_{Hoss}$. Use the same procedure to represent the force by Little Joe, where the ruler marks off a distance of 20 cm. The picture you get will look like the left side of Figure 1. The next step is to use the two arrows representing $\vec{F}_{Hoss}$ and $\vec{F}_{L.Joe}$ to create a parallelogram as is seen on the right in Figure 1. Draw the diagonal that begins at the origin where the tail of the two vectors coincide. Using your ruler and protractor you can measure the length of the diagonal and the angle it makes with the +x-axis. The diagonal is, by definition, the vector sum or $\vec{F}_{net}$!

Of course, most normal people do not carry a ruler and protractor on their person. In practice often the geometric method is used to *approximate* a vector sum. For more accurate work the algebraic method of vector addition is used.

Example One.—*Adding vectors geometrically.*

Use a ruler and protractor to find $\vec{F}_{net}$ in the figure below. Let 1 mm = 1 Newton and place your work to the right of the figure.

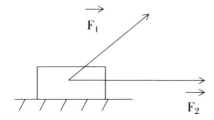

Algebraic Method of Vector Addition.

A new term is required before presenting the algebraic method of vector addition. In Figure 2 is shown a vector $\vec{F}$ with its tail at the origin of a Cartesian coordinate system.

Shown also are what are known as the components of $\vec{F}$. The components are found by drawing line segments—the dashed lines in Figure 2—from the head of $\vec{F}$ to the x-axis and y-axis. Therefore, every vector $\vec{F}$ will have an x-component, F_x and a

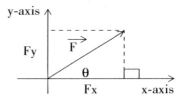

FIG. 2. COMPONENTS (F_X AND F_Y) OF A VECTOR $\vec{F}$.

y-component, F_y. The figure contains a right triangle with sides F_x and F_y, and hypotenuse $\vec{F}$ that makes an angle θ with the +x-axis. On examining the right triangle and remembering some elementary trigonometry we write,

$$\sin\theta \equiv F_y/F \quad \cos\theta \equiv F_x/F \quad \tan\theta \equiv F_y/F_x . \tag{1}$$

Equation (1) gives a way of expressing the components of the vector $\vec{F}$ in terms of its length, F, and its angle, θ:

$$F_x = F\cos\theta \quad \text{and} \quad F_y = F\sin\theta. \tag{2}$$

Using equation (2) to find the components of a vector is often phrased "resolving the vector into its components."

In some situations the components may be known but the length and angle of the vector $\vec{F}$ is desired. From the Pythagorean theorem and the tangent in equation (1) we use,

$$F = \sqrt{(F_x^2 + F_y^2)} \quad \text{and} \quad \theta = \tan^{-1}(F_y/F_x) \tag{3}$$

With this understanding of how to find the components of a vector we can return to the original question, which was, "how do we add two forces algebraically?" That is,

$$\vec{F} = \vec{F_1} + \vec{F_2} = ?$$

$\vec{F}$ is found by a two step process in the algebraic method of vector addition.

Algebraic Method of Vector Addition.

Step One. Find the x and y components of both forces in the sum. That is, using sines and cosines determine

$$F_{1x}, F_{1y}, F_{2x} \text{ and } F_{2y} .$$

Step Two. Add the corresponding components to get the components of the sum. That is,

$$F_x = F_{1x} + F_{2x} \quad \text{and} \quad F_y = F_{1x} + F_{2y} .$$

It is not difficult to prove the geometric and algebraic definitions give consistent results.

Example Two.—*Components of a vector: treasure map.*

A pirate discovers a treasure map while stranded on a desert island. The map is shown below. X marks the location of the loot. Find the x- and y- components of the position vector from the origin to the treasure, and its magnitude and the angle it makes with the +x-axis by using a ruler and a protractor. Use the scale: 1 mm = 100 m.

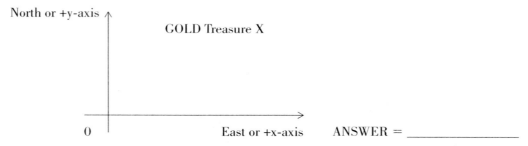

Example Three.—*Adding vectors algebraically.*

Find the x- and y- components of the vector sum of the two force vectors,

$$\vec{F_1} = 100 \text{ N along } x \quad \text{and} \quad \vec{F_2} = 300 \text{ N at } 30° \text{ to the +x-axis.}$$

Solution.

Along x, $100 + 300 \cos 30°$ N $= 100 + 260 = 360$ N and for y, $300 \sin 30° = 150$ N.

$$\vec{F}_{net} = \underline{360 \text{ N along x and } 150 \text{ N along y}}$$

Vector subtraction is also a common operation in physics. Subtraction is defined as adding the negative of a vector,

$$\vec{A} - \vec{B} \equiv \vec{A} + (-\vec{B}).$$

The negative of a vector is a vector of the same length but opposite direction to the original vector. For example, $-\vec{B}$ has the same magnitude as $\vec{B}$ but points in the opposite direction to $\vec{B}$.

This completes our study of vectors for the time being. Our first application of vectors is to the problem of projectile motion.

B. Special Motion: Projectile Motion.

In the everyday world of baseballs and planets there are four types of motion that are very common. These are: free fall, which we already examined, projectile motion, which is the current topic, and later we will consider circular motion and vibrations.

Historically, the motion of projectiles was crucial in the debate between Galileo, who held the heliocentric model of the universe which assumes a stationary sun, and the Aristotelian authorities of his day who held the geocentric model of the universe which assumes a stationary earth. Galileo wrote about taking a stone to the top of a tall tower (e.g. in Pisa) and dropping it. All were in agreement that if the earth is stationary then the stone would hit at the base of the tower. The Aristotelian church fathers of Galileo's day argued against Galileo by saying that if the earth is rotating then as the stone drops the earth moves and leaves the stone behind so that the stone will hit the ground some distance from the base of the tower. On the contrary, Galileo argued that as the stone drops vertically it maintains its constant horizontal motion that it shares with the moving earth, and therefore, this explains why the stone lands at the base of the tower. Then Galileo strengthened his stance further by considering dropping a stone from the crow's nest of a moving sailboat. Even though the sailboat (like the earth) is moving, the stone moves both vertically as it falls but continues to participate in the horizontal motion of the sailboat (earth), thus showing how the stone lands right below the crow's nest.

Examples of projectiles include balls, bombs, etc., i.e. anything that you project into the air that does not go straight up or straight down. We further assume the motion takes place near the surface of the earth so that the acceleration due to gravity, g, can be approximated as a constant. Finally, the affect of friction is ignored. The general problem of throwing a ball is illustrated in Figure 3. This figure is a snapshot at time zero.

It is extremely important in working a projectile motion problem to start with a coordinate system and to know where you are placing your origin of coordinates. Frequently, the

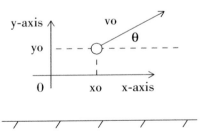

FIG. 3. PROJECTILE MOTION.

origin is placed on the surface of the Earth but not always. The initial velocity of the ball shown in the figure has x- and y- components given by,

$$v_{0x} = v_0 \cos\theta \quad \text{and} \quad v_{0y} = v_0 \sin\theta. \tag{4}$$

The ball has an initial velocity making an angle of θ with the +x-axis and an initial speed denoted, v_0. The initial position vector of the ball has components denoted x_0 and y_0. To understand this problem imagine that a spotlight is placed overhead and the ball casts a shadow on the ground below. As the ball flies through the air, the shadow on the ground is found to move with a constant velocity of $v_{0x} = v_0 \cos\theta$. The shadow has a position from the origin at time t given by the formula for motion with constant velocity, $x(t) = x_0 + v_{0x}t = x_0 + v_0\cos\theta\, t$. The y-component of the motion may also be understood in terms of a shadow. This time, however, we imagine that a spotlight is shone parallel to the ground with the ball casting a shadow on a building. From experiment it is found that the shadow on the building moves with a constant acceleration, $-g$, as in free fall. The y-component of the velocity and position vectors follow from our study of free fall, $v_y(t) = v_{0y} + a_y t$ and $y(t) = y_0 + v_{0y}t + \frac{1}{2} a_y t^2$ where $a_y = -g$, $v_{0y} = v_0 \sin\theta$ and we have assumed the geometry of Figure 3 with the +y-axis pointed up. These equations are used to solve *all* problems involving projectiles and they are summarized in Table 1 below. What remains is to contemplate examples and work homework problems for practice.

Equations of Projectile Motion.

Horizontal, x	Vertical, y
constant velocity	constant acceleration
$a_x = 0$	$a_y = -g$
$x(t) = x_0 + v_{0x}t$	$y(t) = y_0 + v_{0y}t + \frac{1}{2} a_y t^2$
$v_x(t) = v_{0x}$	$v_y(t) = v_{0y} + a_y t$

where $v_{0x} = v_0 \cos\theta$ and $v_{0y} = v_0 \sin\theta$

and +y points up.

TABLE 1. PROJECTILE MOTION.

C. Application: Projectiles.

Refer back to the equations in Table 1 in all of the examples below.

Example Four.—*Trajectory or path of a projectile.*

A marble rests on a horizontal table top. Richard flicks the marble giving it a speed v_0 and the marble flies off the end of the table. Let's place the origin at the point where the marble leaves the table and choose our x-axis horizontal and y-axis vertical, see the figure below. Choose time zero when the marble leaves the table.

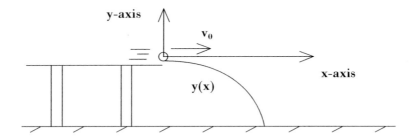

We would like to obtain a mathematical function, $y(x)$, that describes the path (also called the trajectory) of the marble as it flies off the table and eventually hits the floor.

Solution.

From the figure and the above information we identify, $x_0 = y_0 = \theta = 0$, and so $v_{0x} = v_0$ and $v_{0y} = 0$. Using these in Table 1 gives $x = v_0 t$ and $y = -1/2\, g\, t^2$. Solving the first result for time gives $t = x/v_0$, and using this t in the second equation gives our final result (recall from mathematics this is the equation for a *parabola*)

$$y = -1/2\, g\, x^2/v_0^2$$

Example Five.—*Artillery in World War I.*

Big Bertha was a massive artillery gun that was used during WWI. The shell had a range of 62 miles when shot at an angle of 45°. Find (a) the initial speed of the shell and (b) the time it takes for the shell to reach its maximum height. Neglect air friction.

Solution.

(a) Assume the origin is on the ground and that is where the shell leaves the gun. From Table 1 using $x_0 = y_0 = y = 0$ we have,

$$x = v_0\cos\theta\, t \rightarrow t = x/(v_0\cos\theta) \quad \text{and} \quad y = 0 = v_0\sin\theta\, t - \tfrac{1}{2}\, g\, t^2 \rightarrow 0 = v_0\sin\theta - \tfrac{1}{2}\, gt$$

and using the above expression for t in the last expression gives,

$$0 = v_0\sin\theta - \tfrac{1}{2}\, g\, (x/v_0\cos\theta).$$

Solving for v_0,

$$v_0^2 = g\, x/(2\, \sin\theta\, \cos\theta),$$

and putting in the numbers ($x = 62$ miles $\times$ 1610 m/mile = 99820 m and $\theta = 45°$),

$$v_0 = \sqrt{9.8\, (99820)/(2\sin45\, \cos45)} = \underline{989\ \text{m/s}}.$$

(b) Denote the time when the shell is at its maximum height, t^*. At that time the velocity vector of the shell is horizontal and therefore, $v_y(t^*) = 0$. Using this in the y-velocity equation in Table 1, we have

$$v_y(t^*) = 0 = v_0 \sin\theta - gt^*,$$

and this gives for t^*, $t^* = v_0 \sin\theta/g = 989 \sin(45)/9.8 = \underline{71 \text{ s}}$.

Example Six.—*Is it a homerun?*

Babe Ruth hits a ball, and the ball leaves the bat at a height of 1.2 m above the ground with an initial velocity of 25.0 m/s at an angle of 30° above the ground. The ball heads straight for center field where there is a 3 m tall fence that is a distance of 40 m from home plate. Determine whether or not this hit is a homerun.

Solution.

Place the origin on home plate with the x-axis pointed toward center field. We have, $x_0 = 0$, $y_0 = 1.2$ m, $v_0 = 25$ m/s, $\theta = 30°$, and $x = 40$ m, and place these in Table 1 to obtain,

$$x = v_0\cos\theta \, t \text{ and this gives,} \quad t = x/(v_0\cos\theta)$$

$$t = 40/(25\cos(30)) = \underline{1.85 \text{ s}}.$$

This gives for y,

$$y = y_0 + v_0\sin\theta \, t - \tfrac{1}{2} g \, t^2$$

$$y = 1.2 + 25(\sin30) \, 1.85 - \tfrac{1}{2} 9.8 \, (1.85)^2 = \underline{7.53 \text{ m}}.$$

Since $7.53 > 3$ m, this is easily a HOMERUN! Incidentally, it gives comfort to all of us mortals to recall the fact that Babe Ruth struck out more times than he homered.

Example Seven.—*The flight of an electron in a television picture tube.*

An electron emerges from the "electron gun" inside a TV tube with a speed of 1×10^8 m/s in a horizontal direction. The screen of the TV is a distance of 30 cm away. Find how far the electron drops due to gravity as it just hits the screen.

Solution.

Place the origin at the location of the electron as it emerges from the electron gun with +x-axis pointing toward the screen and the +y-axis pointing up. Then we have, $x_0 = y_0 = \theta = 0$, $x = 0.3$ m, and $v_0 = 1 \times 10^8$ m/s. Using these numbers in the $x(t)$ and $y(t)$ equations in Table 1 gives,

$$x(t) = 0 + v_0 t \quad \text{and} \quad y(t) = 0 + 0 - \tfrac{1}{2} gt^2.$$

Solving the $x(t)$ equation for t, $t = x(t)/v_0$, and substituting this in the second equation for t,

$$y = -\tfrac{1}{2} g \, (x/v_0)^2 = -\tfrac{1}{2} 9.8 \, (0.3/10^8)^2 = \underline{-4.4 \times 10^{-17} \text{ m}}.$$

The drop of the electron is utterly negligible—one may safely ignore the effects of gravity.

Example Eight.—*Assassination physics: JFK.*

Courtesy of Associated Press.

Courtesy of Associated Press.

On the tragic afternoon of Friday, November 22, 1963, the president of the United States, John F. Kennedy, was shot in Dallas, Texas by a lone gunman, Lee Harvey Oswald. Oswald was perched on the sixth floor of the Texas School Book Depository from where he fired three bullets from an Italian Mannlicher-Carcano rifle. The first bullet missed, the second (the so called "magic bullet") hit the president in the back and passed on to wound the governor of Texas, John Connally, who was seated in front of the president. The third bullet fatally wounded the president in the head. The diagram below is a sketch of the trajectory of the third bullet. From the references cited below we have:

h = distance from the gun to president = 265.3 ft, y_0 = vertical elevation of gun above the level of the president's head = 70.23 ft and v_0 = initial speed of the bullet = 2000 ft/s. Below use $g = 32$ ft/s^2.

(a) Neglecting air friction and making the approximation that the bullet travels along the straight line from the gun to the president, find the time of flight, *t,* of the bullet.

(b) Use the projectile motion equations to determine the initial angle the bullet makes below the horizontal, the angle θ in the diagram below. This angle is the angle Oswald aimed the gun to hit the president.

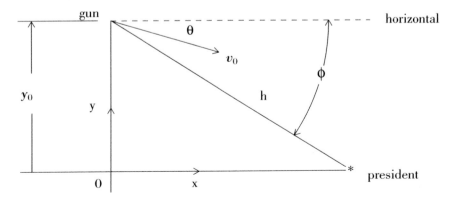

Solution.

(a) Solving, $v_0 = h/t$, for the time t,

$$t = h/v_0 = 265.3/2000 = \underline{0.13265} \text{ s}.$$

This answer is not exact but it should be very close to the actual time of flight.

(b) The relevant projectile motion equation is,

$$y = y_0 - v_0 \sin\theta\, t - \tfrac{1}{2}\, g\, t^2.$$

Substituting in $y = 0$ and solving for $\sin\theta$,

$$\sin\theta = \{y_0 - \tfrac{1}{2}\, g\, t^2\}/(v_0\, t) = y_0/(v_0\, t) - \tfrac{1}{2}\, g\, t/v_0.$$

Placing the above data in along with the answer to (a),

$$\sin\theta = 70.23/(2000 \times 0.13265) - \tfrac{1}{2}\, 32\, (0.13265)/2000 = 0.26472 - 0.001061 = 0.26366$$

or

$$\theta = \sin^{-1}(0.26366) = \underline{15.29°}.$$

According to p. 108 of the *Warren Commission Report* the angle between the line connecting the gun to the president and the horizontal, ϕ in the above diagram, was measured to be 15.35°, a little larger than the answer we found in (b). Oswald had to aim his gun slightly above this line in order to take into account the effect of gravity on the bullet. Incidentally, Oswald used a telescopic lens.

In the year following the assassination the Warren Commission investigated the shooting and concluded Oswald shot the president acting alone. The full Warren Commission deliberations were published in 26 volumes in addition to a one volume summary that is cited below. Dozens of books have been written alleging a conspiracy. Before you believe any of the conspiracy theories, however, I suggest you read the three works cited below. These works leave very little room for doubting the findings of the Warren Commission.

1. *Warren Commission Report* (Longmeadows, 1992). 2. *Reclaiming History*, Vincent Bugliosi (Norton, 2007), and 3. *Case Closed*, Gerald Posner (Random House, 1993). Reference 2, *Reclaiming History*, is a massive (>1500 pages) treatise that supports the Warren Commission conclusion, i.e. Oswald acted alone in killing the president.

D. Special Motion: Uniform Circular Motion.

Another special type of motion is motion in a circle with constant speed. This is called uniform circular motion where uniform indicates the speed is constant. Non-uniform circular motion would have the speed changing. Because all points of a circle are identical, there is no place one could call the beginning or end of circular motion. That which has no beginning or end is eternal. The eternal is perfect. Using this rather lofty language, the ancient Greeks viewed uniform circular motion as the perfect kind of motion. They reasoned, the heavens are perfect, so only uniform circular motion occurs in the heavens.

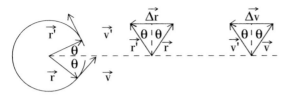

FIG. 4. POSITION AND VELOCITY VECTORS AT
TWO TIMES FOR A PARTICLE IN UNIFORM
CIRCULAR MOTION. THE CHANGE IN POSITION
AND VELOCITY VECTORS ARE ALSO SHOWN.

Coming back down to earth, we now proceed to develop the kinematics of uniform circular motion. The explanation will be based on Figure 4.

In this figure we are looking down on the circular motion of a particle that has a constant speed of $v = |\vec{v}'| = |\vec{v}|$. The radius of the circle is $r = |\vec{r}'| = |\vec{r}|$. Looking on the left in the figure, let's say the particle is at position $\vec{r}$ at an angle θ below the horizontal dashed line. The particle takes a time interval Δt to go from $\vec{r}$ to the position $\vec{r}'$, which is at an angle θ above the dashed line. If we assume Δt is very small then during the time interval the particle will have moved through a displacement,

$$\Delta r = v\,\Delta t, \quad \text{where} \quad \Delta r = |\Delta \vec{r}|.$$

Next, consider the two isosceles triangles to the right in the above figure. The triangles are formed from the position and velocity vectors. Since the triangles have the same angles they are similar triangles, and recall from geometry that for similar triangles the ratio of corresponding sides are equal, that is,

$$\Delta r/r = \Delta v/v.$$

Substituting the former result for Δr in this last equation gives,

$$\Delta r/r = v\Delta t/r = \Delta v/v,$$

and rearranging this gives,

$$\Delta v/\Delta t = v^2/r.$$

The left-hand side of the last result is by definition the acceleration,

$$a = v^2/r \tag{5}$$

Furthermore, from the figure it is clear $\Delta \vec{v}$, and therefore $\vec{a}$, point toward the center of the circle. For this reason the acceleration vector whose magnitude is given by equation (5) is called *cen-tripetal acceleration* which comes from Greek and means "center seeking."

Often times one is given the radius of circular motion and the "period." The *period, T,* is defined to be the time for one trip around the circle. Since a circle has a circumference of $2\pi r$ we may express the speed as,

$$v = 2\pi r/T \tag{6}$$

Example Nine.—*Centripetal acceleration of the Moon.*

The Moon circles the earth with an orbital radius of 3.84×10^8 m and an orbital period (i.e. time for 1 trip around the circle) of about 28 days. From these data determine the (a) speed and (b) centripetal acceleration of the Moon.

Solution.

(a) Using equation (6) we have,

$$v = 2\pi r/T = 2\pi \, 3.84 \times 10^8 \,/(28 \text{ d} \times 24 \text{ hr/d} \times 3600 \text{ s/hr})$$

$$v = \underline{997 \text{ m/s}}$$

(b) Using the answer in (a) in equation (5)

$$a = v^2/r = (997)^2/(3.84 \times 10^8) = \underline{0.00259 \text{ m/s}^2}.$$

Summary.

Two kinds of mathematical objects are routinely encountered in physics, vectors and scalars. The addition of vectors may be found either graphically (head to tail method) or algebraically (adding the components). The motion of a projectile requires an understanding of motion in two dimensions and therefore, a familiarity with vectors. The vertical component of projectile motion is constant acceleration motion while the horizontal component is motion with constant velocity. Vectors are also needed to model circular motion. The center-seeking acceleration is called centripetal acceleration for uniform circular motion.

QUESTIONS.

1. Vector $\vec{A}$ has a length of 10 m and $\vec{B}$ a length of 20 m. What is the maximum length of the sum and the minimum length?

2. Consider the following set of quantities and circle whether the quantity is a scalar or a vector.

(*a*) ten dollars	vector	scalar
(*b*) north by northwest	vector	scalar
(*c*) 10 Newtons south	vector	scalar
(*d*) 24°C	vector	scalar
(*e*) 20 mph north	vector	scalar
(*f*) 2 grams	vector	scalar
(*g*) the reading of your car's speedometer	vector	scalar

3. When two vectors are added together, is the length of the sum equal to the sum of the lengths of the two vectors? Why or why not?

4. A bowling ball and a volleyball both leave the ground with the same speed and angle from the horizontal. Neglecting friction, which ball hits the ground first? Explain.

5. In the flight of a baseball, where is the vertical component of velocity zero? At that point is the speed of the ball zero?

6. A ball is rolled off a horizontal table. In which case will the ball hit the floor first, when it is rolled with a very large initial speed or very small initial speed? Explain.

7. Two balls are rolled off a horizontal table. One is initially moving very fast and the other very slow. Which one hits the floor with the greatest speed? Explain.

8. Two balls are released simultaneously from the same height of 10.0 m above the ground. Ball one is released from rest while ball two has an initial velocity of 10 m/s in the horizontal direction. Determine which ball hits the ground first.

9. A battleship has a gun with multiple barrels and simultaneously fires two shells (with the same initial speeds) at two enemy ships, A and B, and the shells follow the parabolic trajectories as shown. Neglecting air friction, which ship gets hit first, A or B? Hint: consider only the vertical component of the motion.

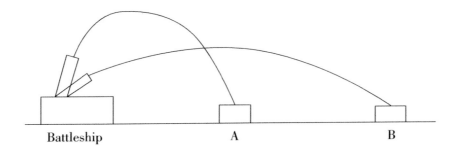

Battleship   A   B

(*a*) A
(*b*) both at the same time
(*c*) B
(*d*) the ship cannot hit both
(*e*) one cannot answer without having numbers supplied

10. The book, *Undaunted Courage* by Stephen Ambrose (Simon and Schuster, 2002), tells the story of how in 1803 President Thomas Jefferson charged Meriwether Lewis and William Clark with the task of exploring the newly acquired northwestern territory. As background we find the following passage on p. 25 about the education of young Meriwether: "An anecdote survived: when told that, despite what he saw, the sun did not revolve around the earth, Meriwether jumped as high into the air as he could, then asked his teacher, 'If the earth turns, why did I come down in the same place?'" Answer young Meriwether's query.

11. A race car driver is driving on a circular track. If he doubles his speed, by what factor does his centripetal acceleration get multiplied?

12. In the figure you are looking down on a marble that is moving along a circular track that is on a horizontal table. When the marble exits the track at point Q, which path does it more closely follow: a, b, c, d, or e?

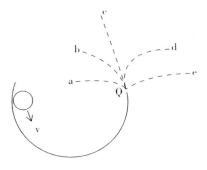

PROBLEMS.

1. A cowboy pulls on a mule with a force of 25.0 N toward the east while another cowboy pulls with a force of 35.0 N toward the north. Using a ruler and a protractor, use the graphical method to find both the magnitude and direction of the total force (i.e. the vector sum of these two forces) acting on the mule by the cowboys.

2. A hot air balloon drifts 10.0 km 60° north of east then the wind shifts and blows the balloon 5.0 km east. Using a ruler and a protractor, use the graphical method to find the sum of these two vectors.

3. In a cross country auto race an automobile moves 5.0 km 30° north of east then 10.0 km 60° west of north. Find (a) the components of both these vectors and (b) the components of the vector sum.

4. In 1954 an African sharp-nosed frog set the world's record distance for three consecutive jumps: 4.0 m 30° north of east, 3.2 m 15° south of east, and 3.6 m 25° south of east. Find (a) the components of these three vectors and (b) the components of the vector sum.

5. Find the length and angle of the vector sum in problem 3.

6. Find the length and angle of the vector sum in problem 4.

7. An airplane is at an altitude of 8.0 km and moving parallel to the ground with a horizontal velocity of 200 mph. If a package is gently released from the plane, determine the time for the package to hit the ground. Neglect air friction.

8. A marble moves with a speed of 2 mph off a table that is 1.0 m tall. Determine the time for the marble to hit the floor. Neglect air friction.

9. For problem 7 find (a) the horizontal distance the package moves after release from the plane until it hits the ground and (b) the components of its velocity vector just before it hits the ground.

10. For problem 8 find (a) the horizontal distance the marble moves after it leaves the table until it hits the floor and (b) the components of its velocity vector just before it hits the floor.

11. The World War I gun called Big Bertha could hurl a projectile with a speed of 1000.0 m/s. Suppose Big Bertha shoots the projectile from ground level at an angle of 30° above the horizontal. Find (a) how far away the projectile lands and (b) the vertical velocity of the shell just before it lands. Neglect air friction.

12. A baseball leaves a bat from ground level with an initial speed of 60 mph at an angle above the horizontal of 30°. Find (a) how far away the ball lands and (b) the vertical velocity of the ball just before it lands. Neglect air friction.

13. Find the maximum altitude of the shell in problem 11.

14. Find the maximum altitude of the ball in problem 12.

15. A basketball leaves the hands of a basketball player with a velocity of 10.0 m/s at an angle of 50° above the horizontal and a height of 3.0 m above the floor. The basketball hoop is 10.0 m away and is at a height of 4.0 m above the ground. Determine the coordinates of the ball when it reaches the hoop and from this decide whether the player makes the shot.

16. A football leaves the foot of a field goal kicker with a velocity of 15.0 m/s at an angle of 40°
above the horizontal and from ground level. The crossbar at the end of the field is 35.0 m away
and is at a height of 4.0 m above the ground. Determine the coordinates of the ball when it reaches
the crossbar and from this decide whether the kicker makes the field goal.

17. Determine the centripetal acceleration of the moon in its orbit around the earth.

18. Determine the centripetal acceleration of the earth in its orbit around the sun.

19. A ferris wheel has a radius of 10.0 m and takes 8.0 s to complete one full revolution. Calculate (a) the speed of a person on the wheel and (b) the person's centripetal acceleration.

20. A crazy rat is placed in a circular room of radius 5.0 m and the rat takes 12.0 s to make one complete revolution around the room. Calculate (a) the speed of the rat and (b) the rat's centripetal acceleration.

Hints and answers to problems.

1) about 40 N at about 55° N of E   2) about 12.5 km at about 40° N of E   3) 4.33 km E, 2.5 km N; 8.66 km W, 5 km N; 4.33 km W, 7.5 km N   4) 3.464 m E, 2.0 m N; 3.091 m E, 0.828 m S; 3.26 m E, 1.52 m S; 9.815 m E, 0.348 m S   5) 8.66 km, 60° N of W   6) 9.82 m, 2.03° S of E
7) 40 s   8) 0.45 s   9) 3580 m, 89.4 m/s, 400 m/s   10) 0.402 m, 0.894 m/s, 4.5 m/s
11) 86.6 km, −500 m/s   12) 62.2 m, −13.4 m/s   13) 12,500 m   14) 8.98 m   15) 2.82 m, No
16) −17 m, No   17) 1.53×0^{-20} m/s^2 18) 2.65×10^{-25} m/s^2 19) 7.854 m/s, 6.17 m/s^2
20) 2.618 m/s, 1.37 m/s^2

ᴄHAPTER IV.
NEWTON'S VIEWS ON MOTION.

Abstract.

Previously we engaged the description of motion by introducing terms such as position, velocity and acceleration. The branch of mechanics that describes motion is called **kinematics**. In this chapter we enter a new area of motion study called **dynamics**. In dynamics the pressing concern is: given the forces acting on an object of a given mass, we seek to find the acceleration, from which the velocity and position can be obtained. The name Isaac Newton figures most prominently in dynamics. We begin with a brief review of his remarkable life followed by Newton's three laws of motion which form the foundation of dynamics.

Definitions. force, mass, weight, tension, normal, friction

Principles. Newton's three laws of motion

Fundamental Equations. Newton's second and third law, spring force

"A truly good person is so precious, and such a wonderful product in our universe of space and stars, that any amount of pain and turmoil are justified by the ultimate emergence of this product."

—Elton Trueblood, Quaker philosopher

Courtesy of Bridgeman-Giraudon/Art Resource, NY.

A. Isaac Newton (1642–1727).

Isaac Newton is considered by many physicists to be the most important physicist in history. His range of accomplishments are astounding in breadth and depth. To Newton we owe our current understanding of how forces account for the motion of systems ranging from everyday objects to planets. He was the first to formulate the law of gravitation, and in so doing he invented calculus as well as explained the nature of tides. Before Newton, the laws of physics were thought to be different for objects on earth (terrestrial physics) from the laws for objects in the heavens (celestial physics). Newton unified physics into one set of laws for all space and time. Newton also introduced a corpuscular model of light and studied rainbows using prisms. Based on his prism investigations he formulated a model of light wherein white light was interpreted

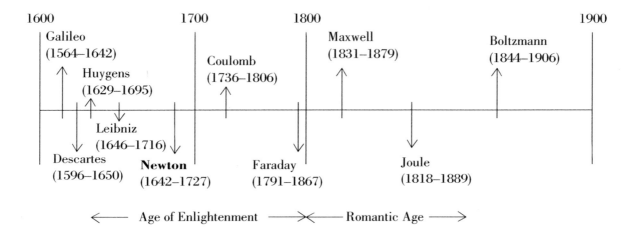

as consisting of all the colors of the rainbow. Many argue that the most important science book ever written was Newton's, *Principia*, written in 1687 (the full title of this work is *The Mathematical Principles of Natural Philosophy*). Unfortunately, in spite of such tremendous success as a mathematical physicist, Newton was not as successful as a human being.

Isaac Newton began his life on Christmas day in 1642 in the English hamlet Woolsthorpe, in Lincolnshire. His parents were farmers but the same could not be said for young Isaac. As a youth he was attracted to mathematics and mechanical toys. Following adolescence, in 1661 he was sent to Trinity College, Cambridge University. He was an excellent but quiet student. Newton made his most important strides in physics during a period of time when the university was closed due to the ravages of the bubonic plague. This was the year 1666 when he was 24 years old and working from home. Afterward he returned to Cambridge and was eventually hired as a professor of mathematics there, replacing his former teacher. He participated in the relatively new Royal Society. Newton became famous worldwide after the publication of the *Principia* in 1687. In 1699 he was appointed master of the mint, and given his interest in chemistry (more accurately, alchemy) he was successful in apprehending some counterfeiters. In 1689 and 1701 Newton was elected to Parliament but his political career was rather uneventful. He was elected president of the Royal Society in 1703 and knighted in 1705. In addition to his many other interests, Newton studied such Biblical prophetic (apocalyptic) books as Daniel and Revelation. Having a suspicious nature, Isaac Newton carried on a decades-long quarrel with the German mathematical genius and philosopher, Gottfried von Leibnitz, over the priority for the invention of the calculus. Isaac Newton died in 1727 and was given a hero's burial in Westminster Abbey.

Newton's contributions to physics were enormous, but in a wider sense his contributions to humanity were even greater. His physics coupled with a deistic religious orientation fueled the development of a century long movement known as the Enlightenment. Reason was the primary path to truth among enlightenment philosophers. By the late eighteenth century many elites had begun to largely base their philosophical views on Newton's physics. The overall viewpoint of the universe that emerged was one in which the world was thought to be a deterministic, closed mechanical system that obeys physical laws. Some carried these lines of thought to the extreme and began thinking of the world as a giant machine, like a watch. Some even said humans are basically machines that lack free will and moral responsibility. This attitude is captured in, for example, the writings of the French scientist, Laplace, who wrote during the enlightenment period,

We ought then to regard the present state of the universe as the effect of its previous state and as the cause of the one which is to follow. Given for one instant a mind which could comprehend all the forces by which nature is animated and the respective situation of the beings who compose it—a mind sufficiently vast to submit these data to analysis—it would embrace in the same formula the movements of the greatest bodies of the universe and those of the lightest atom; for it, nothing would be uncertain and the future, as the past, would be present to its eyes.

There is a word that describes these extrapolations, reductionism. A person engages in reductionistic thinking upon assuming complicated systems can be entirely understood by considering only a few elementary ideas. It is a leap of faith to naively think that physics can account for all aspects of life. Deep philosophical and theological questions will not likely be resolved by making measurements in earth-bound laboratories.

References.

Mathematical Principles of Natural Philosophy (Principia), Isaac Newton (University of California Press, 1962).

Never At Rest, Richard Westfall (Cambridge UP, 1980).

Remarkable Physicists Ioan James (Cambridge UP, 2004).

Great Physicists, William H. Cropper (Oxford UP, 2004).

The Enlightenment Reader, Ed. Isaac Kramnick (Penguin Press).

Physics, the Human Adventure by Gerald Holton and Stephen Brush (Rutgers University Press, 2001).

B. Newton's Laws of Motion.

Imagine a journey to the vacuum of outer space to a place where no stars or planets are nearby. At this isolated place there is only an apple (at rest) and two persons, Moe and Larry. Suppose Moe applies a constant pull on the apple while Larry constantly pulls in the opposite direction. What happens?

The answer to this question depends on whether you follow the opinions of Aristotle or Newton. According to Aristotle (and Newton) a push or pull is called a ***force***. The net force on the apple is found by adding the two forces, keeping in mind if Moe's force is in the positive direction then Larry's is in the negative direction.

$$F_{net} = +F_{Moe} - F_{Larry}$$

If the forces are not parallel then the net force is a vector sum of all the forces acting on the system. For now, let's keep things simple by staying in one dimension.

Aristotle would suggest that this constant net force causes the apple to acquire a constant velocity and thereby undergo what he termed "violent motion." If the net force is positive then the velocity will be positive. If the net force is zero then the apple will remain at rest. Aristotle's opinion can be summarized mathematically by the following equation,

$$F_{net} = m_A v \quad \text{("Aristotle's law")} \tag{1}$$

where v is the apple's velocity and m_A might be named the Aristotelian mass of the apple. This mass is simply a proportionality constant between the net force and the velocity. In this common sense view of motion which is shared by most people, a net force is needed for an object to acquire a velocity. What could be more natural? Objects usually don't acquire a velocity unless we push them. To make a chair move someone has to push it, and after the pushing stops, so does the movement. In the worldview of Aristotle, force causes velocity.

There are situations that violate this simple rule. For instance, if a force is needed to keep an object moving then why does a ball thrown into the air keep moving after leaving the thrower's hand? According to (1) a baseball pitcher would wind up, and the instant the ball left her hand it would fall straight down rather than move horizontally. Free fall is an example of what Aristotle termed "natural motion." Clearly, there is something wrong with (1).

Nevertheless, the Aristotelian system was held until the time of Galileo and Newton. It took the genius of a Newton to overturn equation (1), replacing it with what is now called Newton's second law of motion,

$$\begin{array}{c} \text{Law II} \\ \vec{F}_{net} = m\vec{a} \quad \text{(Newton's second law)} \end{array} \tag{2}$$

where m is called the **mass** of the system and $\vec{a}$ is the acceleration of m. The mass is the proportionality constant between the net force and the acceleration. Traditionally, a standard object was arbitrarily defined to have a mass of 1 kilogram. If a force is applied to this standard and it acquires an acceleration of 1 m/s^2 then that force is defined to be 1 kg m/s^2. Because this latter set of units is rather cumbersome and in order to honor Newton, the unit of force is called the Newton.

$$1 \text{ Newton} = 1 \text{ kg m/s}^2$$

A force of one Newton is about the weight of a typical apple. In the worldview of Newton, force causes acceleration.

But what happened to Newton's *first* law? Newton borrowed heavily from the works of Galileo in establishing his first law and so it is somewhat inappropriate to give Newton the credit for law one. However, it turns out that the first law is only a special case of the second law, corresponding to systems experiencing zero net force. By (2) if the left-hand side is zero, then the acceleration of the apple is zero which implies the velocity is constant. The first law is also called the law of inertia.

Law I *Law of Inertia*

If $\vec{F}_{net} = 0$ then $\vec{v} = $ constant   (Newton's first law)   (3)

Under conditions of zero force, equation (3) implies a body moves with constant speed in a straight line. Our apple in outer space with zero net force acting on it will either remain at rest or move with a constant velocity. Returning to the baseball pitcher example, the pitcher can throw the ball since once it leaves her hand no force is needed to maintain its velocity!

Example One.—*The Three Stooges in space.*

Moe pushes on Curly with a force of 100 N to the right, while Larry pushes with a force to the left of 40 N. Curly has a mass of 50 kg. Find Curly's acceleration.

Solution.

Using (2)

$$F_{net} = ma_x$$
$$F_{net} = 100 - 40 = 60 \text{ N} = 50 \ a_x,$$

solving for a_x

$$a_x = 60/50 = \underline{6/5 \text{ m/s}^2.}$$

Example Two.—*Pulling a sled.*

A boy pulls with a rope that is attached to a 20 kg sled. The rope makes an angle of 30° with the horizontal ground. The force by the rope on the sled is 40 N. Find the acceleration of the sled along the ground. Neglect friction.

Hint: You will need to find the horizontal component of the 40 N force.

Solution.

We are given, m = 20 kg, $\theta = 30°$ and $F_T = 40$ N. The component of the tension force along the (horizontal) x-axis gives rise to the acceleration along the ground,

$$F_{Tx} = F_T \cos\theta = m \ a_x.$$

Solving for the acceleration,

$$a_x = F_T \cos\theta/m = 40 \cos 30°/20 = \underline{1.7 \text{ m/s}^2.}$$

Caution: Make sure your calculator is set to degrees not radians.

Newton's third law of motion is also important in many problems. The third law does not follow from the first two laws but is an independent property of nature. Newton named this law the law of action-reaction. Be forewarned, this phrase is a bit misleading.

The third law examines the process, called an interaction, by which objects exert a force on each other. Suppose Moe pushes on Larry with a force of 10 Newtons to the right. According to the third law, Larry pushes on Moe with a force of 10 Newtons but to the left. So every force is due to something (the agent) and acts on something else (the object). Every force has an agent (that which produces the force) and an object (that which the force acts on). This is summarized below.

	Agent of this force	**Object of this force**
Moe pushes on Larry	Moe	Larry
Larry pushes back on Moe	Larry	Moe

In the first case, the 10 N force points toward the right while in the second case the 10 N force points to the left.

The third law can be written mathematically using vector notation. Vectors are needed since a force has both a magnitude and a direction,

$$\text{Law III} \quad \textit{Action-Reaction}$$
$$\vec{F}_{A \text{ on } B} = -\vec{F}_{B \text{ on } A} \quad \text{(Newton's third law)} \tag{4}$$

Equation (4) implies the two forces are equal in magnitude but are opposite in direction.

The law of action-reaction can be misleading because this language seems to imply first $\vec{F}_{A \text{ on } B}$ occurs, then B retaliates on A at a later time with, $\vec{F}_{B \text{ on } A}$. However, these two forces are simultaneous. It is not a situation of tit for tat. Furthermore, the first force $\vec{F}_{A \text{ on } B}$ has as its object B and agent A while the other force, $\vec{F}_{B \text{ on } A}$, has as its object A and agent B. These two forces do not act on the same object. Every interaction therefore involves two forces of equal size but anti-parallel to each other and with two different agents and two different objects.

Example Three.—*Typing at a keyboard.*

Poindexter pushes on the P key on his computer keyboard. Label the object and agent of the force on the key by Poindexter. Do the same for the force on Poindexter's finger by the key.

Solution.

	Agent	Object
Force by Poindexter on key:	Poindexter	key
Force by key on Poindexter:	key	Poindexter

C. Examples of Some Important Forces.

Problems in mechanics involve a number of everyday forces. Among these we include: weight, tension in a string, spring forces, frictional forces, and the "normal" force. In later chapters, two more forces will be introduced: the electric force and the magnetic force.

Weight.

The weight of a mass m is the gravitational force on m by the earth. We usually denote weight by the symbol F_W. If an object has a mass m and the only force on the object is its weight then we can say,

$$F_{net} = F_W$$

We also know F_{net} = ma and that the acceleration of a freely falling body has a magnitude g (= 9.8 or 10 m/s²). Equating these expressions for F_{net} we find for the weight of a mass m,

$$F_W = mg \quad \text{(weight of mass m, N)} \tag{5}$$

Tension.

The force by a rope is called the tension. In problems with ropes present just remember, you can't push with a rope!

Springs.

Consider a spring resting on a horizontal table top. The spring is neither stretched nor compressed; it is said to be in equilibrium. A contemporary of Isaac Newton, Robert Hooke made laboratory observations that concluded, if we pull the spring a distance x from its equilibrium position, the spring will pull back with a force proportional to x. Stating Hooke's law mathematically leads to,

$$F_{elastic} = -kx \tag{6}$$

where k is called the spring constant of the spring (large k is characteristic of a stiff spring). The minus sign in (6) is needed to give the correct direction of the spring (elastic) force.

Friction.

When two surfaces are in contact they exert a frictional force on each other that is parallel to the plane of contact. In more advanced courses two "laws of friction" are introduced: static friction where the two objects are not in relative motion and kinetic friction when they are in relative movement. In this text we will not introduce the laws of friction. Unless otherwise stated, assume friction is not present. If friction is present you will be given the value of the friction force in Newtons.

Normal Force.

The normal force is a force between an object and the surface the object lies on. The word normal is a mathematical phrase that means perpendicular and so it is not meant to suggest other forces are somehow abnormal. A normal force is present when a book rests on a horizontal surface

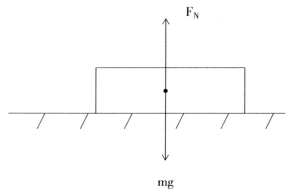

FIG. 1. THE FREE-BODY DIAGRAM OF A BOOK
RESTING ON A HORIZONTAL TABLE: GRAVITY
AND THE NORMAL FORCE ARE SHOWN.

like the floor, as in Figure 1. The book experiences a downward force due to the gravitational attraction of the earth, mg. This is its weight. Since the book is pushing down on the floor, by Newton's third law, the floor pushes up on the book. The upward force is vertical and makes an angle of 90° with the floor. The normal force is the upward force, F_N.

D. Applications: Newton's Laws.

Let's begin this section with an analogy. The PC was first mass-produced by IBM in the early eighties. Later the Macintosh entered the market in the mid-eighties. At that time most people found the Macintosh easier to use. Why? The reason is no matter what application one performed on a Macintosh (word processing, spreadsheets, etc.), the procedure was similar because of the mouse, menus, and windows. Before windows, one had to memorize many archaic keyboard commands to run an IBM PC. In short, the Macintosh made many different problems appear similar.

We can make an analogy of this situation to physics problem solving. Solving a problem in Newtonian mechanics is made easier by using the "window" I call the Newton's law ritual. Master this straightforward recipe that can be followed for all Newton's laws problems and you will find such problems easier to solve. Why? Because the ritual makes all problems seem similar.

The Newton's Law Ritual.

1. Draw a picture for the problem and identify the system.

2. Make a ***free-body diagram*** by placing all forces acting on the system onto the figure in step one above. Depending on the problem, you may need to use Newton's third law.

3. Introduce an x-y coordinate system, and resolve all of the forces into their x- and y-components.

4. Introduce Newton's second law for the x- and y- dimensions,

$$\Sigma \, F_x = m \, a_x \quad \text{and} \quad \Sigma \, F_y = m \, a_y$$

5. Solve the linear equations found in step four for the unknowns of the problem (normally the unknowns are forces or acceleration).

6. Make sure your answer has the proper units and is reasonable.

This ritual will only become transparent by using it to solve numerous problems. Before we look at some examples, a warning: *As always in physics, you will gain problem-solving skills only after you have practiced solving problems on your own. Read our examples, but you must do your homework to make the subject your own. "Be doers of the word and not hearers only."*

Example Four.—*Pushing boxes.*

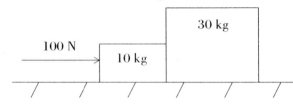

A constant 100 N horizontal force is applied to the system of boxes in the diagram. Neglecting friction, find (a) the acceleration of the boxes, and (b) the force by the 10 kg box on the 30 kg box.

Solution.

(a) The net force on the system (both boxes) we equate to ma_x,

$$F_{net} = ma_x.$$

Solving for the acceleration,

$$a_x = F_{net}/m = 100/40 = \underline{2.5 \text{ m/s}^2}.$$

(b) Considering the 30 kg box as the system, there is only one force (to the right) acting on it, F. Note: One can not assume F is 100 N. Using Newton's second law for the 30 kg box and the acceleration found in (a),

$$F_{net} = ma_x$$

or

$$F = 30\,(2.5) = \underline{75 \text{ N}}.$$

Extra: Apply Newton's second law to the 10 kg box to find the force on the 10 kg box by the 30 kg box. Answer: $\underline{-75 \text{ N}}$ (as required by Newton's third law)

Example Five.—*The elevator as a miracle weight loss scheme.*

A woman stands on a set of ordinary bathroom scales placed on the floor of an elevator. Her mass is 75 kg. (a) Find the woman's weight in Newtons. Next, find the reading on the scales assuming the elevator is (b) going up with an acceleration of magnitude 2 m/s², (c) going down with the same magnitude acceleration as in (b), (d) moving with constant velocity, (e) in free fall.

Solution.

Orient our +y-axis pointing down toward the earth. Then the net force acting on the woman will be her weight acting down, mg, and the scales pushing up, F_s. By the second law,

$$F_{net} = ma_y$$

$$mg - F_s = ma_y \quad \text{("elevator equation")}$$

Solving this for the scale force, which, in magnitude, will equal the reading on the scales by Newton's third law,

$$F_s = m(g - a_y) = m(10 - a_y).$$

All sections of this problem will use this final expression to obtain values for F_s.

(a) Use $a_y = 0$ in the expression above,

$$mg = 75(10) = \underline{750 \text{ N}}.$$

(b) Use $a_y = -2$ m/s^2, since the elevator is speeding up in the negative direction,

$$F_s = m(10 - a_y) = 75(10 - -2) = 75(12) = \underline{900 \text{ N}}.$$

(c) Use $a_y = +2$ m/s^2

$$F_s = m(10 - a_y) = 75(10 - 2) = 75(8) = \underline{600 \text{ N}}.$$

(d) Since v_y is constant, use $a_y = 0$

$$F_s = mg = 75(10) = \underline{750 \text{ N}}.$$

(e) Use $a_y = +10$ m/s^2

$$F_s = m(10 - a_y) = 75(10 - 10) = 75(0) = \underline{0 \text{ N}}.$$

Example Six.—_Inclined plane._

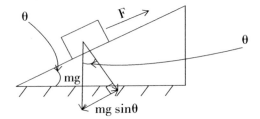

A 140 kg refrigerator is to be pulled up an incline that makes an angle of 30° with the horizontal. How large a force, applied parallel to the incline, must be exerted to accelerate the refrigerator up the incline at 1 m/s^2?

Solution.

See the diagram. Choose a +x-axis that points up and along the incline. The net force on the refrigerator along the +x-direction consists of the applied force, F, and the component of gravity down the incline, mg sinθ, which gives with the second law,

$$F_{net} = ma_x$$

$$F_{net} = F - mg \sin\theta = ma_x.$$

Solving for the applied force that gives $a_x = 1$ m/s^2,

$$F = mg \sin\theta + ma_x$$

$$F = 140 (10) \sin 30° + 140 (1) = 1400/2 + 140$$

$$F = \underline{840 \text{ N}}.$$

Example Seven.—*Parachuting and terminal speeds with D. B. Cooper.*

This is an interesting story. In 1971 D. B. Cooper boarded an airline carrier in Oregon. Cooper passed a note to the flight attendant. With this note, he managed to extort $200,000 from the airline, and his getaway plan was to parachute out of the plane. (a) Assuming the total mass of Mr. Cooper (plus the parachute) is 100 kg and air friction is 50 N, find the acceleration of Mr. Cooper. (b) A more accurate model assumes the air friction to vary linearly with the velocity,

$$F_f = -bv, \quad \text{where } b = 15 \text{ N/(m/s)}.$$

Under this scenario, the friction increases in magnitude as Mr. Cooper accelerates downward toward Earth. Eventually, the friction balances the weight of Mr. Cooper (+parachute). The speed at balance is called the **terminal speed**, v_T. When he reaches terminal speed, thereafter he falls at this constant speed. Determine the terminal speed of Mr. Cooper. (Raindrops also reach a terminal speed, otherwise it would not be safe to go outside when it is raining.) The fate of Mr. D. B. Cooper is unknown to this day and remains one of the most famous unsolved crimes of the twentieth century.

WANTED: DEAD OR ALIVE

(If you have seen this man, report it immediately to the FBI. There is a reward.)

Solution.

(a) Choosing the +y-axis to point up, the net force on Cooper is air friction, F_f (up), and gravity, mg (down), with the second law we have,

$$F_{net} = ma_y$$

$$F_{net} = F_f - mg = 50 - 100(10) = 100a_y$$

The acceleration is then,

$$a_y = -950/100 = \underline{-9.5 \text{ m/s}^2}.$$

(b) Again from the second law, but this time at terminal speed the acceleration vanishes,

$$F_{net} = ma_y$$

$$bv_T - mg = m\,0$$

This gives for the terminal speed,

$$v_T = mg/b = 100\,(10)/15 = 1000/15 = \underline{66.7 \text{ m/s}}.$$

[Note, converting this to mph we have

$$66.7 \text{ m/s } (1 \text{ mile}/1610 \text{ m}) (3600 \text{ s}/1 \text{ h}) = 149 \text{ mph}.$$

This is a little bigger than typical terminal speeds, 120 mph. Also, this assumes the parachute did not open and so D. B. died on impact.]

Summary.

The foundation for motion is Newton's three laws of motion. Without a doubt F=ma is the most famous equation in all of physics (with E=mc^2 a close second). Some common forces include weight, tension, friction, normal and spring forces. This chapter presents numerous examples that illustrate the application of the equations of motion. Mathematically, the task involves solving simultaneous equations.

QUESTIONS.

1. I exert a force on a refrigerator but it does not move. Explain why this occurs.

2. A 200 N force acts on a 10 kg box of books and the box accelerates at only 5 m/s^2. Explain why this occurs.

3. A horse pulls on a cart and the cart pulls back on the horse with a reaction force of equal size. How then can the cart accelerate?

4. Why is it easier to pull a lawn mower than to push it?

5. Two balls of mass m and 2m are dropped simultaneously from the Leaning Tower of Pisa. Ignoring air friction, will the balls hit the ground at the same time? Explain.

6. You are sitting in your chair and not moving. Make a free-body diagram for your body.

7. If there is no friction between your feet and the ground would you be able to run? Explain

8. How does the net force on the first car of a subway train compare with the net force on the last car of the subway if the train is moving with a constant velocity?

9. How does the net force on the first car of a subway train compare with the net force on the last car of the subway if the train is moving with a constant acceleration?

10. Explain the physics behind why water flies off a wet dog when it shakes.

11. When you stop your car suddenly and are not wearing your seat belt why do you move forward?

12. What kind of motion is produced by a non-zero constant force?

13. A glider plane is moving due north when a force pointed due west acts on the plane. What is the direction of the acceleration of the plane?

14. The maximum acceleration of a particular car is 3.5 m/s². If the car is now towing an identical vehicle, what is the maximum acceleration? (Neglect wind friction.)

15. An astronaut is floating freely in the vacuum of outer space. Is his mass the same as when he is on earth or is his weight the same?

16. A parachutist has reached terminal velocity. What is her acceleration?

17. Does the terminal speed of a falling parachutist increase, stay the same, or decrease when he opens the parachute?

18. Explain why if you push on a stationary car and it doesn't budge that this does not violate Newton's laws of motion.

19. You push on a wagon with a constant horizontal force of 150 N and it moves horizontally with a constant velocity. What is the net force on the wagon?

20. A heavy fullback runs head on into a skinny defensive end. Which person experiences the larger force? Explain.

21. You hold a 2-gram diamond stationary in your hand. What is the net force on the diamond?

22. You drop a 2-gram diamond. What is the net force on the diamond as it falls, neglecting friction?

23. What force causes a race car to accelerate?

24. If you are in an elevator that is accelerating up is the force on your feet by the floor larger or smaller than your weight?

25. Is the plant below in equilibrium? Explain

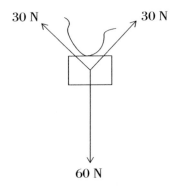

30 N   30 N

60 N

PROBLEMS.

(Reminder: in all problems assume $g = 10$ m/s².)

1. The net force applied to a mass is plotted against the acceleration of the mass below. Find the value of the mass.

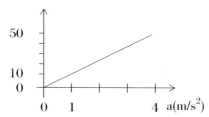

2. A 2,000.0 kg car has a maximum acceleration of 3.0 m/s². What net force acts on the car in causing this acceleration?

3. A 500.0 kg snowmobile has a maximum acceleration of 4.0 m/s². What net force acts on the snowmobile in causing this acceleration?

4. The car in problem 2 is towing a second car of twice its mass. What would its maximum acceleration be now?

   (*a*) 2.5 m/s^2

   (*b*) 2.0 m/s^2

   (*c*) 1.5 m/s^2

   (*d*) 1.0 m/s^2

   (*e*) 0.5 m/s^2

5. The snowmobile in problem 3 is towing a second snowmobile of twice its mass. What would its maximum acceleration be now?

   (*a*) 0.5 m/s^2

   (*b*) 0.8 m/s^2

   (*c*) 1.3 m/s^2

   (*d*) 1.7 m/s^2

   (*e*) 2.3 m/s^2

6. A woman weighs 600.0 N and is riding an elevator from the 1st to the 6th floor. What is the mass of the woman?

7. As the woman in problem 6 approaches the 6th floor its upward velocity decreases from 8.0 to 2.0 m/s in 3.0 s. Assuming a constant acceleration, determine the value of her acceleration. (Let up be the positive direction.)

8. As the woman in problem 6 approaches the 6th floor her upward velocity decreases from 7.0 to 1.0 m/s in 3.0 s. Assuming a constant acceleration, determine the value of her acceleration. (Let up be the positive direction.)

9. For problem 7 what is the force exerted by the elevator floor on the woman during this 3.0 s interval?

    (a) 120 N

    (b) 480 N

    (c) 600 N

    (d) 720 N

    (e) 1200 N

10. For problem 8 what is the force exerted by the elevator floor on the woman during this 3.0 s interval?

    (*a*) 120 N

    (*b*) 480 N

    (*c*) 600 N

    (*d*) 720 N

    (*e*) 1200 N

11. A rope will break if its tension exceeds 3,000 N. Calculate the maximum possible acceleration of a 1,500 kg automobile that is pulled by the rope, ignoring frictional forces.

12. A string will break if its tension exceeds 10.0 N. Calculate the maximum possible acceleration of a 0.5 kg box that is pulled by the string along the floor, ignoring frictional forces.

13. Answer problem 11 assuming the rope is inclined at 30° to the horizontal.

14. Answer problem 12 assuming the string is inclined at 30° to the horizontal.

15. The lower left chamber of the heart pumps blood such that 80.0 grams of blood is accelerated from rest to a speed of about 0.45 m/s in 0.2 s. Assuming constant acceleration, find (a) the acceleration and (b) the force by the heart on this mass of blood.

16. A 50.0 gram arrow traveling at 60.0 m/s hits a bale of hay and stops after entering 0.3 m into the hay. Assuming constant acceleration, find (a) the acceleration and (b) the force by the bale on the arrow.

17. Find the acceleration of the masses in the system shown below where the masses are attached to each other with a rope and the rope hangs over the pulley (the circle with an *x*). Also, find the tension in the rope. The masses are $m_1 = 10$ kg and $m_2 = 20$ kg.

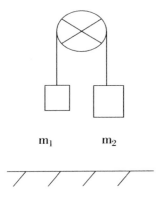

18. A 30.0 kg boy hangs from a rope which passes over a pulley. A 40.0 kg mass is attached to the other end of the rope (see picture in problem 17). Find the acceleration of the boy and the tension in the rope.

19. During a head-on collision, the person in the front seat of the car (constantly) decelerates from 13.3 m/s to rest in 0.1 s. Find (a) the person's deceleration and (b) the force on the person by his seat belt given his mass is 70.0 kg.

20. A baseball of mass 0.150 kg enters the catcher's mitt at an initial speed of 50.0 m/s. The baseball is stopped in a distance of 16.0 cm. Find (a) the constant acceleration and (b) the force on the ball by the mitt.

21. A 3.0-gram penny released from the top of the Sears Tower in Chicago lands on the head of a pedestrian 460 m below. Just before the penny hits the person's head it has a downward velocity of 25 m/s. The person's head stops the penny in a distance of 1.00 mm. Find (a) the constant acceleration of the penny as it is coming to rest and (b) the force by the penny on the person's head. Note: some skull bones fracture under a force of 900 N.

22. A 3.0-gram penny released from the top of the Empire State Building in New York City lands on the head of a pedestrian 430 m below. Just before the penny hits the person's head it has a downward velocity of 23 m/s. The person's head stops the penny in a distance of 1.00 mm. Find (a) the constant acceleration of the penny as it is coming to rest and (b) the force by the penny on the person's head. Note: some skull bones fracture under a force of 900 N.

23. A 100.0 kg refrigerator is pushed on a frictionless incline by a force of 80.0 N that is parallel to the incline. The incline makes an angle of 30.0° with the horizontal. Determine the acceleration of the refrigerator. Explain.

24. Two crates are at rest on an ice rink floor when a boy pushes on the crates with a force F. Let $m_1 = 10.0$ kg, $m_2 = 20.0$ kg and $F = 100$ N in the sketch below. Find (a) the acceleration of the crates and (b) the force crate 1 exerts on crate 2. Compare your answer to the answer to the next problem.

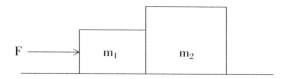

25. Two crates are at rest on an ice rink floor when a boy pushes on the crates with a force F. Let $m_1 = 10.0$ kg, $m_2 = 20.0$ kg and F = 100 N in the sketch below. Find (a) the acceleration of the crates and (b) the force crate 2 exerts on crate 1. Compare your answer to the answer to the previous problem.

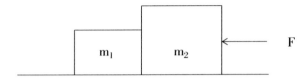

26. A skydiver is being pulled down by the Earth with a force of 970 N. If there is also an air resistance force of 400 N on the diver, what additional force would be needed to maintain constant speed?

27. If a 50.0 kg skydiver has a downward acceleration of 5 m/s² then what is the value of the force of air resistance acting on the diver?

Hints and answers to problems.

1) 12.5 kg   2) 6000 N   3) 2000 N   4) d   5) c   6) 60 kg   7) –2 m/s²   8) –2 m/s²   9) b 10) b   11) 2 m/s²   12) 20 m/s²   13) 1.73 m/s²   14) 17.3 m/s²   15) 2.25 m/s² 0.18 N 16) –6000 m/s² 300 N   17) Hint: You will need to review the algebraic method of solving two equations with two unknowns. 3.33 m/s² 133 N   18) Hint: You will need to review the algebraic method of solving two equations with two unknowns. 1.43 m/s² 343 N   19) –133 m/s² 9310 N 20) –7813 m/s² 1172 N   21) –3.125 × 10⁵ m/s² 938 N   22) 2.645 × 10⁵ m/s² 794 N 23) –4.2 m/s²   24) 3.33 m/s² 66.7 N   25) 3.33 m/s² 33.3 N   26) 570 N   27) 250 N

CHAPTER V.
ROTATIONAL MOTION AND GRAVITATION.

Abstract.

In this chapter we encounter two firsts of physics: the first fundamental force in nature, the gravitational force, and the first field theory of physics, the gravitational field. The second fundamental force, the electromagnetic force, will be introduced later when we study electrical charges. In total there are four fundamental forces of nature; the other two are beyond classical physics since they are only found in the subatomic world. The other major topic of this chapter is circular motion. Recall the ancient Greeks believed circular motion is perfect. Perfect motion pertains only to *uniform* circular motion where the circulating particle has a constant speed. In this chapter we extend our previous study of rotation by introducing several new terms. The first of these is torque which is the twisting ability of a force. A torque produces a change in the angular velocity and angular momentum of a system. These terms will also be explained.

Definitions. gravitational force and field, angular position, angular displacement, angular velocity, angular acceleration, moment of inertia, angular momentum of a circulating particle, and torque by a tangential force

Principles. superposition principle for force and field, Kepler's three laws of planetary motion

Fundamental Equations. Universal force of gravitation, gravitational field of a particle, and Newton's second law in rotational form

A. Fundamental Force: Newton's Universal Force of Gravitation.

It was commonly believed during the time of Isaac Newton in the seventeenth century that material objects could only influence each other by making physical contact. Any viewpoint that posited material bodies could exert forces on each other without contact was a conjecture that was strenuously dismissed as "action at a distance." Action at a distance means one body can exert a force on another body without touching and without there being anything in between the bodies. Many contemporaries of Newton found action at a distance to be reminiscent of spiritualism or to use the language of the day, reminiscent of the "occult arts." One of Newton's contemporaries, Rene Descartes, about whom we will learn more in a later chapter, vigorously opposed anyone who suggested the existence of non-contact forces. His explanation of how astronomical bodies are able to exert forces on each other involved an elaborate theory that invoked the presence of vortices (whirlpools or tornados) in the so called ether. Descartes' "ether" should not be confused with the ether of the ancient Greeks. According to scientists of the time, the ether was an invisible, mass-less fluid filling all space. Going against these views, Isaac Newton formulated his law of universal gravitation which postulates all matter attracts all other matter by a gravitational force, a decidedly non-contact force. When pressed by the Cartesians about such an apparently "mystical" like force, Newton responded with the famous phrase, "I do not feign hypotheses." By this he meant, he did not know how a gravitational force acts across the vacuum of space but all observations suggest that it does and therefore, Newton chose not to make up some fanciful speculative theory about how gravity really works. During the seventeenth century most persons followed the Cartesian vortex theory of gravitation instead of Newton's gravity law.

Eventually Newton's gravitational theory was adopted though and now his universal law of gravitation is one of the foundations of classical physics. The law is "universal" because it assumes the same force law holds in the terrestrial and celestial realms. In contrast with ancient Greek thinking, heaven and Earth are governed by the same physical laws according to Newtonian physics.

But exactly how does this force work? Suppose we have two particles of mass, m_1 and m_2, a distance r apart. Newton postulated the gravitational force one particle exerts on another is proportional to the product of their masses,

$$F \approx m_1 m_2.$$

This means larger masses exert larger forces on each other. Furthermore, he assumed the force is inversely proportional to the square of the distance between the masses, r,

$$F \approx 1/r^2.$$

This implies as the masses get farther and farther apart, the r in the denominator gets larger and the force diminishes. Two masses that are far apart attract each other weakly compared to when they are near each other. Finally, the direction of the force vector is determined from the assumption the gravitational force between two masses is always attractive. The attractive nature is a feature of gravitation that makes it fundamentally different from electrical forces since electrical charges can repel or attract each other depending on their signs. Combining both of the above features gives the mathematical statement of the gravitational force law.

Newton's Universal Law of Gravitation.

$$F = Gm_1m_2/r^2 \quad \text{(always attractive)} \tag{1}$$

where

$$G = 6.67 \times 10^{-11} \text{ N} - m^2/\text{kg}^2$$

Equation (1) introduces one of the fundamental constants of nature, the universal law of gravitation constant, G. In the eighteenth century Henry Cavendish measured this constant in a rather delicate experiment. Equation (1) is our first example of what is called an inverse-square law. Later, the electric force will be another example. Lastly, Newton also assumed the gravitational force obeys his third law of motion.

Example One.—*Force by the Sun on Earth.*

How large a force does the Sun exert on the Earth?

Solution.

We will need the mass of both the Sun and Earth in addition to their separation. From the flyleaf we gather these data:

$$M_{sun} = 1.989 \times 10^{30} \text{ kg}$$

$$M_{earth} = 5.974 \times 10^{24} \text{ kg}$$

$$\text{distance between the Sun and Earth} = r = 1.46 \times 10^{11} \text{ m.}$$

Putting these numbers into equation (1),

$$F = GM_{sun}M_{earth}/r^2$$

$$F = 6.67 \times 10^{-11} \times 1.989 \times 10^{30} \times 5.974 \times 10^{24}/(1.46 \times 10^{11})^2$$

$$F = 3.718 \times 10^{22} \text{ N}$$

An important situation arises if instead of two particles exerting gravitational forces on each other we have three or more particles. How does the gravitational force work then? A fundamental principle called the *superposition principle* shows us how to go beyond two particle situations. According to this principle the total gravitational force on a mass by a collection of particle masses is found by first finding the force on the mass by only one particle of the collection using equation (1), ignoring all the others. Then you repeat this procedure for every particle in the collection, each time using equation (1) for the force while ignoring the other particles in the collection. Finally, the total force is the vector sum of all of these forces. Without the superposition principle the law of gravitation would be practically useless. This principle is best illustrated by an example.

Example Two.—*The force on the Moon by the Earth and the Sun.*

Place the Sun at the origin and the Earth on the x-axis as shown in the diagram below. Find the forces on the Moon in the position shown. The data we need are:

$$M_{sun} = 1.989 \times 10^{30} \text{ kg} \quad \text{Sun-Earth separation} = 1.5 \times 10^{11} \text{m}$$

$$M_{earth} = 5.974 \times 10^{24} \text{ kg} \quad \text{Moon-Earth separation} = 3.84 \times 10^8 \text{ m}$$

$$M_{moon} = 7.36 \times 10^{22} \text{ kg}$$

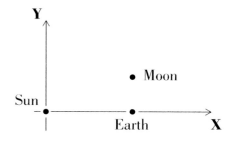

Solution.

Let's first find the magnitude of the forces on the Moon. The Earth pulls on the Moon with a force along the −y direction with a force of magnitude given by,

$$F_{ME} = GM_{earth}M_{moon}/r^2_{earth-moon}$$

$$F_{ME} = 6.67 \times 10^{-11} (5.974 \times 10^{24}) (7.36 \times 10^{22})/(3.84 \times 10^8)^2$$

$$\underline{F_{ME} = 1.99 \times 10^{20} \text{ N}, \quad \text{along } -y \text{ direction}}$$

Next we find the force on the Moon by the Sun. The direction of this force is along the line connecting the Sun and the Moon and the vector force points toward the Sun. The Sun-Moon separation is the hypotenuse of the right triangle in the above figure and therefore, using the Pythagorean theorem,

$$r^2_{sun-moon} = (1.5 \times 10^{11})^2 + (3.84 \times 10^8)^2 \approx 2.25 \times 10^{22}$$

The magnitude of the force on the Moon by the Sun is then,

$$F_{MS} = GM_{sun}M_{moon}/r^2_{sun-moon}$$

$$F_{MS} = 6.67 \times 10^{-11} (1.989 \times 10^{30})(7.36 \times 10^{22})/2.25 \times 10^{22}$$

$$\underline{F_{MS} = 4.34 \times 10^{20} \text{ N, along the line connecting the Sun to Moon.}}$$

The force on the Moon by the Sun is more than twice that by the Earth. Why doesn't the Moon orbit the Sun rather than the Earth?

The total force vector on the Moon is found using the principle of superposition to add the vectors,

$$\vec{F}_{tot} = \vec{F}_{ME} + \vec{F}_{MS}$$

Adding these vectors will be left as an exercise for the student.

Up to this point we have contemplated the gravitational force between two particles or the force on a particle by a system of particles. However, suppose we want to know the force of gravity by the Earth on an apple near the Earth's surface. Neither the Earth nor the apple is a particle and so it would appear we are ill equipped to solve this simple problem. Newton was able to extend his theory of gravitation between particles to find gravitational forces acting between extended mass distributions. In order to solve this more general problem Newton invented the integral calculus.

B. The Gravitational Field: A Field Theory.

Action at a distance assumes the space surrounding a mass is not affected by the mass. Field theory assumes just the opposite, that is, for any particle having mass the region of space surrounding the particle is altered. At each point of the surrounding region a "field" is said to be created by the mass.

The presence of a field at any point in space is determined by the field's affect on a test mass, m_{test}. By a test mass we mean a particle with such small mass that it has negligible affect on the mass that created the field in the first place. If I place a test mass at a point in space, a field is known to be present if the test mass experiences a gravitational force there. The bigger the force that is experienced by the test mass, the bigger the field at that point in space. The definition of the **gravitational field** at a point follows,

$$\vec{g} = \text{gravitational field} \equiv \vec{F}(\text{gravitational force on test mass})/m_{\text{test}}. \qquad (2)$$

By equation (2) the direction of $\vec{g}$ is the same direction as the gravitational force $\vec{F}$ acting on the test mass and this points from m_{test} toward the mass that creates $\vec{g}$. The reason for this direction is the gravitational force is always attractive and as a consequence the field is parallel to this force.

For an arbitrary collection of masses the gravitational field produced is very complicated. It is wise to start with the simplest distribution of mass, a point mass m, and find the field m produces a distance r away. From the definition of $\vec{g}$ given in equation (2) we find the field by placing a test mass, m_{test}, a distance r from m and use the law of gravitation to find the force on m_{test} by m.

$$\vec{g} = \vec{F}/m_{\text{test}} = [Gmm_{\text{test}}/r^2]/m_{\text{test}} \text{ , points toward } m.$$

Since m_{test} is in the numerator and denominator, it cancels out. The field produced by a particle of mass m at a distance r away is accordingly,

Gravitational field of a point mass m
$$\vec{g} = Gm/r^2, \text{ points toward } m. \qquad (3)$$

Equation (3) is an important result—nearly as important as equation (1) for the force of gravity. Notice several things. First, the units of $\vec{g}$ are those of acceleration, m/s². Second, $\vec{g}$ depends only on two things: the mass m that produces the field and the distance from the mass. Because r^2 is in the denominator, the field declines rapidly with increasing distance away from m. Gravity fields weaken as you go farther away from their source. Finally, it is important not to confuse g and G, as the next example will clearly show what a big mistake that would be.

Example Three.—*Gravitational field produced by the Earth at its surface.*

What is the value of the gravitational field at the Earth's surface? Approximate the Earth as a particle concentrated at its center and measure distances from the center of the Earth.

Solution.

We need: $M_{\text{earth}} = 5.974 \times 10^{24}$ kg   and $R_E = $ radius of Earth $= 6.38 \times 10^6$ m

Using these in equation (3),

$$\vec{g}_E = GM_E/R^2_E, \text{ points toward center of Earth.}$$

$$\vec{g}_E = 6.67 \times 10^{-11}(5.974 \times 10^{24})/(6.38 \times 10^6)^2$$

$$\vec{g}_E = \underline{9.8 \text{ m/s}^2, \text{ points toward center of Earth.}}$$

This result should look familiar, as it is the acceleration due to gravity! When you measure the acceleration due to gravity in a physics experiment, you are also measuring the gravitational field in the laboratory.

The gravitational field produced by a collection of particles is also found from the superposition principle: the field produced by each particle, as if acting alone, is determined, and the total field is the vector sum of all these fields.

C. Torque on and Angular Momentum of a Simple System.

Often problems involving gravitation involve masses that are moving in circles. This is certainly the situation for the motion of astronomical bodies such as the planets in our solar system. According to Kepler's first law of planetary motion the planets move in elliptical orbits around the Sun but since the ellipses are very close to being circular it is reasonably accurate to approximate the orbits as circles. We are led once again to return to the case of motion in a circle, the Greek's idea of perfect motion.

As discussed previously, the ancient Greeks also believed there exists a being called the prime mover who spins the outer shell that contains the stars. The prime mover exerts a tangential force on the star shell and we ask, what effect should such a force have? This "spinning force" creates a **torque** which we now define more precisely.

To simplify the situation, imagine a particle of mass m that moves in a circle of radius r. There are two special cases: uniform and non-uniform circular motion. In uniform circular motion only one force is at work, the force that is directed toward the center of the circle which produces the centripetal acceleration of the particle. This force could arise due to the attractive force of gravity. For example, the mass m could be the orbiting Earth while the Sun is at the center of the circle, attracting the Earth. To take another example, attach a rock to a rope and twirl the rock in a horizontal circle. In this case the force that maintains the circular motion is the tension in the string. Whatever the nature of the force that produces the centripetal acceleration, this force does no work on the mass m since at every instant the force is always perpendicular to the displacement of the mass. If no work is done then the speed of the particle remains constant in compliance with the work-kinetic energy relation of the next chapter.

For non-uniform circular motion, in addition to the force pointing toward the center of the circle, there is another force that points tangent to the circle, just like the prime mover of the Greeks (see Figure 1). The tangential force will cause the circulating mass to speed up or slow down. The tangential force causes greater spinning speed and we say it produces a torque on the mass it acts on. The torque, τ, produced by the tangential force, $F_{tangential}$, is defined

$$\tau \equiv F_{tangential} \; r. \tag{4}$$

In equation (4) r is called the moment arm or lever arm of the force. The units for torque are N-m. An important observation is, the greater the moment arm, the larger the torque, that is, the

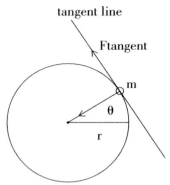

FIG. 1. FORCES ON A PARTICLE OF MASS *m* MOVING IN A CIRCLE OF RADIUS *r*. THERE IS A FORCE ALONG THE TANGENT LINE TO THE CIRCLE AND A FORCE POINTING TOWARD THE CENTER OF THE CIRCLE.

greater the ability of the force to produce a change in speed. For instance, you may be familiar with a torque wrench. This is a wrench that is very long to provide a large lever arm and torque. Such wrenches are used to loosen tight bolts on an automobile engine.

Equation (4) and Figure 1 assume the force is applied along a tangent to the circle. In more advanced presentations of physics, this restriction is removed and the force can be applied at any angle to the tangent line. Even in those more general situations, only the component of the force along the tangent exerts a torque, though.

Rotational motion has a full-blown vocabulary to describe the kinematics where most linear terms have the adjective, "angular," attached as a prefix. If we measure the angle from the horizontal radius in Figure 1 over to the particle, this angle is called the **angular position** of the mass *m*. Angles in rotational kinematics are expressed in radians rather than degrees, where the following conversion factor must be kept in mind,

$$180° \equiv \pi \text{ radians.}$$

An **angular displacement**, $\Delta\theta$, is just a change in angular position and if this occurs over a time interval, Δt, then the average angular velocity, ω_{avg}, is written,

$$\omega_{avg} \equiv \Delta\theta/\Delta t \quad \text{(rad/s).}$$

As in one dimension, the instantaneous **angular velocity** is

$$\omega \equiv \Delta\theta/\Delta t \quad (\Delta t \text{ is very small).} \tag{5}$$

If ω changes, as it does when the motion is non-uniform circular motion, then there is an **angular acceleration** (rad/s²) given by,

$$\alpha \equiv \Delta\omega/\Delta t \quad (\Delta t \text{ is very small).} \tag{6}$$

Note that angular acceleration is not the same as centripetal acceleration (v^2/r) since centripetal acceleration points toward the center of the circle. Moreover, in uniform circular motion centripetal acceleration is non-zero but angular acceleration is zero.

Finally, there is a rotational generalization for mass too, which is called rotational mass or **moment of inertia**, I, which for our particle *m* moving in a circle is given by,

$$I \equiv m r^2 \quad \text{(particle of mass } m\text{).} \tag{7}$$

The units for moment of inertia are kg-m². Large values of I mean the particle is massive and moves in a large radius circle. Putting all of this together, there is a rotational version of Newton's second law,

Newton's Second Law (Rotational Form)

$$\tau_{net} = I\,\alpha. \tag{8}$$

Initially, all of this extra vocabulary for circular motion may seem a bit daunting and unnecessary. To absorb all the new jargon, it is helpful to think in terms of analogies between linear and rotational quantities. These are summarized below (note the last entry will be introduced in a short while).

Linear	Rotational
x	θ
Δx	$\Delta\theta$
v	ω
a	α
m	I
F	τ
p	L

The above discussion seems to be rather restricted since it pertains only to the case of a single particle moving in a circle. And yet, the results are remarkably relevant to much more complicated situations. For instance, a common problem in rotation involves a system known as a rigid body. As one might guess, a *rigid body* is basically a very hard object—no vibrations can occur. A rotating rigid body then can be viewed as a collection of particles, all of which are executing circular motion of varying radii. The above development for a single particle in circular motion is then applicable to that of a rotating rigid body. The major difference is, the moment of inertia of the rigid body is not given by equation (7) since that equation assumed the body was a particle. For rigid bodies there are tables that give the moment of inertia based on the geometry of the body (sphere, cylinder, rod, etc.) and where the axis of rotation is situated. If you take a more advanced physics course you will find such tables listed in your textbook.

All of the kinematic and dynamic concepts introduced to analyze motion of a particle in one dimension may be generalized to study rotational motion, even the linear momentum of a particle has a generalization known as **angular momentum,** L (the last entry in the table above). Returning once again to Figure 1, the linear momentum of a mass m is $\vec{p} \equiv m\vec{v}$ where $\vec{v}$ is the velocity. The angular momentum of the circulating particle in the figure has a magnitude defined by,

$$L \equiv pr = mvr = I\omega \text{ (rigid body).} \tag{9}$$

In more advanced work it is useful to define angular momentum as a vector quantity like linear momentum $(m\vec{v})$. There is even a conservation law for angular momentum but this would take us beyond the scope of the present textbook.

Example Four.—*Torque on a jar of jelly.*

A jar of jelly has the shape of a cylinder with radius 4 cm. A tangential force of 20 N is applied to the jar in order to open it. Find the torque on the jar by this force.

Solution.

First, convert 4 cm to meters then use this in equation (4),

$$\tau = F_{\text{tangential}}\, r$$

$$\tau = 20 \times 0.04 = \underline{0.8 \text{ N-m}}.$$

Example Five.—*Spinning a bicycle wheel.*

A bicycle wheel can be viewed as a hoop with radius 20.0 cm, of negligible thickness, and mass 600 grams. Assuming the wheel starts from rest, what tangential force must you apply to give the wheel a constant angular acceleration of 2.00 rad/s²? Neglect friction.

Solution.

We will use equation (7) to obtain the moment of inertia of the wheel, and then use this result in equations (4) and (8) to solve for the force.

$$I = 0.6 \text{ kg } (0.20 \text{ m})^2 = 0.024 \text{ kgm}^2$$

$$\tau_{\text{net}} \equiv F_{\text{tangential}}\, r = I\,\alpha = 0.024\,(2.00) = 0.048$$

Solving for the force by dividing this last result by *r* gives,

$$F_{\text{tangential}} = 0.048/0.2 = \underline{0.24 \text{ Newtons}}$$

Example Six.—*Angular momentum of the planets: Kepler's first and second laws.*

Find the torque exerted by the Sun on every one of the planets in our solar system. Even though *Kepler's first law* states the orbits are elliptical, assume they are circles. What implication does your answer have for the orbital angular momentum of the planets?

Solution.

To solve this problem you might be tempted to search for the mass of the Sun and planets, and look up the radius of each planet's orbit. However, the solution is much simpler. Since the gravitational force on each planet points toward the center of its circular orbit, there is zero torque by the Sun. The gravitational force is only keeping the planets in their circular orbits without speeding them up or down. But according to equation (8) if the net torque on a planet is zero then we see it will have zero angular acceleration. Finally, this means all of the following quantities are constant: *m*, *v* and *r*. Using equation (9) therefore the angular momentum (mvr) of a planet is also constant. This finding is an example of the general law: the principle of conservation of angular momentum. One consequence of this principle is Kepler's second law of planetary motion that states the radius from the Sun to the planet sweeps out equal areas in equal time intervals. Although not obvious, this law is a direct consequence of angular momentum conservation.

D. Applications: Gravitation.

Suppose a very large mass **M** is stationary and a much smaller mass m is orbiting **M** in a circle of radius r with constant speed. Since m is executing uniform circular motion, m has a centripetal acceleration that points toward the center of the circular orbit. Assume the force holding m in its orbit is the gravitational attraction by **M**. We also know that m obeys Newton's second law. Therefore,

$$F = GMm/r^2 = ma$$
$$= mv^2/r$$

This gives,

$$v = [GM/r]^{1/2} \qquad (10)$$

Equation (10) is remarkable since it gives the speed an object must have to establish a circular orbit of radius r around a mass **M**. It is sometimes called the *orbital equation*. In short, it says a small radius orbit (r small) around **M** requires a large speed (v large) for the orbiting particle.

But we also know the speed is the circumference of the circle divided by the time for m to make one circle, T, called the ***period*** of the motion,

$$v = 2\pi r/T.$$

Equating the last two equations for v gives,

$$[GM/r]^{1/2} = 2\pi r/T.$$

Squaring this and solving for T^2 leads to an historically famous result known as Kepler's third law of planetary motion,

$$T^2 = 4\pi^2 r^3/GM. \qquad (11)$$

In words, equation (11) expresses the fact that the period gets larger as the radius of the orbit grows. Consequently, the outer planets that have a large orbital radius (large r) take longer (large T) to go around the Sun than the inner planets that have a smaller orbital radius.

Example Seven.—*Geosynchronous orbits of a satellite.*

How high above the Earth's surface must a satellite be placed so that the satellite remains above the same point? Such an orbit is called a geosynchronous orbit.

Solution.

The distance from the center of the Earth to the satellite denote r, the radius of the Earth, R_E (= 6.38×10^6 m), and the height of the satellite above the Earth's surface, h. Then,

$$r = R_E + h.$$

The period for the satellite, T, will need to be one day in order for it to stay above one point of the surface of the Earth. Hence, the speed of the satellite must be,

$$v = 2\pi r/T.$$

Using Newton's second law, the centripetal acceleration formula and the law of gravitation just as we did above, we arrive once again at equation (11),

$$T^2 = 4\pi^2 r^3/GM_E,$$

where instead of M being the mass of the Sun, it is that of the Earth, M_E. Rearranging this to find r^3,

$$r^3 = T^2 GM_E/4\pi^2.$$

Take the cube root to get,

$$r = (GM_E/4\pi^2)^{1/3} T^{2/3}.$$

Substituting in numbers with $M_E = 5.974 \times 10^{24}$ kg and T = 1 d $\times$ 24 hr/d $\times$ 60 min/hr $\times$ 60 s/min = 86,400 s gives,

$$r = (6.67 \times 10^{-11} \times 5.974 \times 10^{24}/4\pi^2)^{1/3} (86,400)^{2/3}$$

$$r = 21,611 \times 1,954 = 42,227,894 \text{ m}$$

$$h = r - R_E = 42,227,894 - 6,380,000 = \underline{35,848,000 \text{ m}}$$

or, h is about <u>22,000 miles</u> above the surface of the Earth.

Summary.

The gravitational force and field are introduced. The force is an inverse-square law. We continue a study of rotation by defining angular velocity, angular acceleration, moment of inertia and torque. The torque is a measure of the twisting ability of a force. The moment of inertia of a system depends on both its mass and how its mass is distributed in space relative to an axis of rotation. With this background one can state the rotational form of Newton's second law of motion which involves torque, moment of inertia, and angular acceleration.

QUESTIONS.

1. Is a force needed to keep a particle moving in a circle? If so, what is the direction of the force?

2. If the distance between two planets is tripled the new gravitational force divided by the original force is

   (a) 3

   (b) 9

   (c) 1/3

   (d) 1/9

   (e) 1/2

3. If the mass of each of two point masses doubles then by what factor does the force between the two masses increase?

   (a) 1

   (b) 2

   (c) 3

   (d) 4

   (e) you cannot answer without more numerical information

4. Suppose a point mass M is at the origin of coordinates and point mass m at $x = a > 0$. In what region(s) of the x-axis is there a place where the total gravitational field due to M and m add to zero?

   (a) $x < 0$

   (b) $0 < x < a$

   (c) $x > a$

5. Saturn has a mass 95.1 times that of Earth and Saturn has a gravitational field at its surface with the value 9.05 m/s². From this determine the ratio of the radius of Saturn to that of Earth. Note: As usual, for Earth use $g = 10$ m/s².

6. Would you weigh more, less, or the same on the Moon? (The gravitational field on the surface of the Moon is 1/6 that of its value on the surface of the Earth.)

7. Suppose the universal gravitational "constant" G was in fact decreasing with time. Assuming the radius of the Earth's circular orbit around the Sun stays the same, how would this change the time for one revolution around the Sun? Hint: See Kepler's third law.

8. Two people attract each other gravitationally. Why don't they therefore accelerate toward each other? or do they?

9. Circle the statement below that is true. The gravitational force acting between two particles
   (*a*) is independent of the distance between them

   (*b*) obeys the law of superposition

   (*c*) is inversely proportional to the distance between them

   (*d*) can be shielded by the presence of an intervening mass

10. The universal constant of gravitation (G) is
   (*a*) different depending where you are in the universe

   (*b*) found from measuring the speed of light

   (*c*) equals g at the Earth's surface

   (*d*) is found by measuring the force of attraction between two known masses of a known separation

11. Historically Isaac Newton thought about the motion of the Moon around the Earth. Newton would claim the Moon does not fall to Earth because
   (*a*) it has zero net force acting on it

   (*b*) it is in Earth's gravitational field

   (*c*) it is beyond the influence of Earth's pull

   (*d*) it experiences forces due to the Sun and other planets that balance the force on it by Earth

   (*e*) the Earth's gravitational force is what is causing the Earth's centripetal acceleration

12. The Earth exerts a force of 1 Newton on a typical apple. What is the force the apple exerts on the Earth?

13. In previous chapters we used the formula mg for the weight of a mass m. In this chapter the weight of m is given by GMm/r^2 where M is the Earth's mass. Are we being inconsistent? Explain.

14. Why is Newton's law of gravitation called universal?

15. What is the difference between weight and mass?

16. If the radius of a circular orbit is to increase by a factor of four, by how much must the speed of the orbiting body change? Hint: see the orbital equation.

17. Certain nineteenth-century geological theories postulated that the Earth has been shrinking in radius as it slowly cools. If indeed this occurred, how would this alter the value of g at Earth's surface?

18. When writing about the ultimate cause of gravity, Newton said "I do not feign hypotheses." What did he mean by this?

19. Describe the force on a mass m that is moving with constant speed in a circle.

20. Perhaps you have observed a motorcycle at an amusement park that enters a spherical cage and moves in a vertical circle (see figure below). Assuming the motorcycle is moving counterclockwise in uniform circular motion, at the points A, B, C, D in the figure, indicate the direction of the velocity and acceleration vectors as well as all force vectors acting on the motorcycle.

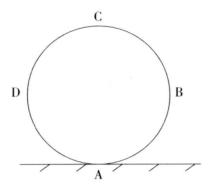

21. A popular ride at amusement parks is the "rotor." People enter a cylindrical room and place their backs up against the walls of the room. The room then begins spinning. Next, the floor is lowered and people remain stuck to the walls as the room spins. Make a diagram of a person that is pinned to the wall of this ride and indicate all of the forces acting on the person. Is friction required for this ride to work? Explain.

22. Describe the forces, torques, and moments of inertia involved when two children are at play on a teeter-totter.

23. A child sits on the floor of a spinning merry-go-round. What forces are acting on the child?

24. Is the angular velocity of a point on the Earth's equator the same as a point near the Earth's poles? How about its speed?

25. What is the angular acceleration of the Earth in its rotation? in its revolution?

26. Explain how the spin-dry cycle of a washing machine works.

27. Where on the Earth's surface would your centripetal acceleration be largest?

28. Recall the *period* of circular motion is the time to go around once. The *frequency* is the inverse of the period. What is the frequency of Earth's rotation? revolution?

29. Estimate the frequency of motion for a person on a ferris wheel. (see previous problem)

PROBLEMS.

1. An apple (mass of about 0.10 kg) is on a rocket that is a distance of 50.0 km above the surface of the Earth. Determine the gravitational force on the apple by the Earth. You will need to look up the mass and radius of the Earth—see the flyleaf of this book.

2. A girl of mass 40.0 kg is in a rocket ship an altitude of 35.0 km above the surface of the Earth. Determine the gravitational force on the girl by the Earth. You will need to look up the mass and radius of the Earth—see the flyleaf of this book.

3. Romeo has a mass of 75.0 kg and Juliet a mass of 45.0 kg. Romeo serenades Juliet in the courtyard below her (bed) room window—a distance of separation of 20.0 m. What is the force of attraction between these two lovers and how does that force compare to the weight of a typical apple (1 N)?

4. Mars has a mass that is 0.1074 that of Earth. Assume Earth and Mars are a distance of 78×10^6 km apart. How far from the center of the Earth would one need to be so that the net gravitational force due to Earth and Mars would add to zero?

5. Venus has a mass that is 0.815 that of Earth. Assume Earth and Venus are a distance of 42×10^6 km apart. How far from the center of the Earth would one need to be so that the net gravitational force due to Earth and Venus would add to zero?

6. Jupiter has a radius of 7.1×10^4 km. The gravitational field at the surface of Jupiter is 22.9 m/s². From this determine the mass of Jupiter in kg.

7. The Sun has a radius of 6.96×10^5 km. The gravitational field at the surface of the Sun is 274 m/s². From this determine the mass of the Sun in kg.

8. The radius and mass of the Moon are 1.74×10^6 m and 7.36×10^{22} kg. Find the value of the Moon's gravitational field at the surface of the Moon. What is the ratio of the Moon's gravitational field at its surface to that of the Earth's gravitational field at its surface?

9. A mayonnaise jar has a circular lid of radius 5.0 cm and it is found that a tangential force of 10.0 N is required to begin to cause the lid to rotate. What torque is exerted on the lid?

10. The cork of a bottle of wine is circular of radius 0.5 cm and it is found that a tangential force of 5.0 N is required to begin to cause the cork to rotate. What torque is exerted on the cork?

11. Continuing problem 9, suppose the moment of inertia of the mayonnaise jar lid is 1.5×10^{-4} kgm². Determine the angular acceleration of the lid under the torque in problem 9.

12. Continuing problem 10, suppose the moment of inertia of the cork is 0.5×10^{-4} kgm². Determine the angular acceleration of the cork under the torque in problem 10.

13. A pirate with a mass of 90.0 kg stands on the end of a 2.0 m long plank. What torque is needed to keep him from falling in the shark-infested water below?

14. The hula hoop was invented in 1948 by Mellin and Knerr in a garage. They got the idea for the toy from schoolchildren in Australia who made hoops out of bamboo and spinned the hoops around their waists. Mellin and Knerr brought the hula hoop to the United States market where it became a national obsession during the 1950s. By 1958 20,000 hula hoops per day were produced and more than 15 million were sold that year. Suppose the radius of a hula hoop is 75.0 cm and the mass is 200 grams. Compute the moment of inertia of the hula hoop about its center. You may use the point mass formula for moment of inertia since all of the mass is at the same distance from the center. (Source: *The Old Farmer's Almanac*, pp. 147–148, 2006).

15. In the second of the *Pirates of the Caribbean* films (2006) a rather large wheel is introduced. (You will recall, actor Johnny Depp [**Captain** Jack Sparrow] rides the wheel down a mountain side.) Assuming the radius of the wheel is 3.0 m and the mass is 100.0 kg, find the moment of inertia of the wheel about its center. You may use the point mass formula for moment of inertia since all of the mass is at the same distance from the center.

16. Find the angular velocity of the Earth in its orbit around the Sun. (Assume the orbit is a circle.)

17. Find the angular velocity of the Earth as it rotates on its axis.

18. Use Kepler's third law to determine the period (in years) of orbit for the "planet" Pluto. (Pluto is a distance of 5900×10^6 km from the Sun.)

19. Use Kepler's third law to determine the period (in years) of orbit for the planet Mars. (Mars is a distance of 228×10^6 km from the Sun.)

20. (a) What orbital radius must a satellite of Earth have in order for its period to be 0.5 days? (b) How high (in miles) is such a satellite above the Earth's surface?

21. (a) What orbital radius must a satellite of Earth have in order for its period to be 27 days? (b) Do we have a particular Earth satellite in mind?

22. What speed must a projectile have in order for it to establish a circular motion around the Earth at an altitude corresponding to the height of Mt. Everest? Neglect air friction. Mt. Everest is 8853 m above sea level. Give your answer in m/s and mph.

23. Two satellites 1 and 2 of the same mass are going around the Earth in concentric orbits. Satellite 2 has an orbital radius twice that of satellite 1. What is the ratio of the force on 2 to that acting on 1?

   (*a*) 1/8

   (*b*) 1/4

   (*c*) 1/2

   (*d*) 1/√2

   (*e*) 1

Hints and answers to problems.

1) 0.968 N   2) 389 N   3) 5.63 × 10^{-10} N   4) 5.87 × 10^{10} m   5) 2.21 × 10^{10} m   6) 1.73 × 10^{27} kg   7) 1.99 × 10^{30} kg   8) 1.62 m/s^2 9) 0.5 Nm   10) 0.025 Nm   11) 3300 s^{-2} 12) 5000 s^{-2} 13) 1800 Nm   14) 0.113 kgm^2 15) 900 kgm^2 16) 1.99 × 10^{-7} 1/s   17) 7.26 × 10^{-5} 1/s   18) 248 y   19) 1.88 y   20) 2.6616 × 10^7 m   20.25 × 10^6 m   21) 3.8 × 10^8 m Same as distance to the Moon   22) 17,700 mph   Hint: use the orbital equation   23) b

ℜCHAPTER VI.
THINGS THAT DON'T CHANGE IN MOTION.

Abstract.

Momentum and energy are important mechanical properties of a system. We examine how to calculate and use these two new ideas to solve problems that heretofore would be, in many instances, nearly impossible to solve using Newton's laws of motion. Historically, these ideas emerged over a long period of time starting with an examination of simple systems of colliding balls. Descartes, Huygens and Leibniz figure prominently in the early development of these new concepts, although energy conservation was not fully developed until the mid-nineteenth century. The ability of a force to produce work, impulse, and power are also studied herein.

Definitions. impulse, momentum, internal and external forces, completely inelastic collision, work, dot product, kinetic energy, gravitational potential energy, total mechanical energy, elastic collision, and power

Principles. The conservation of momentum and conservation of energy

Fundamental Equations. impulse-momentum relation and the work-energy relation

Two of nature's conservation laws, the conservation of momentum and the conservation of energy, are presented in this chapter. Other conservation laws include conservation of electric charge and angular momentum. The derivation of momentum and energy conservation utilizes Newton's laws of motion. In fact, the conservation laws are wholly based on Newton's laws, so one might naturally ask, what is the use of these two new laws? Indeed, any result we find based on conservation will be in complete agreement with what we would have found based on Newton's laws. The pragmatic answer is, conservation laws are useful. It is somewhat surprising to find there are many problems in physics that would be extremely difficult to solve using Newton's laws but which become relatively easy to solve using the mechanical conservation laws. Just like a carpenter who has various tools to use, it is useful for the physicist to have more than one approach to problem solving.

A. Descartes, Huygens, and Leibniz.

Herein we give a brief summary of highlights of the lives of three seventeenth century pioneers in the physics of conservation laws: Descartes, Huygens, and Leibniz. All three of these individuals' lives overlapped with and significantly influenced the great Isaac Newton.

The idea that in a world of continual change, some things never change, is an old notion. In physics one of the earliest manifestations of this idea was developed during the study of collisions.

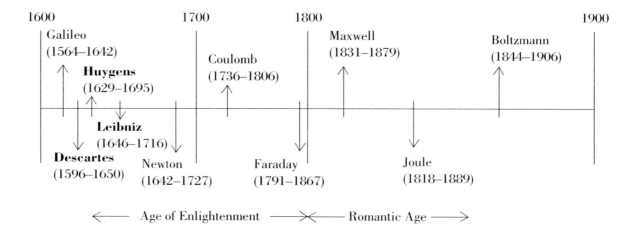

1600   1700   1800   1900

Galileo
(1564–1642)
  Huygens
  (1629–1695)
Coulomb
(1736–1806)
Maxwell
(1831–1879)
Boltzmann
(1844–1906)

Leibniz
(1646–1716)
Descartes
(1596–1650)   Newton
              (1642–1727)
Faraday
(1791–1867)
Joule
(1818–1889)

←——— Age of Enlightenment ———✕——— Romantic Age ——→

It was the year 1666 when members of the new Royal Society of London met and the members were amazed as they observed the collision between two hardwood pendulum bobs. A great deal of discussion and controversy ensued during the next several years as the members tried to explain their observations. Why did the first ball stop and the second one rise to the same height of the first ball? The eventual explanation and continued development of conservation principles started with the views of Descartes, Huygens, and Leibniz. Descartes and Leibniz were philosophers of major impact while Huygens is mostly known for his work in physics.

Courtesy of Erich Lessing/Art Resource, NY.

Rene Descartes (1596–1650).

"A man is incapable of comprehending any argument that interferes with his revenues."

—Descartes

Rene Descartes is often cited as the father of both modern philosophy and modern mathematics. He was born in 1596 near Tours, France. His life spanned a period of enormous religious bigotry and political turmoil in Europe. In those days there were giants in the land: Descartes outlived Galileo by eight years and Newton was eight when Descartes died. The family of Descartes was part of the French nobility, although they were not especially wealthy. Most of Rene's life was spent in and out of bed due to his frequent sicknesses. Early on it was apparent that Rene was exceptionally curious about all things, although he was not viewed as overly precocious. At the age of eight, Descartes began a rigorous Jesuit college education that was focused primarily on the humanities. He remained at the college until 1612. The rector of the college took an early liking to Rene, and knowing of his health problems, allowed him to stay in bed as late as he pleased before coming to the classroom. Those mornings of rest led to a lifetime of intense meditation. Although, for the most part he was a loyal Catholic, Descartes had a skeptical and rational mind which might have arisen as a reaction to the extreme dogmatic intellectual climate he found himself in. Indeed, he is most famous because of his oft-repeated question, "how do we know anything?" Descartes' greatest love was mathematics since he felt among all fields mathematics is the area where one can deduce proofs and therefore gain certain knowledge. Descartes' major mathematical contribution was the invention of analytic geometry—a fusion of algebra with geometry—which is most commonly encountered in the Cartesian coordinate system. In philosophy Descartes is famous for invoking the Latin phrase "Cogito ergo sum," which translated means, "I think, therefore I am." He wrote *Meditations* wherein he envisioned a malicious demon who tries to deceive him about everything at every moment. Descartes' life was a quest for certain knowledge. He wanted to know what could not be doubted and eventually concluded that his own existence was beyond doubt. Moreover, Descartes desired to fashion a rational philosophical system that encompassed all aspects of life and was beyond doubt. It is to Descartes we owe the vision of all knowledge as a tree with the roots being metaphysics, and the trunk physics and the other sciences the branches. Descartes sought to convince his contemporaries to loosen their hold on Aristotle's philosophy in order to seek truth by reason alone rather than relying on authorities.

Following college Rene engaged in a short period of raucous living in Paris, after which "to get a little peace Descartes decided to go to war." It was during a lull in the action in 1619 that the soldier Descartes experienced three dreams which led to a religious and scientific reawakening and became a watershed for his life. Out of these night thoughts emerged analytic geometry and Descartes' further resolve to rationalize the world of nature. Descartes created a dualistic philosophy wherein science governs the material world including human bodies while a completely separate realm of spirit and human mind has its own distinct laws which are best left to the thoughts and disputations of philosophers and theologians. This was a convenient arrangement for someone like Descartes who embraced both science and religion. In this dualism, science and religion are separate and therefore, cannot be a threat to each other. Eventually many intellectuals embraced Cartesian dualism and like Descartes came to think of the material world as essentially a giant machine. Some speculated that even animals may be like machines.

On a more human level, although Descartes was attracted to the opposite sex, he never married. For twenty years he roamed over Holland as a vagabond philosopher-scientist. In 1634 at the age of thirty-eight he was at work on the final revision of his masterpiece *Traite du monde (Discourse on Method)*, which was to be a summary of his wide-ranging discoveries in science and thoughts on philosophy and religion. Hearing of how Galileo was treated by the inquisition because of his heretical Copernican opinions, Descartes chose to steer clear of a similar fate. His thoughts contained much more potentially controversial material of a religious nature than the works of Galileo.

Descartes, who also embraced the Copernican viewpoint, wisely chose not to publish *Le Monde*. His decision was not out of cowardice but resulted more from his loyalty to the Catholic faith and therefore, his unwillingness to contradict the views of the Pope. The publication was delayed until 1637. The last days of his life were spent tutoring a Swedish royal, Queen Christina, whereupon he contracted a lung inflammation that did not respond to the state-of-the-art medicine of the time— bleeding by leeches. He died in 1650 at the age of 54.

It remains to answer the question, why is Descartes important to physics? Descartes made three major contributions to physics: first, the law of refraction in optics which also included studies of the rainbow; second, the idea that the whole universe is filled with vortices in the ether which explains the attraction of heavenly bodies for one another; and third, Descartes' belief that in the beginning God created a fixed amount of motion in the universe, and so this fixed amount could not be depleted. The vortex model conflicted with the later proposed universal law of gravitation. The model became quite popular even in Newton's day, however. The third contribution forms the seed of the idea of a conservation law. Descartes argued that it would be impious to believe that the amount of motion given to the world by God in the beginning somehow becomes depleted over time. Rene posited that which is fixed (conserved) is the product of mass times speed, however. He almost had it right. It remained for his friend, Huygens, to make an important correction. Although Rene Descartes was a brilliant mathematician and philosopher, most of his work in physics was eventually discarded except for the idea of conservation.

Courtesy of Bettmann/Corbis.

Christiaan Huygens (1629–1695).

Of the three individuals under discussion here, the Dutch physicist Huygens, who was a contemporary of Newton, made the most lasting and important contributions to physics. But his name is not as recognizable by most people as Descartes and Leibniz. Perhaps this can be attributed to his narrower intellectual pursuits and comparatively less focus on philosophical ideas. We begin with his major work in physics, which was primarily work in mechanics, and conclude with a short recap of his life.

Huygens is credited with being the first person to derive the formula for centripetal acceleration, v^2/r. Huygens, along with several others, also made strides in the mid-seventeenth century by his analysis of the collisions of hard balls. This work was prompted by an ingenious demonstration at the Royal Society of London in 1666 involving two pendula in close proximity. (This device is now a familiar lecture demonstration but with five pendula rather than just two.) Over a period of several years people analyzed colliding pendulum bobs and from this analysis Huygens arrived at some fundamental discoveries. He postulated that in elastic collisions a quantity mv^2 (later called vis viva by Leibniz) was conserved for the system of balls. With this discovery we can attribute the conservation of kinetic energy in elastic collisions to the work of Huygens. Moreover, by 1669 Huygens realized that Descartes' definition of quantity of motion (mass times speed, mv) had to be changed to mass times velocity (momentum, $m\vec{v}$) in order to have the correct law of conservation of momentum. Additionally, Huygens' work with pendula led to his development of the pendulum clock. The pendulum clock had profound implications for society at large (e.g. applications to navigation) since previously the art and science of time keeping had been crude.

Outside of mechanics, Huygens developed a wave theory of light based on what later became known as Huygens' principle. Huygens' principle is an important idea that is useful to this day. The principle provides a different perspective on light propagation in contrast to the particle model espoused by Newton. Unfortunately, partly due to the stature of Newton, Huygens' wave model was largely ignored in his day but it was later found to be a fruitful principle of wave propagation.

But what do we know of the life of Huygens outside of his physics pursuits? In contrast to Newton, Huygens came from a wealthy family. His brilliant and influential father was a career diplomat in service to the Dutch royalty. Huygens' father, Constantin, exhibited a keen interest in mathematics as attested to by his close friendship with Rene Descartes who thought highly of his broad ranging intellectual pursuits. Christiaan's extraordinarily intelligent mother also came from a privileged background. Huygens and his brother were home schooled by a private tutor until Christiaan was age 16 (1645). Although his schooling concentrated on the arts and languages, he was especially interested in fashioning mechanical models and showed promise in his geometrical abilities. Christiaan was a sensitive, delicate and sickly child who made a lasting impression on Descartes. In 1645 Huygens entered the University of Leyden, studying law and mathematics; he was an excellent pupil. In 1655 he visited Paris for the first time. His interest in physics began in about 1650 with his major scientific accomplishments made during the next sixteen years. Huygens' abilities in physics were nearly on par with those of Newton. In 1664 he left Paris to return to his homeland, after which he went back to Paris in 1666 to remain there for the next seventeen years. During this period he made numerous contacts with scientists in London who were members of the Royal Society of London. One of those he met was Isaac Newton. For many of the years he lived in Paris Christiaan was president of the Paris Academy. In spite of his association with the Paris Academy, Huygens was more impressed by the work of London's Royal Society. It was in 1673 that he made his most important contributions to horology, i.e. the science of clock making. By 1670 his chronic poor health seems to have deteriorated even further. Hence, not many years thereafter he returned to The Hague. By 1680 his health problems had taken a toll on his scientific endeavors. Huygens never married, although on several occasions he was involved in romantic attachments. During the seventeenth century Huygens was second only to Newton in his accomplishments in natural philosophy, having been most influenced by the mechanistic philosophy of his family's close friend, Rene Descartes.

Courtesy of Bildarchiv Preussischer
Kulturbesitz/Art Resource, NY.

G. W. Leibniz (1646–1716).

Leibniz has been called a "universal genius." He was born in Leipzig, Germany and died in Hanover, Germany. As a youth he taught himself several languages while studying history. Leibniz received a baccalaureate in 1663 followed by a doctorate in law in 1667. He later developed an interest in philosophy and natural philosophy (physics). Our man served as a diplomat in Paris from 1672 to 1676. Best known for his contributions to mathematics and philosophy, he desired to subsume all thought to symbolic logic and mathematics. It was during his diplomatic period in Paris, 1675–1676 to be exact, that Leibniz invented calculus. Independently, Isaac Newton also developed calculus and this became fuel for a prolonged public feud between Leibniz and Newton, virtually following them to the grave.

On the personal level, Leibniz was reportedly not a very pleasant individual. Indeed, several not uncommon traits of German philosophers in that day was their somewhat arid and rather hard to follow writing style, which Leibniz shared with his German colleagues. It has been said that Leibniz had a public philosophy that at times bordered on being shallow as exemplified by his famous phrase: "this is the best of all possible worlds." Some of his opponents countered his optimism with the statement, "this is the worst of all possible worlds," arguing there is just enough good present to make the maximum amount of evil. On the other hand, Leibniz had a more private philosophy that was quite profound. His thought was deeply influenced by the philosophies of Aristotle and Descartes. Leibniz posited that all substances consist of a hierarchy of point like monads, immortal souls. Monads could not interact; they only appeared to. The world has a "pre-established harmony" between monads, given by God, and which gives the appearance but not the reality of monad interactions. The dominant monad is our soul and yet each person consists of many monads. Leibniz was an idealist thereby denying the existence of matter. He believed in human free will. Moreover, he devoted much time to shoring up the standard arguments for the existence of God. He maintained there are an infinite number of possible worlds, i.e. worlds that are logical, and God created the best of these possibilities. Hence, our world is the one world with the most harmony and the greatest surplus of good over evil. His philosophy had elements of determinism but more than anything else his views were rational, emphasizing a law of contradiction and a law of sufficient reason.

Although Leibniz was interested in physics, this was not his main area of concentration. He did, however, have some ideas that are worth pointing out and that make his views relevant to this chapter. Like the Greeks, he did not believe in the vacuum since for Leibniz a vacuum denies that

God created as much good as possible. During his diplomatic era in 1672 at age 26 in Paris he met Huygens who taught him the mathematics underlying the pendulum. In 1673 he visited London and met English mathematicians at the newly founded Royal Society. By analyzing the simple act of tossing a stone vertically, Leibniz is credited with providing physics with two of its most useful concepts, kinetic and potential energy. In fact, Leibniz named the quantity studied by Huygens, mv^2, "vis viva" (living force), and he argued that as a stone ascends it loses vis viva only to gain potential (stored) energy. From this point it is only a short step to surmise that the total energy—kinetic plus potential, at all times is conserved (neglecting friction).

He left London to return to Paris and after concluding his diplomatic work there in 1676 he left Paris. For a short period of time he used his diplomatic skills—with no luck—to attempt a unification of the various factions of the Christian church. The last twenty-five years of his life were devoted to philosophy. Leibniz died in relative obscurity only to be rediscovered later.

References.

Remarkable Physicists, Ioan James (Cambridge UP, 2004).

Great Physicists, William H. Cropper (Oxford UP, 2004).

The Project Physics Course, Rutherford, Holton, and Watson (Holt, Rhinehart and Winston, 1970).

Physics, the Human Adventure, Gerald Holton and Stephen Brush (Rutgers University Press, 2001).

Men of Mathematics, E. T. Bell (Simon and Schuster, 1965).

A History of Philosophy, Frederick Copleston (Image, 1963).

A History of Western Philosophy, Bertrand Russell (Simon and Schuster, 1945).

Thinking Through Philosophy, Chris Horner and Emrys Westacott (Cambridge UP, 2000).

B. Impulse and Momentum.

Consider a particle of mass m that is restricted to move in one dimension along the x-axis (the proceeding is easily generalized to include vectors). Newton's second law for *m* acted on by a net force F_{net}, which is parallel to the x-axis, is familiar to us already,

$$F_{net} = ma.$$

The net force causes the mass to undergo an acceleration and from our studies of kinematics we know precisely what is meant by the acceleration of the mass.

$$a = \Delta v/\Delta t. \quad (\Delta t \text{ is very small}).$$

Combining these last two equations,

$$F_{net} = m\Delta v/\Delta t,$$

and this can be rearranged by multiplying both sides by Δt to obtain,

$$F_{net}\Delta t = m\Delta v \quad (\Delta t \text{ is very small}). \tag{1}$$

This new expression is really only a restatement of Newton's second law based on the definition of acceleration. Equation (1) suggests we define two new terms, linear momentum and impulse:

$$p \equiv mv \text{ (\textbf{\textit{linear momentum}} of } m) \quad \text{and} \quad J \equiv F\Delta t \quad (\textbf{\textit{impulse}} \text{ of force over a very small } \Delta t).$$

Several comments are in order. First, the impulse of a force depends both on the value of the force and the time interval over which the force acts, Δt. Above we assumed the time interval to be very small. However, if the force is constant (which occurs often in elementary physics) then the time interval does not have to be very small. Second, it is useful to remember: *a force causes an acceleration but as equation (1) indicates, an impulse causes a momentum change.* Third, for dimensions greater than one, both p and J become vector quantities since $\vec{v}$ and $\vec{F}_{net}$ are vectors and multiplying these vectors by the scalars m and Δt yields vectors. Armed with these two new definitions, equation (1) can be restated as an important principle of physics,

$$\textit{Impulse-Momentum Relation}$$
$$\vec{J}_{net} = \vec{F}_{net}\Delta t = \Delta\vec{p} = m\Delta\vec{v} \quad (\Delta t \text{ is very small}) \tag{2}$$

(If $\vec{F}_{net}$ is constant then Δt does not have to be very small.)

Since equation (2) is only a restatement of Newton's second law one might justifiably ask, what good is it? Equation (2) is *not* going to lead to results that are different than would be found using the second law. There are several reasons for the significance of equation (2), though. One is, equation (2) is *useful* in describing the forces involved when objects collide with each other. This usefulness is illustrated by the next two examples.

Example One.—*The guillotine (Oh no!).*

Courtesy of Bridgeman-Giraudon/Art Resource, NY.

From pp. 10 and 169 of the *Encyclopedia of Crime*, Oliver Cyriax, Colin Wilson and Damon Wilson (Overlook Press, 2006) we find some rather curious background for this example. **If you are squeamish, just skip this example and go on to the next.**

The guillotine gets its name from the Frenchman Dr. Guillotin, who suggested this form of execution to the French Revolutionary Council in 1789. Dr. Guillotin, who did not actually invent the device (the inventor was a Dr. Louis), was described by a contemporary as "devoid of either talent or repute." The device, however, was considered a much more humane form of execution than the previously preferred mode, i.e. torture. Before this invention, only the nobility were afforded the luxury of execution by decapitation. Reportedly, the guillotine works so fast that the victim's lungs still contain their last inhaled air and as a consequence, a peculiar whistling noise is emitted *after* the parting of the ways. The French became so enthralled by this invention that on many occasions large crowds accompanied executions. The device even became somewhat of a "quasi-religious totem." The guillotine was finally abolished in 1981. Let us move on to guillotine physics.

Suppose the mass of the falling blade is 2.0 kg and the blade falls from a height of 4.00 m before encountering the obstacle that will bring it to rest. If the blade is in contact with the obstacle for 0.01 s in coming to a final rest, find the force experienced by the obstacle.

Solution.

To unpack this rather morose tale, we will first determine the speed of the blade immediately after the 4 m drop. Using the shortcut equation (no pun intended!) from our study of kinematics in one dimension,

$$v^2 = v_0{}^2 + 2a_y(y - y_0).$$

Placing the origin at the initial location of the blade, aiming the y-axis downward, and assuming the blade starts from rest we have: $y_0 = 0 = v_0$ and $a_y = g = 10$ m/s², $y = 4$ m and taking the square root,

$$v = \sqrt{(2gy)} = \sqrt{(2*10*4)} = 8.94 \text{ m/s}.$$

The force is determined by dividing equation (2),

$$F_{net}\Delta t = \Delta p = m\Delta v,$$

by Δt and putting in the numbers for the other quantities,

$$F_{net} = m\Delta v/\Delta t = 2 \text{ kg } (0 - 8.94 \text{ m/s}^2)/0.01\text{s}.$$

$$\underline{F_{net} \approx 1800 \text{ N}} \quad \text{(about the weight of 1800 apples).}$$

For those still reading, you can gain even further gory details from the above source.

Example Two.—*A nightmare: Falling out of a plane <u>without</u> a parachute.*

Consider two scenarios where a mass m undergoes a collision that takes it from a velocity of v to rest. In both cases the momentum change of the mass and the impulse acting on the mass are the same,

$$\Delta p = 0 - mv = J_{net}.$$

Even though the impulse is the same that does not mean the force experienced by the mass is because the time interval for the two cases might be different. In one case the force might be large and the corresponding time interval small while the opposite holds in the other case, therefore,

$$J_{net} = F_{net\,\Delta t} = F_{net}\Delta t = 0 - mv = -mv.$$

This important result is relevant in many everyday occurrences and is the physics behind why boxers wear boxing gloves and cars come equipped with seatbelts and airbags. If you ever have to fall from a great height, make sure you roll as much as possible when coming in contact with the ground. For instance, there is a story in the 1996 *Guinness Book of World Records* about a Royal Air Force rear gunner who had to bail out of his bomber, without a parachute. Unfortunately, the bomber was at an altitude of 5500 m. The gunner obtained a terminal speed of 54 m/s but survived the fall because his motion ($\Delta p = -mv$) was stopped relatively slowly (large Δt) due to his passing through branches of a pine tree combined with his landing on a pile of snow of thickness 46 cm. By making Δt large, the force his body experienced in being brought to a stop was small, F_{net}. The gunner received only minor injuries. On the other hand, we read also of a less fortunate individual. In 1972 a flight attendant was onboard a Yugoslavia DC-9 airplane that blew up at 10,160 m. This person received numerous broken bones and was in a coma for 27 days followed by an 18-month hospitalization. No report was made of the surface that caused her to come to rest but she did survive (at least until she was given the medical bills).

Another reason for the significance of equation (2) is it leads to one of the most fundamental ideas in physics, a conservation law for motion.

C. Constancy of Momentum.

One of the fundamental questions addressed by the ancient Greeks was the question: why does the world change rather than stay the same? Is your idea of a perfect world a dynamic world in which things are continually changing or a static world where nothing changes? At its foundation, motion is about change, and therefore mechanics is the study of changes. In our development of mechanics so far, change has been a central idea—just glance back and notice all the Δ's we have used throughout the past chapters.

But another approach to mechanics is to concentrate not on the changing quantities of motion but rather to focus on a few things that do not change amid the complexities of moving systems. This new perspective is encapsulated in the three conservation laws of mechanics, the conservation of angular momentum (see the previous chapter), momentum and energy. As usual in discussing a new topic in physics, we begin with the simplest of systems—a single particle. According to the impulse-momentum relation of equation (2), if the net force on the particle is zero then its momentum will not change. Since the mass of a particle is constant, this means its velocity must not change. This should sound familiar—it is Newton's law of inertia (law one) that states a free particle ($F_{net} = 0$) moves in a straight line with a constant speed. Momentum conservation (constancy) for a particle is then an idea that is not new.

But what about more complicated systems? Here one can also use momentum conservation with one proviso, the system must be isolated. Newton's laws of motion for a system of particles leads to the general conservation of momentum summarized in the box below.

Conservation of Momentum.

If a system is isolated ($\vec{F}_{net}^{\,ext} = 0$) then its momentum $\vec{P}$ is constant.   (3)

Conservation Law Ritual.

Step One. Define the system and make sure *momentum* is conserved.

Step Two. Add up the *momentum* at the initial and final times.

Step Three. Equate the *momenta* in step two and solve for the unknown.

The "ritual" outlined in equation (3) is a step-by-step procedure for using the conservation of momentum principle. All conservation laws use this same procedure, only the quantity that is conserved differs. For example, the conservation law of energy uses this ritual but with the substitution *momentum* → *energy*.

To understand the more complicated version of momentum conservation, assume there are two particles in our system. A particle in a two-particle system can experience two classes of forces: an internal force which is a force by the other particle within the system and external forces. According to equation (3) it is *only* the external forces that cause the momentum of a system to change— you can ignore the internal ones. So, we add up all of the external forces acting on particle one and do the same for particle two, then add the total external force on one and the total external force on particle two to get the grand total (i.e. net) external force on the system. If the grand total of the external forces adds to zero, then the momentum of the system is constant. However, what precisely do we mean by the momentum P of the system? The momentum of a system is defined as the vector sum of the momenta of each particle in the system:

$$\vec{P} \equiv \vec{p_1} + \vec{p_2} = m_1\vec{v_1} + m_2\vec{v_2} \quad \text{(momentum of a system)} \tag{4}$$

If there is a third particle in the system, just place $\vec{p_3} = m_3\vec{v_3}$ in the sum on the right of equation (4).

To take a more concrete situation, suppose the two particles are billiard balls on a pool table. The balls can collide with each other (an internal force) but the balls may also experience an external force such as air friction. If friction is negligible then the momentum of the two adds to a constant vector, as in equation (4). But you object, the balls experience a normal force and a gravitational force by earth and these are external forces! If the table is level the normal and gravitational forces add up to zero. For a tilted table the normal and gravitational forces no longer cancel out and the momentum of the system is no longer constant.

Momentum conservation is particularly useful in analyzing colliding particles. An especially important type of a collision is a ***completely inelastic collision***, where the two colliding bodies stick together following the collision.

Example Three.—*Big Bertha meets Slim Jim.*

Big Bertha has a mass of $M = 200.0$ kg and her significant other, Slim Jim, has a mass of $m = 50.00$ kg. While skate boarding Bertha races across the parking lot with a speed of $v = 10.0$ m/s. Slim, who is at rest initially on his skate board, awaits her embrace. When Bertha collides with Jim the couple go off in each other's arms with a common final velocity, *V.* Determine the final velocity of the pair.

Solution.

This is an example of a completely inelastic collision. The system is our pair of love birds. Neglecting friction, there are no external forces acting on the two, and so the momentum of the system is conserved. The momentum before their collision is only that of Bertha since Jim is initially at rest.

$$P_i = Mv = 200 \times 10 = 2000 \text{ kgm/s.}$$

After the collision the momentum of the pair is

$$P_f = (M + m)V = (200 + 50)V.$$

Conserving the momentum gives $P_i = P_f$,

$$2000 = 250V.$$

Solving for the unknown V,

$$V = 2000/250 = \underline{8 \text{ m/s.}}$$

Example Four.—*Bumper cars at Disney.*

Henry rides in a bumper car moving with a speed of 5.0 m/s. The total mass of Henry plus his car is 400.0 kg. Junior is in front of Henry moving with a speed of 4.0 m/s straight away from Henry. The total mass of Junior plus his car is 300.0 kg. Henry's car bumps into Junior's car in a head-on collision and an observer measures Henry's speed after the collision, finding a value of 3.0 m/s. What is the speed of Junior's car after the collision, v?

Solution.

Once again we neglect friction and use momentum conservation for the system of cars.

$$P_i = P_f$$
$$400 \times 5 + 300 \times 4 = 400 \times 3 + 300v$$
$$3200 = 1200 + 300v$$
$$2000 = 300v$$
$$v = 2000/300 = \underline{6.7 \text{ m/s.}}$$

Example Five.—*The running back meets the tackle.*

In a game of football a running back (mass 125.0 kg) moving with a speed of 5.0 m/s collides head on with an initially stationary tackle of mass 200.0 kg. Determine their common final velocity, V, immediately after the collision.

Solution.

Treating the pair as an isolated system, momentum conservation gives for this completely inelastic collision,

$$125 \times 5 + 0 = (125+200)V,$$

$$625 = 325V$$

$$V = 625/325 = \underline{1.92 \text{ m/s}}.$$

D. Work, Kinetic, and Gravitational Potential Energy.

For an isolated system the momentum of the system is conserved. But another quantity that is conserved is the energy of the system. Energy is probably the single most important concept of physics and therefore, it deserves a careful look. This is how we shall proceed. First, we will introduce the concept of work. In physics you learn what work means. When a force does work there are two possible outcomes: an increase in motion energy (kinetic energy) or an increase in position energy (potential energy). The energy of a system is the sum of all forms of energy (kinetic plus potential) within a system. Let us begin.

The momentum of a particle can be changed by a force acting on the particle over an interval of time, see equation (2). But instead of focusing on the time interval over which the force acts, consider the spatial interval over which the force acts, i.e. the displacement of the particle. Assume the simple case of a particle restricted to motion only along the x-axis that is acted on by a single force, F, which is parallel to the x-axis. Further, suppose F is a constant. Under these conditions, physicists define the **work**, W, by the force F during the particle displacement, Δx, as the product of force and displacement,

$$W \equiv F\Delta x, \quad F = \text{constant and parallel to } \Delta x. \tag{5}$$

Clearly, the units for work are N-m and we define 1 N-m = 1 Joule. Work is therefore associated with a force and a displacement. Large forces acting over long distances do a lot of work.

The above definition is rather restrictive. In some cases, the force remains parallel to the x-axis but varies in magnitude. This situation is beyond the level of our course, since to treat variable forces properly would require the introduction of integral calculus.

In this book we will only be concerned with the work done by constant forces. If the constant force is not parallel to the x-axis then equation (5) can not be used. Let the displacement of the particle be denoted $\Delta \vec{r}$ and the constant force $\vec{F}$ where these two vectors are at an angle θ to each other. For this more general situation we define *work* as

$$W \equiv \vec{F} \cdot \Delta \vec{r} \equiv |\vec{F}| \, |\Delta \vec{r}| \cos\theta, \quad \vec{F} = \text{constant, and makes an angle } \theta \text{ with } \Delta \vec{r}, \tag{6}$$

where we have used a mathematical multiplication operation between the two vectors called the dot or scalar product. This definition has several unusual features that distinguish physics work from how work is defined in the everyday world. For instance, since the cosine can be positive or negative, equation (6) allows for work to be either positive or *negative*. In particular, if θ is 180° then cos180° = −1 and W is then negative. That is, if the force is in one direction but the displacement is in the opposite direction, then the force does negative work. On the other hand, if θ is 90° then the force does zero work, it is workless. Moreover, if the displacement is zero, so is the work. You could push on a wall all day long but unless the wall moved, you did zero physics work. Indeed, physics work is quite often in conflict with the common use of this term. It is time for a few examples.

Example Six.—*Loading a toy gun.*

A toy gun is spring loaded. Estimate how much work is done in loading the gun with a plastic bullet.

Solution.

Although we must push in on the bullet against the force of the spring, and we know spring forces are not constant, let's approximate the constant force needed to load the gun as about 2.0 N. Assume we slowly push the bullet in a distance of 10.0 cm in loading the gun. The approximate amount of work required is then,

$$W = F\Delta x = 2 \times 0.10 = \underline{0.2\ J}.$$

Example Seven.—*Work by Sisyphus.*

In ancient Greek mythology the characters depicted in this figure were especially evil during their lifetime. Tantalus, where we get the phrase to tantalize, was punished by being placed in a lake while at the same time he was inflicted with a raging thirst. Whenever he tried to drink from the lake the waters would recede from him. Ixion's punishment was to spend eternity chained to a rotating wheel, as shown. Sisyphus had to push a huge marble rock up a hill only to have it slide back down again, after which he had to push it back up again, over and over again forever.

Suppose the marble slab has a mass of 1000.0 kg and the hill is an incline making an angle of 30° with the horizontal. Assuming the slab moves with constant velocity, find out how much work Sisyphus would do in pushing the slab a distance 100.0 m along the incline. Neglect friction.

Solution.

The component of the force of gravity on the slab that is parallel to the incline is

$$mg\sin\theta,$$

and this is the size of the (constant) force Sisyphus must exert to push the slab along the incline. Using equation (5) with the x-axis parallel to the incline,

$$W \equiv F\Delta x = mg\sin\theta\Delta x = 1000(10)\sin 30° 100 = \underline{500,000\ J}.$$

To proceed, the following summary be helpful.

$$
\begin{array}{lll}
F_{net} & \text{causes} & a \\
F_{net}\Delta t & \text{causes} & \Delta p \\
F_{net}\Delta x & \text{causes} & \underline{\quad ? \quad}
\end{array}
$$

To answer this last question, again apply a constant force parallel to the x-axis to a particle of mass m. Further, assume the constant force is the net force on m, and that m has position x_1 and velocity v_1 when the force is first applied and x_2 and v_2 when the force stops being applied to the particle. The work done by the net force is called the net work,

$$W_{net} \equiv F_{net}\Delta x.$$

However, we also know, $F_{net} = ma$ (Newton's second law), and using this gives,

$$W_{net} = ma\Delta x = ma(x_2 - x_1).$$

Since the net force is constant, the acceleration is constant and from an earlier chapter recall the shortcut equation,

$$v^2 = v_0{}^2 + 2a(x - x_0).$$

Rearranging this gives,

$$x = x_0 + (v^2 - v_0{}^2)/2a.$$

This can be used to find

$$W_{net} = ma(x_2 - x_1) = ma\{[x_0 + (v_2{}^2 - v_0{}^2)/2a] - [x_0 + (v_1{}^2 - v_0{}^2)/2a]\}.$$

Simplifying this gives,

$$W_{net} = ma\{(v_2{}^2 - v_1{}^2)/2a\}.$$

Cancelling the "a" from this last result yields the famous *work-kinetic energy relation*.

Work-Kinetic Energy Relation
$$W_{net} = \tfrac{1}{2}mv_2{}^2 - \tfrac{1}{2}mv_1{}^2 \equiv K_2 - K_1$$
$$\text{where kinetic energy } K \equiv \tfrac{1}{2}mv^2 \tag{7}$$

The work by the net force creates a speed change. The work adds energy to the particle, and in this case, the energy is manifested by an increase in the speed of the particle. For this reason,

kinetic energy is called the energy of motion. All moving masses possess kinetic energy. Moreover, all moving masses can be used to perform work, for example, by their collision with another system they can exert forces and produce displacements, thereby doing work on the system.

Kinetic energy can do work and more generally, all forms of energy can be converted into work. ***Energy*** is defined as the ability to do work and is perhaps the most important concept in all of science. To give some indication of how the meaning of words change with time, consider the definition of energy given in the original (1769) version of the *Encyclopaedia Britannica*: "**Energy**, a term of Greek origin, signifying the power, virtue, or efficacy of a thing. It is also used, figuratively, to denote emphasis of speech."

Returning to equation (7) we can now fill in the question mark from above,

$$F_{net} \quad \text{causes} \quad a$$
$$F_{net}\Delta t \quad \text{causes} \quad \Delta p$$
$$F_{net}\Delta x \quad \text{causes} \quad \Delta K.$$

Although equation (7) was derived under the special conditions of a constant net force, the result is valid even when the force is variable and even when the force makes an angle with the displacement.

Example Eight.—*Kinetic energy of a baseball.*

Major league baseball pitchers can heave a baseball with a speed of 100 mi/hr. Assuming the baseball has a mass of 0.25 kg, determine the kinetic energy of the ball.

Solution.

We first must convert mi/hr to m/s,

$$100 \text{ mi/hr} \times (1{,}610 \text{ m/mi}) \times (1 \text{ hr}/3{,}600 \text{ s}) = 44.72 \text{ m/s}.$$

Therefore the kinetic energy is,

$$K = \tfrac{1}{2} mv^2 = \tfrac{1}{2} \tfrac{1}{4} (44.72)^2 = \underline{250 \text{ J}}.$$

Example Nine.—*Kinetic energy of an automobile.*

A car has a mass of 2,000 kg and is moving with a speed of 70.0 mi/h. Find its kinetic energy.

Solution.

Using the same procedure as in the previous example,

$$K = \tfrac{1}{2} 2000(70 \times 1610/3600)^2 = \underline{980{,}000 \text{ J}}.$$

Our discussion remains incomplete, however. In the above development it was assumed the net force acts on a particle and the particle moves horizontally across a floor. No other forces were present. Now suppose instead of applying a horizontal force, we apply a constant external force in the vertical dimension. Here, in addition to the external force, the constant gravitational force by the Earth (i.e. the weight) will act on the particle. Suppose the external force is just a little bit bigger than the weight mg, then the particle will slowly increase in elevation, say from height y_1 to height y_2, where we have placed the origin of the y-axis on the level ground and pointed the y-axis up away from Earth. In this case the work by the external force against the gravitational force is,

$$W_{ext} = F_{ext}\Delta y = mg\,(y_2 - y_1).$$

The external force has done work on the particle and therefore added energy to the particle but the particle does not have any increase in kinetic energy to show for it. Where did the energy by the external work go? We say the energy has been stored in the earth-m system and define this increase in stored energy as an increase in ***gravitational potential energy***,

$$\Delta U_g = U_g(y_2) - U_g(y_1) \equiv W_{ext} = -W_g = mg(y_2 - y_1).$$

In the last step we made use of the fact that the external work is the negative of the work by the gravitational force. At first it seems strange to define a quantity by its change rather than its value, i.e. why define ΔU_g rather than U_g? The reason is, the change in U_g is associated with the change in position that was present in the displacement and work. One may eliminate the change in potential energy and thereby make potential energy absolute by introducing a reference location where one arbitrarily defines the potential energy to be zero. The surface of the Earth is commonly chosen as the reference location or baseline, and with this we have an absolute gravitational potential energy.

Gravitational Potential Energy

$$U_g = mgy \ \ \text{or} \ mgh. \quad (\text{assume } U_g \equiv 0 \text{ at } y = h = 0). \tag{8}$$

It is important to note, the gravitational potential energy, mgh, is only valid provided the gravitational force (weight) of the mass m is viewed as constant. This is true only if the mass stays near the surface of the Earth. For distances far above Earth, the universal force of gravitation must be used and the formula for gravitational potential energy must be generalized by use of integral calculus, but we will stay near the Earth's surface.

Finally, the gravitational potential energy may be called position energy since it involves the location of the parts of a system.

E. Constancy of Energy.

A force can increase the kinetic energy of a mass if it is applied parallel to the ground, and it can increase the gravitational potential if it is applied vertically. In the general situation, a mass m can move in any direction relative to the Earth. Suppose the only force acting on the mass is its weight, *mg*. The system (m + Earth) is called isolated. Then we have associated with the displacement of the mass in any direction, an amount of work given by,

$$W_{net} = \Delta K \text{ but also } W_{net} = -\Delta U_g.$$

Equating these,

$$\Delta K = -\Delta U_g,$$

which gives,

$$\Delta K + \Delta U_g = 0.$$

This gives us the most important conservation law of physics and the most important principle in physics.

Conservation of Energy.

For an isolated system with no friction present,

$$\Delta E = 0$$
$$E_i = E_f \qquad\qquad (9)$$

where

$$E \equiv K + U_g$$

Conservation Law Ritual.

Step One. Define the system and make sure *energy* is conserved.

Step Two. Add up the *energy* at the initial and final times.

Step Three. Equate the *energies* in step two and solve for the unknown.

Equation (9) suggests that as a mass *m* moves it will have variable amounts of kinetic and gravitational potential energies but its total energy will remain constant. For example, as its kinetic energy increases, its potential energy must decrease and vice versa. The "ritual" in equation (9) is a step-by-step procedure for using the conservation of energy principle. All conservation laws use this same procedure, only the quantity that is conserved differs. For example, the conservation law of momentum discussed earlier in this chapter uses this ritual but with the substitution *energy* $\rightarrow$ *momentum*.

Example Ten.—*A monster of a roller coaster.*

Cedar Point Amusement Park in Sandusky, Ohio has *17* roller coasters, which is more than any other park in the world, according to their web site. To quote, "Top Thrill Dragster reaches a stratospheric

420 feet tall and tops out at an unheard-of speed of 120 mi/hr. This new steel screamer helped Cedar Point reclaim the title of owning the tallest and fastest roller coaster in the universe." If you look closely you will see the riders at the top of the coaster in the picture below. The vertical drop is 400 ft.

Courtesy of Associated Press.

Courtesy of Associated Press.

Let's see if we believe them based on energy conservation. Equate the gravitational potential energy of a person at the top of the dragster to the person's kinetic energy at the bottom, and solve for the person's speed in mi/hr at the bottom. Are they telling the truth about the speed at the bottom? Neglect friction.

Solution.

Let h represent the initial height off the ground at the top of the roller coaster, h = 400 ft $\times$ 0.3048 m/ft = 122 m. The initial energy of the person of mass m is all gravitational potential energy since we assume the person starts from rest.

$$E_i = U_g = mgh.$$

At the bottom of the drop the gravitational potential energy has been converted entirely to kinetic energy,

$$E_f = \tfrac{1}{2}\,mv^2.$$

Assuming energy conservation, we equate the last two expressions,

$$E_i = E_f$$

$$mgh = \tfrac{1}{2}\,mv^2.$$

Notice the mass m is a common factor and therefore we divide both sides by m and solve for v to obtain,

$$v = \sqrt{(2gh)} = \sqrt{(2 \times 10 \times 122)} = 49.4 \text{ m/s} \times 1 \text{ mi/hr}/0.447 \text{ m/s} \underline{- 111 \text{ mi/hr}}.$$

This is slightly smaller than their quote of 120 mi/hr but perhaps the coaster had a slight kinetic energy at the top of the hill. If so, this could explain the slight (9 mi/hr) difference we have found.

F. Applications: Constancy of Momentum and Energy.

As already mentioned, one of the earliest applications of conservation laws was to the analysis of collisions. For an isolated system of two particles the momentum of the system is conserved. If the two balls collide in what is called an ***elastic collision***, then the kinetic energy of the system is also conserved. For example, to an excellent approximation the collision of two steel balls is elastic.

Example Eleven.—*Down at the pool hall.*

A cue ball has a mass equal to that of the eight ball. The cue ball moving with a velocity of v strikes the initially stationary eight ball head on. Prove that following the collision the cue ball is at rest and the eight ball moves with velocity v. Neglect friction.

Solution.

The two balls, each of mass m, form an isolated system, and therefore the total momentum is conserved. Also, we can assume the collision is elastic given the hardness of the balls, therefore, the total kinetic energy is also conserved. Writing the conservation laws,

$$mv + 0 = mv' + mv'' \text{ (momentum conservation)}$$

$$\tfrac{1}{2} mv^2 + 0 = \tfrac{1}{2} mv'^2 + \tfrac{1}{2} mv''^2 \text{ (kinetic energy conservation)},$$

where v' is the velocity of the cue ball after the collision and v'' is that of the eight ball. The mass m can be divided out, and we have

$$v = v' + v'' \quad \text{and} \quad v^2 = v'^2 + v''^2.$$

Solving the first equation for v'',

$$v'' = v - v'$$

and using this in the second equation gives,

$$v^2 = v'^2 + (v - v')^2 = v'^2 + v^2 - 2vv' + v'^2$$

or

$$0 = 2v'^2 - 2vv' = 2v'(v' - v).$$

This last result has two solutions,

$$v' = 0 \quad \text{and} \quad v' = v.$$

We choose the solution $v' = 0$ (why?), which then gives from above $v'' = v$.

Example Twelve.—*Playing with marbles.*

A street urchin is playing with two marbles. The first marble has a mass m while the second marble has a mass $M > m$. Assume M is initially at rest and m has a velocity v before it collides head on with M. Obtain algebraic equations for the velocity of m after the collision, v', and that of M afterwards, v''.

Solution.

The conservation laws give,

$$mv + 0 = mv' + Mv'' \quad \text{and} \quad \tfrac{1}{2}mv^2 + 0 = \tfrac{1}{2}mv'^2 + \tfrac{1}{2}Mv''^2.$$

Solve the first equation for v'' and substitute that result into the second equation. One arrives at a quadratic equation in the variable, v'. As an exercise for the student, use the quadratic formula to arrive at the final result,

$$v' = v\,(m - M)/(m + M).$$

Actually there are two solutions for v'; we leave it to the reader to determine the proper choice between the two solutions. Substituting this expression for v' into the first equation gives an expression for v''. Notice, if $m = M$ then we get the same result for v' (i.e. 0) as we found in the previous example.

G. Power.

So far we have discussed the addition of energy to a system by doing work on the system. Either the work will cause an increase in kinetic energy or potential energy or possibly both. However, no mention has been made of the time involved in doing the work. Power is the *rate* of adding energy to a system. The average power delivered to a system involves how much energy is added by doing work on a system, ΔW, and how long it takes to add the energy, i.e. the time interval, Δt, involved. This can be expressed mathematically,

$$P_{ave} \equiv \Delta W/\Delta t. \tag{10}$$

If the time interval is very small, then the average power is called simply the **power** delivered by the force doing the work. One Joule of work delivered to a system every second is called one *Watt* of power. James Watt was one of the early developers of the steam engine during the Industrial Revolution of the 1800s.

Example Thirteen.—*Power by a baseball pitcher.*

Estimate the average power delivered to a baseball by a major league pitcher.

Solution.

Recall from an earlier example that a pitcher in the pros typically throws a baseball with a speed of 100 mi/hr. We found for a 0.25 kg ball this gives the ball a kinetic energy of 250 J. The time interval involved would be the time for a pitcher to wind up and throw the ball, about 2 s. This gives,

$$P_{ave} = 250 \text{ J/2 s} = \underline{125 \text{ W}}.$$

Summary.

Three contributors to the physics of this chapter are profiled: Descartes, Huygens, and Leibniz. We find that a force acting over a time interval gives rise to the concept of impulse. The impulse by the net force on a particle causes a change in the momentum of the particle—this is called the impulse-momentum relation. For an isolated system the momentum is constant or conserved. A force acting over a displacement gives rise to the notion of work. The work by the net force on a particle causes a change in the kinetic energy of the particle—this is called the work-kinetic energy relation. In some systems, namely isolated systems and those systems without frictional forces present, the total energy of the system is constant. The total energy includes both the energy of motion (kinetic) and the energy of position (potential) or the stored energy. Energy conservation is the most fundamental principle of physics. Finally, the rate in which energy is added to a system is called the power input into the system.

QUESTIONS.

1. Which of the following has the greatest momentum?

   (a) 0.4 kg baseball moving at 20.0 m/s

   (b) 0.6 kg bowling ball moving at 8.0 m/s

   (c) 4000.0 kg dump truck moving at 2.0 m/s

   (d) 2000.0 kg Ferrari moving at 60.0 m/s

   (e) 30,000 kg spacecraft moving at 0.1 m/s

2. Which of the following produces the greatest change in momentum?

   (a) 100.0 N force acting for 0.1 s

   (b) 1 N force acting for 5,000 s

   (c) 1000.0 N force acting for 0.01 s

   (d) 0.1 N force acting for 100.0 s

   (e) 10,000 N force acting for 0.001 s

3. The picture below represents a collision between two pool balls as seen from above.

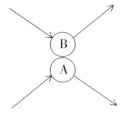 The arrows represent the momentum vectors of the balls before and after the collision. Which set of vectors best represents the direction of the change in momentum of each ball?

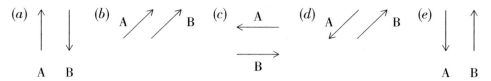

4. The Craters of the Moon is a place in Idaho that is used for astronaut training. Suppose a fully suited astronaut jumps off one of the craters and has a speed of 7.0 m/s just before hitting the surface. If on the Moon the astronaut jumps onto the Moon surface and hits the Moon surface with the same speed of 7.0 m/s, how will the impulse on the Moon compare with the impulse on the Earth?

5. A car of mass m experiences a net impulse of 1,000 N-s while a car of mass $2m$ experiences the same net impulse. How does the final speed of the more massive car compare to the final speed of the car of mass m?

6. A constant force is applied to a block that resides on a horizontal frictionless surface (see diagram). The block is initially at rest. The force acts for a certain interval of time and gives the block a final speed. To reach the same final speed with a force that is only half as big, the force must be exerted on the cart for a time interval

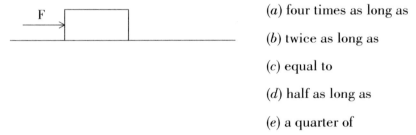

(a) four times as long as

(b) twice as long as

(c) equal to

(d) half as long as

(e) a quarter of

that for the stronger force.

7. A woman jumps off the roof of a house. Explain why it is better for her to land on her feet and bend her knees rather than to land on her feet with her legs stiff.

8. A huge truck runs into the back of a small car. Which vehicle experiences the greater force? the greater impulse? the greater momentum change? Treat the system as isolated.

9. If a rifle and the bullet in the rifle had the same mass then the rifle would recoil with the same speed as the bullet. Explain why this is true.

10. The momentum of a particle in free fall is not conserved. Why is this not a violation of the law of conservation of momentum?

11. If two particles move along the x-axis, how can the total momentum of the system be zero?

12. Two identical balls reside on a frictionless horizontal table. Ball 2 is initially at rest and ball 1 has an initial velocity of v to the right. Ball 1 collides head on with ball 2. Use the appropriate physics to argue that ball 2 moves to the right with the same velocity v after the collision and ball 1 is at rest after the collision.

13. Why do bungee jumpers use elastic ropes when jumping rather than ropes that do not stretch? Explain based on ideas from this chapter.

14. Use Newton's laws of motion to explain why in the collision of two particles that are isolated the total momentum of the system is conserved.

15. You are an astronaut out in free space on a spacewalk to repair the ship. You have in your hands a bag full of massive rocket parts. The cord holding you to the spacecraft snaps and you are at rest at some distance from the stationary ship. Explain what you could do to get back to the ship based on the physics of this chapter.

16. Suppose rain falls vertically into an open cart rolling along a straight horizontal track with no friction. As a result of the accumulating water, the speed of the cart

    (*a*) increases

    (*b*) does not change

    (*c*) decreases

    (*d*) can not be found without numbers

    (*e*) depends on where this occurs

17. Can kinetic energy ever be negative? Can work ever be negative? Explain.

The next three questions pertain to the diagram below where two hockey pucks are on a frictionless surface and we are looking down from above. Puck A has mass m and B a mass $4m$ and two equal forces F push on the pucks all the way to the finish line.

---------------------- Finish line

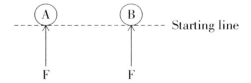

18. Which puck has the greater kinetic energy upon reaching the finish line?

(*a*) Puck A (*b*) Puck B (*c*) They both have the same kinetic energy (*d*) not enough information.

19. Which puck reaches the finish line first?

(*a*) Puck A (*b*) Puck B (*c*) they arrive at the same time (*d*) not enough information.

20. Which puck has the greater momentum upon reaching the finish line?

(*a*) Puck A (*b*) Puck B (*c*) They both have the same momentum (*d*) not enough information.

21. Two marbles are dropped to the ground from the top of a ladder. One of the marbles has twice the mass of the other. Neglect friction. Just before hitting the ground, the heavier marble has

(*a*) the same kinetic energy as the lighter one

(*b*) twice as much kinetic energy as the lighter one

(*c*) half as much kinetic energy as the lighter one

(*d*) four times as much kinetic energy as the lighter one

(*e*) not enough information to determine

22. Compare the work done to lift a mass m a vertical distance h without appreciably changing its kinetic energy to the work done in moving m up the incline below without appreciably changing its kinetic energy. Neglect friction.

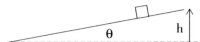

23. Two cars of equal mass are moving such that the first car has twice the speed of the second car. Therefore, the ratio of the kinetic energy of the first car to that of the second car is

(*a*) 1/2

(*b*) 1/4

(*c*) 2

(*d*) 4

(*e*) not known

24. A bowler lifts a bowling ball from the floor up to a rack. Given the weight of the ball, what else must be known to determine how much work is done by the bowler?

25. When a firefighter slides down a fire pole, what happens to his gravitational potential energy?

26. Which of the following is conserved as a ball falls freely in a vacuum: the ball's kinetic energy, gravitational potential energy, momentum, or mechanical energy?

27. Explain the energies present and how the energies are transformed in the motion of a simple pendulum.

28. Galileo argued for the law of inertia based on a double incline (see sketch below).

He argued that when a block is released from a height of h on the incline on the left, the block returns to the same height h on the incline on the right, even if the angle θ of the incline on the right is made very small. As the θ approaches zero, the block continues to move forever toward the right. Explain why the block always "remembers" to return to its initial height, h.

29. Another argument of Galileo stated that a ball falling from A in the figure below will have the same speed independent of path (AB, AC, AD, AE). This assumes the absence of friction. Use energy ideas to prove this assertion.

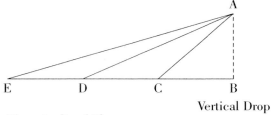

Vertical Drop

Three Inclined Planes

30. Suppose a golf ball is rolled toward a heavy bowling ball initially at rest. The golf ball bounces elastically straight back from the bowling ball. After the collision, which of the balls has the larger momentum and which has the larger kinetic energy? Show your reasoning. One makes an approximation to solve this.

31. A light bulb is on for two hours one night. The next night the light bulb is on for three hours. The ratio of energy usage by the bulb the second night to that of the first night is

(*a*) 1

(*b*) 2

(*c*) 3

(*d*) 1/2

(*e*) none of the above

32. Use the power given for the following two activities to answer these questions. Note: 1 calorie = 0.239 Joules

Activity	Power Consumption
brisk walk	3.5 calories per minute
sleeping	1.3 calories per minute

(a) How many minutes must you walk to consume the same energy as that in a candy bar which has 280 calories?

(b) How many calories are consumed by your body during an eight hour night's sleep?

PROBLEMS.

1. How fast would a 5-gram cockroach have to move to have the same momentum as a 2,000.0 kg car moving at 30.0 m/s?

2. Benjamin Franklin objected to the corpuscular theory of light by saying that a corpuscle (particle) of light travels at the large speed of 3×10^8 m/s and this would have the same effect as a 10.0 kg ball fired from a cannon at a speed of 100.0 m/s. What did Franklin assume for the mass of the light corpuscle?

3. A 150-gram baseball traveling at 50.0 m/s is hit by a baseball bat and rebounds with a speed of 55.0 m/s. Find (a) the initial momentum of the ball and (b) the change in momentum of the ball.

4. A 0.5-kg hammer drives a nail into a wall. Suppose the hammer is moving with a speed of 3.0 m/s as it just encounters the nail and it is brought to rest by moving the nail a distance of 3.0 cm. (a) Find the average acceleration of the hammer and (b) the average force on the nail.

5. A professional boxer hits his opponent on the head. Assume the glove and hand have a total mass of 0.3 kg and is moving with a speed of 2.5 m/s just before hitting the person in the head. If the stopping distance of the glove is 4.0 cm, find (a) the average acceleration of the glove and (b) the average force on the person's head.

6. The game of billiards originated no later than the middle ages in Europe. This game illustrates well the physics of collisions. Suppose a 0.20-kg cue ball moving with a speed of 1.0 m/s hits the cushion of a billiard table. The ball rebounds in the opposite direction with the same speed. Assuming the collision time is 0.005 s, find the average force on the table.

7. This is not for the squeamish. A 75.0 kg prisoner is brought to the gallows and the noose is attached to his head. (a) If he drops freely a distance of 2.0 m before the rope becomes taut, how fast will he be traveling just as the rope begins to tighten? (b) Assuming it takes 0.1 s to stop him after the rope becomes taut, calculate the average force by the rope on the man in bringing him to rest in peace. Give your results in Newtons and pounds (1 N = 0.225 pounds).

During the 1800s in Britain the "Committee of Inquiry" into prison hangings recommended a maximum force of 1,260 pounds. This inquiry resulted from an especially gruesome hanging conducted by the famous executioner James Berry. To pry further into this dark topic, see *Encyclopedia of Crime*, Cyriax, et al., p. 33. Fortunately, not many nations continue to execute by hanging.

8. Bonnie and Clyde were a couple of bank robbers and murderers who became famous after their rampage during the US Great Depression in the 1930s. They met their doom on May 23, 1934 in an ambush by law enforcement officials in Louisiana. A total of 187 bullets hit their jalopy. Assuming this avalanche of bullets hit the car over a time interval of 10.0 s and each bullet had a mass of 2.0 grams and was moving with a velocity of 1,500 m/s, find the average force on the jalopy by the bullets.

To read further about their exploits, consult *Encyclopedia of Crime*, Cyriax, et al., pp. 41−43. In 1967 a major motion picture was produced titled *Bonnie and Clyde*, that glamorized the couple. The beautiful actress Faye Dunaway and handsome actor Warren Beatty played the pair—the real Bonnie and Clyde looked much different than the actors. The tagline of the movie was, " they're young . . . they're in love . . . and they kill people."

9. A 10,000 N-s impulse stops a car in 0.1 s. Find the average force on the car.

10. Each 0.17 s approximately 80 grams of blood is pumped by the heart. Assuming the blood starts at rest and acquires a speed of 0.6 m/s, what is the average force on the blood?

11. A baseball bat is in contact with a 150-gram baseball for 1.3 ms. If the ball has an initial speed of 45.0 m/s and the average force on the ball by the bat is 9,000 N, what is the final speed with which the ball leaves the bat?

12. Two roller skaters, Tom and Jerry, stand stationary and very close to each other. Tom has a mass of 55.0 kg while Jerry's mass is 70.0 kg. Tom holds a 500-gram ball and tosses it horizontally with a speed of 2.0 m/s and Jerry catches the ball. What is the final velocity of (a) Tom and of (b) Jerry? Ignore any effects of gravity.

13. At a circus two ice skaters stand stationary a short distance apart. The first skater has a mass of 60.0 kg and the second a mass of 45.0 kg. The first skater tosses a 20.0-kg child horizontally at a speed of 4.0 m/s toward the second skater. What is the final velocity of (a) the first skater and of (b) the second skater? Ignore any effects of gravity.

14. A 5.0-kg gun rests on a frictionless horizontal surface. The trigger of the gun is pulled and a 5.0-gram bullet leaves the barrel with a horizontal velocity of 300.0 m/s. Find the recoil velocity of the gun.

15. The US population is about 300×10^6 people. If the average mass of a person is 65.0 kg and each person in the US simultaneously jumped off the ground with a speed of 5.0 m/s, what would the recoil velocity of the (5.98×10^{24} kg) Earth be?

16. A 2.0-gram marble moves with a speed of 3.0 m/s and hits head-on an initially stationary 4.0-gram marble. After the collision the 4-gram marble is observed moving with a velocity of 1.0 m/s in the same direction as the initial direction of the 2.0-gram marble. What is the final velocity of the 2.0-gram marble? Treat the system as isolated.

17. A 1,800 kg black tank moves with a speed of 12.0 m/s and hits head-on an initially stationary 2,200.0 kg white tank. After the collision the 2,200 kg tank is observed moving with a velocity of 2.0 m/s in the same direction as the initial direction of the 1,800.0 kg tank. What is the final velocity of the 1,800.0 kg tank?

18. A man of mass 65.0 kg runs with a speed of 10.0 m/s and jumps onto a surfboard of mass 10.0 kg. Neglecting friction, with what speed does the man plus surfboard skim across the water?

19. Sisyphus pushes on a marble slab with a constant force of 500.0 N. The force is parallel to an incline that makes 30° with the horizontal. Find how much work is done by Sisyphus in moving the slab 100.0 m along the incline.

20. In building a pyramid an ancient Egyptian slave pushes with a constant 300.0 N on a slab of rock. The rock moves up an incline that makes 20° with the horizontal. The constant force is applied parallel to the incline. How much work is done by the Egyptian in moving the slab 100.0 m along the incline?

21. A waiter picks up a 0.75 kg tray lifting it slowly a vertical distance of 1.0 m. He then carries the tray while he walks 10.0 m with a constant velocity across a horizontal floor. Next, he slowly lowers the tray a distance of 0.5 m in order to place it on a counter. For each step of this process find the work done by the waiter.

22. Assuming the Moon orbits the earth in uniform circular motion, compute the work done by the Earth on the Moon in one month— the time for one complete orbit around the Earth.

23. A major league pitcher throws a 0.3 kg baseball with a speed of 50.0 m/s. How much kinetic energy does the ball have?

24. A 1,500-kg automobile moves with a speed of 30.0 m/s. How much kinetic energy does the car have?

25. A 0.5-kg rock is released from rest from the top of the 55.0-m tall Leaning Tower of Pisa. (a) Compute how much work is done on the rock by the force of gravity for the total trip down to the ground and (b) use your answer to (a) to compute the kinetic energy of the rock just before hitting the ground. (c) Use the answer to (b) to determine the speed of the rock just before hitting the ground. Ignore air friction.

26. A 2.0-kg particle is shot from ground level straight up with a speed of 30.0 m/s. Use the work-kinetic energy relation to predict how high above ground the particle will go before falling back down. Neglect air friction.

27. An 80.0-kg basketball player jumps 0.8 m straight up above the floor. Use the work-kinetic energy relation to find how fast the player was moving off the floor. Neglect air friction.

28. A 60.-kg girl on a bicycle is traveling at 12.0 m/s on a horizontal surface when she stops pedaling as she starts up a hill that is inclined 15° with the horizontal. Find (a) her kinetic energy at the bottom of the hill and (b) how far along the incline she travels in coming to rest. Ignore friction.

29. A 5,000-kg trolley car in San Francisco is pulled a distance of 250.0 m along a hill that is inclined 10° from the horizontal. Compute the increase in gravitational potential energy of the trolley.

30. An ancient Egyptian of mass 55.0 kg climbs to the top of a 1,000 m tall pyramid. How much of an increase in gravitational potential energy occurred for this person?

31. A boy mounts a sled at the top of a 50.0 m tall snow-covered hill. The boy plus sled have a total mass of 80.0 kg and start from rest. Use energy conservation to find the speed of the sled at the bottom of the hill.

32. A roller-coaster car has a mass of 200.0 kg and starts from rest at point A below. Given A is 30.0 m above the ground and C is 10.0 m from the ground, determine the speed of the car at C.

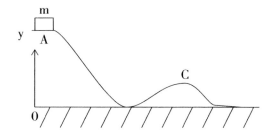

33. In this chapter we presented gravitational potential energy, U_g. Another form of potential (stored) energy is that of a compressed (or stretched) spring—this is called ***elastic potential energy***. If the spring is compressed (or stretched) a distance x from its equilibrium then the elastic potential energy is

$$U_{el} = \tfrac{1}{2} k x^2,$$

where k is a measure of the stiffness of the spring called the spring constant. Imagine a spring that has a value of k of 10,000 N/m and that has been compressed a distance of 10.0 cm. (a) How much elastic potential energy is in the spring? (b) If a 5.0-gram marble is placed next to the end of the compressed spring and the spring is released, the marble shoots across a (frictionless) horizontal surface as a result of the action of the spring. How fast is the marble traveling as it moves across the floor far from the spring?

34. Suppose in the previous problem the spring is aimed vertically. About how high up does the marble go?

35. A 0.2-kg croquet ball with an initial speed of 2.0 m/s collides head-on with a stationary 0.1-kg baseball. After the collision, the balls travel in the same direction and the croquet ball has a speed of 1.0 m/s while the baseball has a speed of 2.0 m/s. Are momentum and kinetic energy conserved in this collision?

36. A 4.0-kg toy truck with a speed of 5.0 m/s collides head-on with a stationary 1.0-kg toy car. After the collision, the toys are locked together and move with a speed of 4.0 m/s. (a) Is momentum conserved? (b) What is the difference between the final and initial kinetic energy of the system? (c) Is kinetic energy conserved?

37. A 60.0 Watt light bulb consumes how many Joules of energy in 10.0 hours?

38. A 1,600.0 kg car starts from rest on a horizontal road and accelerates in 5.0 s to a speed of 60.0 mi/hr. Find the average power input to the car.

39. In one of the writings of Huygens the following observation is made. To paraphrase, if you start a simple pendulum with the bob at rest in the horizontal position, then when the bob gets to the bottom of its swing the tension in the string, F_T, will be three times the weight of the bob, i.e. $F_T = 3mg$. Prove this.

40. A block of mass $3m$ moves on a frictionless surface toward the right with a speed of v. Another block of mass m moves with the same speed but toward the left. Assuming this collision is elastic and the collision is head-on, find the velocity of the two masses after the collision.

Hints and answers to problems.

1) 27 million mi/hr   2) 3.3 μkg   3) 7.5 kgm/s and -15.8 kgm/s   4) Hint: Use work-energy relation or shortcut eq., -150 m/s and 75 N   5) Hint: Use work-energy relation or shortcut eq., 78.1 m/s^2 and 23.4 N   6) 80 N   7) Hint: Use work-energy relation or shortcut eq., 6.32 m/s and 1076 lbs   8) 56.1 N   9) 100,000 N   10) 0.28 N   11) 33 m/s   12) -0.18 m/s and 0.014 m/s   13) -1.33 m/s and 1.23 m/s   14) -0.3 m/s   15) -1.63×10^{-14} m/s   16) 1 m/s   17) 9.56 m/s   18) 8.67 m/s   19) 50,000 J   20) 30,000 J   21) 7.5 J, 0 , -3.75 J   22) 0   23) 375 J   24) 675,000 J   25) 275 J, 275 J, 37.4 m/s   26) 45 m   27) 4 m/s   28) 4320 J and 27.8 m   29) 2.17 MJ   30) 5.5×10^5 J   31) 31.6 m/s   32) 20 m/s   33) 50 J and 141 m/s   34) 1,000 m   35) yes and no   36) yes and -10 J   37) 2.16×10^6 J   38) 115,000 W   39) Hint: use energy conservation and apply Newton's second law to the bob at the bottom of its swing.   40) 0 and 2v to the right.

Chapter VII.
WAVE MOTION AND LIGHT.

Abstract.

We have lent considerable attention to motion with constant acceleration, either in one or two dimensions. In this chapter we open with an instance where acceleration is *not* constant. In vibratory motion all three basic kinematic quantities change with time, x, v_x and a_x. Examining vibrations is interesting in its own right but a knowledge of vibrations is also essential to understanding wave motion. Broadly, we introduce two kinds of waves: traveling and standing waves. Other outstanding properties we examine include the reflection and refraction of light. With this background we cover the properties of light: diffraction, interference, dispersion and polarization.

Definitions. period of vibration, frequency, wavelength and speed of waves, wave function, traveling and standing waves, nodes and antinodes, harmonics, angle of reflection and refraction, virtual and real images, interference, diffraction, dispersion, index of refraction, and polarization

Principles. superposition principle, laws of reflection and refraction

Fundamental Equations. wave relation, Snell's law of refraction

A. Special Motion: Vibrations.

A pendulum bob moves back and forth over the same region of space. The wings of a mosquito undergo the same kind of repetitive motion. Nature exhibits innumerable instances of motion that is repetitive. It is to such repetitive motion that we now turn. Vibratory motion is any motion that repeats itself over the same region of space. A pattern is repeated over and over. The time for one complete vibration is called the ***period*** of the motion. The **frequency** of vibration, f, is the number of vibrations per second and is therefore, $f = 1/T$. The units of frequency are $1/s = s^{-1} \equiv 1$ Hertz.

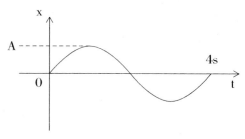

FIG. 1. POSITION VERSUS TIME FOR A PARTICLE ATTACHED TO A SPRING.

For example, in Figure 1 is shown the position of a mass attached to a spring versus time. The mass is moving up and down along the x-axis in the figure and the period is 4 s.

The special kind of vibratory motion displayed in Figure 1 is called simple harmonic motion (SHM). A mass on a spring is a case of SHM. In all cases of SHM, the position of the mass may be represented mathematically, using

$$x = A \sin(2\pi t/T + \delta), \tag{1}$$

where the period T is inside the sine function. In using Equation (1) it is important to note that the angles must be in radian measure, where $180° = \pi$ radians. Equation (1) implies that the initial position of the mass, $x_0 = x(0)$, is given by setting t equal to zero,

$$x(0) = A \sin \delta.$$

Since the sine function has a maximum value of 1, the maximum value of position is given by,

$$x_{max} = A,$$

where A is called the amplitude of vibration. Finally, the argument of the sine function is known as the phase of the function, and so the constant δ appearing in (1) is called the phase constant of the motion. The phase constant should be expressed in radians.

Equation (1) leads to a velocity and acceleration that also vary in time, in a similar manner. However, it is beyond this course to study these in detail.

Example One.—*A mass on a horizontal spring and Hooke's law.*

A 300-gram mass, m, is attached to a horizontal spring. Initially the spring is relaxed and the position of the mass is denoted, $x = 0$ (see (a) below). Suppose the spring is stretched by an amount x as shown below in (b). Robert Hooke found the spring force acting on the mass is proportional to x; this is known as Hooke's law.

$$F = -k\,x \text{ (Hooke's Law)}$$

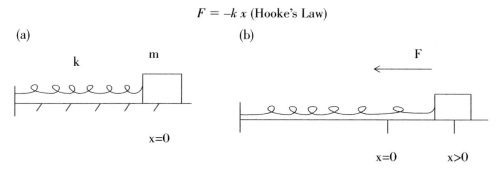

The minus sign is needed to give the right direction for the spring force.

Ignoring friction, Newton's second law for m becomes,

$$-k\,x = m\,a.$$

Once the mass is released it will oscillate and so x will change. According to the above equation, this means the acceleration will also change. This is one of the few situations in this course we will encounter where acceleration is not constant. Using calculus it is found there is a relationship between the above variables and the period of vibration,

$$2\pi/T = \sqrt{k/m}.$$

(a) A force of 1.1 N is required to pull the mass m a distance of 1 cm to the right. Determine the value of the spring constant using Hooke's law.

(b) Use the spring constant found in (a) to find the period and frequency of vibration of the mass m.

Solution.

(a) Rearrange Hooke's law to solve for k (don't worry about the minus sign) and change x to meters,

$$k = F/x = (1.1 \text{ N/1 cm})(100 \text{ cm/m}) = \underline{110 \text{ N/m}}.$$

(b) Solving for the period, T, above and converting m to kg,

$$T = 2\pi \sqrt{m/k} = 2\pi\sqrt{(300 \text{ grams} \times 1 \text{ kg/1000 grams})/110 \text{ N/m}}$$

$$T = 2\pi\sqrt{0.3 \text{ kg/110 N/m}}$$

$$T = \underline{0.328 \text{ s}}.$$

Also, $f = 1/T = \underline{3.05 \text{ Hz}}.$

B. Special Motion: Traveling and Standing Waves.

Everyone is familiar with water waves, sound waves and waves of light to mention only a few everyday examples. Energy is present in any wave phenomenon because work had to be done to establish the wave. The wave transports energy but it also transports momentum from place to place. In all cases (except one) waves need a medium to propagate through. For water waves the medium is water, air is the medium for sound waves, and a string is the medium for waves on a string.

String waves are especially easy to visualize. Imagine a taut horizontal string coincident with the x-axis. If one plucks the string, this disturbs it from its equilibrium and the ensuing simple wave that is created is called a pulse. The pulse travels down the length of the string. Consider a point of the string at position x. Before the pulse arrives at x, that point of the string is in equilibrium and not moving. To introduce the mathematics of waves we use a y-coordinate axis to measure the vertical displacement of the string from equilibrium. A pulse can be described by a mathematical function, known as the **wave function**, $y(x)$, as illustrated in Figure 2(a). The moving pulse is an example of a **traveling wave**. By continually plucking the string, a wave train is created. The most important example of a traveling train of waves is the sinusoidal wave where $y(x)$ is the well known sine function. For instance, later we will find that light is a sinusoidal traveling wave.

In Figure 2(b) the wave function for a sinusoidal wave is plotted versus t for the point of the string with $x = 0$ while in (c) y versus x at $t = 0$ is shown. The amplitude of the wave, A, is the maximum displacement of the wave from equilibrium, as shown in the figure. The **period** of the wave, T, is the time for one complete oscillation, as illustrated in (b), while the distance for one vibration is called the **wavelength**, λ, as shown in (c). The **frequency**, f, of a wave is the inverse of the period, $1/T$. If 1 vibration takes 1 s then the frequency is 1 s^{-1}, which is called 1 Hertz.

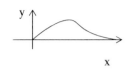

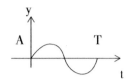

FIG. 2. (A) PROFILE OF STRING THAT LIES ALONG THE X-AXIS.

(B) WAVE FUNCTION OF STRING VERSUS TIME. THE PERIODIC WAVE HAS A PERIOD T.

(C) WAVE FUNCTION OF STRING VERSUS POSITION. THE WAVELENGTH OF THE WAVE IS λ.

From these definitions we arrive at one of the most fundamental equations of wave theory, the wave relation. For an observer located at one point of the string, it is clear that one wavelength of the wave passes that point in a time interval of one period. The ***wave speed*** of the wave is therefore,

$$v \equiv \Delta x/\Delta t = \lambda/T = \lambda f \quad \text{(wave relation)} \tag{2}$$

In future physics courses you will learn how to express the wave function as a function of both x and t.

Another classification scheme for waves is to categorize waves as transverse or longitudinal. In a transverse wave, such as string waves, while the pulse(s) travel horizontally along the string (the x-axis) the string itself (the medium) moves vertically (along the y-axis). Most waves in nature are transverse but sound is a very important example of the other category of waves, longitudinal. In a sound wave moving along the horizontal direction we find that the medium (air) also travels along the horizontal direction but in vibratory motion.

Now that we have some background on describing how a wave moves in a medium we can consider a slightly more complicated scenario where we have two waves occupying the medium. An important question comes to mind: what does the wave function look like if there are two waves present? The answer to this question is as one might guess: the total wave function is the sum of the individual wave functions. This is called the *superposition principle*, and this principle underlies the physics of many phenomena involving waves.

$$y = y_1 + y_2 \quad \text{(superposition principle)} \tag{3}$$

Example Two.—*The Slinky.*

"What walks down stairs, alone or in pairs, And makes a slinkity sound? A spring, a spring, a marvelous thing, Everyone knows it's Slinky . . . It's Slinky, it's Slinky, for fun it's a wonderful toy. It's Slinky, it's Slinky, it's fun for a girl and a boy.

—*(a rather corny) Advertising Jingle*

Our story begins in Philadelphia in the year 1945. A marine engineer named Richard James was investigating how to reduce vibrations on ships onset by firing guns or storms at sea. Richard noticed one of his steel springs fell off a table and "walked away" from him. He shared this observation that evening with his wife Betty telling her that this might make a good toy. They followed this line of thinking, developed the concept, and named the toy, Slinky. Since then about 250 million Slinkies have been sold to the public. Your mission, should you accept it, is to purchase a Slinky and investigate the relationship between speed of the pulses and the wavelength and frequency. Also, demonstrate that it is possible to set up both transverse and longitudinal waves with the Slinky. Once we have introduced standing waves below, you may also create standing waves on your Slinky. With a friend you may set up wave interference on the Slinky by having the friend create a pulse at one end while you create a pulse at the other. Go ahead, learn everything you can learn about vibrations and waves with this relatively inexpensive physics toy!

This tale has an unusual ending. It seems Mr. Richard James was wound a bit too tight (pardon the pun). In about 1960, Richard James suffered from an emotional crisis and deserted his wife, six children, and the Slinky Empire to join a Bolivian religious cult. Undaunted, Betty James took over as the Slinky CEO and rescued the company from the debts left by her husband's gifts to his religion. She moved the company to its current Hollidaysburg (≈ Philadelphia) location and began an advertising campaign using the famous Slinky jingle. Richard James died in 1974.

Sources: *The 2006 Old Farmer's Almanac*, pg. 146. and http://inventors.about.com/od/sstartinventions/a/slinky.htm

---

Example Three.—*Constructive and destructive interference.*

Two identical triangular pulses start at opposite ends of a string and move in opposite directions. Use the superposition principle to sketch the resultant pulse when the triangles meet in the middle assuming (a) the pulses both have positive wave functions (constructive interference) and (b) one of the pulses has a positive wave function and the other a negative (destructive interference).

Solution.

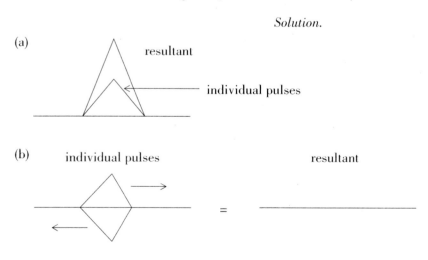

To give another application of the superposition principle in action we turn to what are known as **standing waves**. Imagine a taut horizontal string that has one end attached to a wall. If a man jiggles the other end of the string traveling waves are produced. Once a wave reaches the wall, it reflects off the wall. Therefore, at any point of the string there are two traveling waves—one moving to the right (incident wave) and the other to the left (reflected wave). The total wave function of the string is given by equation (3). Suppose further, the man jiggles in such a way that the traveling waves produced are sinusoidal. In general, the total wave function of the string wave is rather random looking. However, for certain frequencies of jiggling, the string vibrates in a beautiful pattern known as a normal mode or a harmonic, as illustrated in Figure 3. Points of the string in Figure 3 that never move are called *nodes*, while points where the string has a maximum vibration amplitude are *anti-nodes*. The standing wave patterns are called *harmonics*.

FIG. 3. STANDING WAVE ON A STRING —
THE THIRD HARMONIC IS SHOWN.

Often it is of interest to determine the values of the jiggling frequencies which give rise to the harmonics. Denote the length of the string by L. From Figure 3 we see the nth harmonic ($n = 1, 2, 3, \ldots$) contains n "bumps," where one bump has a length of $\lambda/2$. Therefore,

$$L = n\,\lambda/2 \quad \text{where } n = 1, 2, 3, \ldots$$

Solving this for the wavelength,

$$\lambda = 2L/n,$$

which, with the wave relation ($f = v/\lambda$), gives the normal mode or harmonic jiggling frequencies,

$$f = (v/2L)\,n, \quad n = 1, 2, 3, \ldots \tag{4}$$

The quantity in parenthesis in Equation (4) is the fundamental or first harmonic frequency. A harmonic has a frequency that is an integer multiple of the fundamental frequency. Given the wave speed on the string, v, and the length of the string, L, we use Equation (4) to obtain the jiggling frequencies needed to create the harmonics.

Example Four.—*Standing waves on a guitar string.*

A guitar string has a length of 75 cm and waves on the string travel with a speed of 100 m/s. Use (4) to find the frequency of the three lowest harmonics of the string.

Solution.

First, let's find the fundamental frequency using (4) with $n = 1$ and $L = 0.75$ m.

$$f(1) = (100/1.5) = \underline{66.7 \text{ Hz}} \quad \text{(first harmonic or fundamental)}$$

The next two harmonics are found by multiplying this result by 2 and 3, respectively.

$$f(2) = 2\,f(1) = \underline{133 \text{ Hz}} \quad \text{and} \quad f(3) = 3\,f(1) = \underline{200 \text{ Hz}}$$

C. Reflection and Refraction of Light.

The mystery of light has occupied a central place in the history of physics. During the 1600's Isaac Newton believed light consisted of tiny particles which he dubbed corpuscles. Huygens, a contemporary of Newton, argued that light is a wave rather than a series of particles. Given the stature of Newton it is not surprising that the particle model prevailed from his time through the eighteenth century. The particle model was slowly replaced by the wave model beginning with the influential interference experiments of Thomas Young in the early nineteenth century. The theoretical work of James Clerk Maxwell during the 1860s added to the emerging consensus that light is best described as a wave. The current model of light, which forms one of the foundations of modern physics, did not emerge until the twentieth century. However, our text only concerns classical (pre-twentieth century) physics and so we will not address the history of theories of light further.

Fortunately, one can understand a wide range of phenomena without worrying about whether light is a wave or a particle. There are two basic laws of optics that can be used to understand an array of phenomena, the law of reflection and the law of refraction.

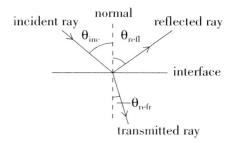

FIG. 4. INCIDENT, REFLECTED, AND REFRACTED (TRANSMITTED) RAYS OF LIGHT. THE NORMAL IS PERPENDICULAR TO THE INTERFACE THAT SEPARATES THE TWO MEDIA.

The law of reflection is something everyone is familiar with who has ever played a game of pool (billiards). Suppose a ray of light begins in a medium (e.g. air) and then encounters another medium (e.g. glass). The ray is (partially) reflected when it reaches the interface of the two media. The normal (perpendicular) to the interface is defined as illustrated in Figure 4.

In Figure 4 three angles are present: the *angles of incidence, reflection,* and *transmission* (refraction). Each of these angles is measured from the appropriate ray to the normal to the interface. In terms of these angles the law of reflection reads,

$$\theta_{inc} = \theta_{refl} \quad \text{(law of reflection)} \tag{5}$$

Most phenomena involving mirrors may be explained based on equation (5).

Example Five.—*Reflection off a plane mirror.*

Imagine an object that is shaped like an arrow and that emits light from each point of the object. We place this object in front of a plane mirror a distance, s_o (the object length), away from the mirror. The tip of the

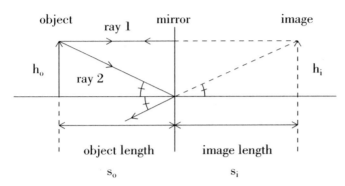

arrow emits light in all directions; there is an infinite number of rays emerging from the tip. From this vast number of rays, consider just two rays, known as the principal rays. The first principal ray emerges along the horizontal direction while the second is as shown in the figure. The first ray reflects straight back and the second ray obeys the law of reflection.

Next, we extend the two reflected rays back into the mirror—the extended rays are dashed lines in the figure. The tip of the image is found where the two extended rays intersect. The image length, s_i, is the distance from the mirror to the image. (In this case the image is called virtual and so we adopt the sign convention, $s_i < 0$. See below for further discussion of virtual images.) Let h_o and h_i represent the height of the object and image, respectively. Clearly, using θ_i to denote the incident angle for ray 2,

$$\tan\theta_i = h_o/s_o = h_i/{-s_i}.$$

The magnification, *M*, of the object is defined as

$$M \equiv h_i/h_o,$$

and so we have,

$$M = -s_i/s_o.$$

For a plane mirror it is found $M = 1$. The image above is called a **virtual image** since if a screen were placed behind the mirror where this virtual image is located, the image would not appear on the screen. (Equivalently, for a virtual image the rays appear to diverge from the image.) For **real images** the image would appear on the screen and the rays converge to the image. All of the terminology we have introduced for a plane mirror carries over to the description of non-planar mirrors.

The second law of optics is not quite as straightforward as the law of reflection. This law results from the observation that light changes speed when it goes from one medium into a different medium. Figure 5 assumes light slows down as it encounters a different medium. The short horizontal line segments called wave fronts correspond to crests of the waves. The distance between two crests (or wave

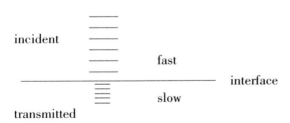

FIG. 5. LIGHT CHANGES SPEED AS IT GOES FROM ONE MEDIUM INTO ANOTHER.

fronts) is one wavelength and so in the figure the wavelength is shorter in the bottom medium and longer in the top medium. We know from experiment that the frequency of the light does not change in going from one medium to another. From the wave relation, $v = f \lambda$, shorter λ therefore implies smaller wave speed, v.

Physicists introduce a function that characterizes the speed of light in a medium. Using c to represent the speed of light in vacuum and v the speed in the medium, the **index of refraction** of the medium, n, is defined as,

$$n \equiv c/v \quad \text{(index of refraction)} \tag{6}$$

Light travels faster in vacuum than in any other media and as a consequence, by (6) the index of refraction is always greater than 1. Further, the index is positive and is dimensionless since it is the ratio of two speeds. Air has an index of refraction of 1, glass is about 1.5 and water is around 1.33.

The second law of optics makes use of the index of refraction concept. As light moves from one medium into another its change in speed causes the ray to bend, as illustrated in Figure 4 where a refracted (transmitted) ray is sketched. The transmitted (refracted) angle, $\theta_t \, (= \theta_{refr})$, is once again measured from the normal to the interface. The law of refraction (transmission), also called Snell's law, is found from experiment to involve the index of refraction of the incident and transmitted media and the angles of incidence and refraction shown in Figure 4.

$$n_{inc} \sin \theta_{inc} = n_t \sin \theta_t \quad \text{(law of refraction)} \tag{7}$$

Example Six.—*Is it a diamond or what?*

The shady character Snidely Whiplash claims he has a diamond. Although his sample looks like a piece of glass, you are willing to test his character by determining the index of refraction of the sample. Given a laser, a pencil and paper and a protractor, describe how you will vindicate(?) Snidely.

Solution.

Shine the laser on the diamond. Using the protractor, measure the angles of incidence and transmission for the light. Use equation (7) to solve for the transmitted index,

$$n_t = n_{inc} \sin \theta_{inc}/ \sin \theta_t$$

Finally, compare the value you find for n_t to the known index of refraction of diamond.

Snell's law may be rewritten in the following informative way,

$$\sin\theta_t /\sin\theta_{inc} = n_{inc}/n_t.$$

Consider the case where light is in an incident medium that has an index of refraction less than the transmitted medium, i.e. $n_{inc} < n_t$. For example, light is in air and goes into water or glass.

Using the above rearrangement of Snell's law and the fact that the sine function increases with increasing angle we get,

$$\sin\theta_t < \sin\theta_{inc} \quad \text{which implies} \quad \theta_t < \theta_{inc}.$$

Therefore, light as it moves from a smaller index of refraction medium (e.g. air) into a larger index medium (e.g. water or glass) gets bent toward the normal once inside the larger index medium. The example below illustrates the opposite case.

Example Seven.—*Fish in the water.*

A fish is at the bottom of a clear pond. Determine the angle of refraction for the ray shown in the figure, given the index of refraction of water is 1.33 and the incident angle inside the water is $\theta = 45°$.

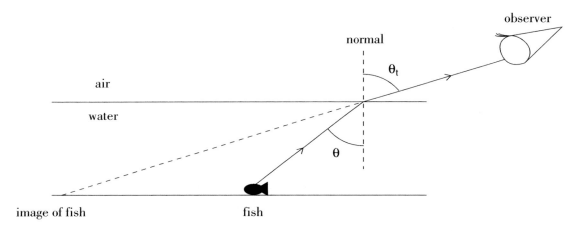

Solution.

Snell's law gives $\sin\theta_t = n_{inc} \sin\theta_{inc} / n_t = 1.33 \sin 45°/1 = 0.94$,

and taking the inverse sin, $\theta_t = \sin^{-1}(0.94) = \underline{70.1°}$.

Notice in this case the light is going from a higher index of refraction medium (water) into a lower index medium (air), and the light is bent away from the normal giving, $\theta_t > \theta_{inc}$. By tracing the refracted ray back into the water—the dashed line in the figure, one finds the apparent location of the fish, i.e. its image. For the same reason, a straw inside a glass of water appears to be bent.

Although we will not prove this, it turns out that the law of refraction may also be used to understand thin lenses. For a simple lens we need to know what is meant by its focal length, f. Imagine a set of parallel rays encountering a thin lens. After the rays pass through the lens they converge to a point called the focal point of the lens. The distance from the lens to the focal point is the quantity f. (We are assuming the lens is converging, there are diverging lenses but that is another story.) For an object in front of a converging lens the distance between the lens and the object is called the object length, s_o. The image that is formed behind the lens is at a distance from the lens called the image length, s_i. These three variables, s_o, s_i, and f, are related by the thin lens formula: $1/s_o + 1/s_i = 1/f$. Moreover, it is not difficult to prove that the lens magnification formula is the same as the one for the plane mirror above. Indeed, one of the beauties of physics is the amazingly few fundamental principles!

D. Other Properties of Light: Diffraction, Interference, Dispersion, and Polarization.

In this section we will deviate substantially from our previous presentation. To understand the properties of light waves known as interference and diffraction one begins with the principle of superposition from the previous section of this chapter. Here we will not examine the detailed mathematics but only show the patterns that are observed in the laboratory.

Diffraction is the fanning out of light that occurs when light passes through an opening. Suppose the light has wavelength, λ, and the opening in an opaque screen has a diameter d. If the value of d is much larger than λ then the light passes straight through the opening and appears on a wall behind the apparatus. This is what occurs if you shine a flashlight through an open door leading into a dark room as in Figure 6(a). One observes a beam on the wall. However, if d is about the size of λ then the light is bent when passing through d and one observes a diffraction pattern on the wall as in Figure 6(b).

In Figure 6(c) a picture of a diffraction pattern appears. Notice the alternating bands of bright spots separated by dark spots. The detailed explanation of this effect is based on how the light from various portions of the opening add together at the wall.

Another effect obtains when there are two openings in the screen. Double-slit ***interference*** occurs when light from one of the slits (openings) adds to light coming from the other slit. Figure 7 shows the distinct interference pattern of light. Although it may be difficult to tell the difference between the diffraction and interference patterns (Figure 6(c) and Figure 7), a careful study indicates the patterns are not the same.

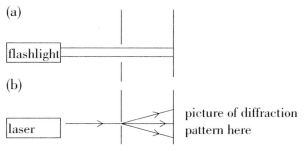

(a)

flashlight

(b)

laser

picture of diffraction pattern here

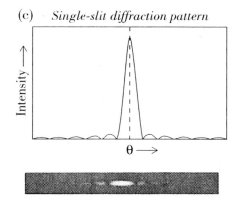

(c)   *Single-slit diffraction pattern*

Intensity $\longrightarrow$

$\theta \longrightarrow$

FIG. 6. DIFFRACTION OF LIGHT. IN (A) THE LIGHT IS HARDLY BENT SINCE THE OPENING IS VERY WIDE WHILE IN (B) THE LIGHT IS STRONGLY BENT AS IT PASSES THROUGH THE NARROW SLIT. IN (C) IS SHOWN AN ACTUAL DIFFRACTION PATTERN WITH A GRAPH OF THE INTENSITY (BRIGHTNESS) OF THE LIGHT.

FIG. 7. ACTUAL TWO-SLIT
INTERFERENCE PATTERN IS
SHOWN.

Interference (and diffraction) patterns also occur when water waves pass through two openings in a break wall. In the early 1800s Thomas Young based his wave theory of light on the fact that the pattern of light was similar to the pattern of water waves.

Another result is associated with the formation of rainbows. Isaac Newton studied light using prisms in order to understand how rainbows are produced. Newton used a prism to create a rainbow from sunlight ("white light") in his laboratory, and then he used a second prism to make the rainbow convert back into white light. Based on these observations Newton developed the white light theory which says white light is composed of all the colors (wavelengths) of the rainbow. In Figure 8 is shown a prism and a white light source. The light enters the prism on one side and exits on the other. It is clear that different colors or wavelengths are refracted through different

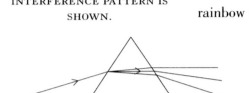

white light   rainbow

prism

FIG. 8. A RAY OF WHITE LIGHT IS
DISPERSED INTO A RAINBOW BY A PRISM.

angles of refractions—thus forming the rainbow. By Snell's law we can therefore state that the index of refraction of the prism must vary with the wavelength, an effect known as ***dispersion***. Hence, in a dispersive medium different wavelengths of light will travel with different speeds.

(a)   (b)

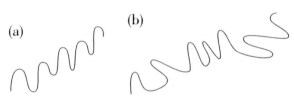

FIG. 9. (A) POLARIZED LIGHT IS SHOWN WHERE
THE ELECTRIC FIELD VECTORS ALL LIE IN THE
SAME PLANE. (B) UNPOLARIZED LIGHT HAS
ELECTRIC FIELD VECTORS IN MANY
DIFFERENT PLANES.

Notice from the figure that dispersion occurs at both air-prism interfaces.

The last topic we consider is ***polarization***. Figure 9(a) shows a polarized light wave. All the vibrations of the light occur in one plane. In general, light waves are unpolarized as in (b). Later we will learn more about the structure of light waves and find that light vibrations can be polarized by shining the light through a polarizing medium as in polarized sunglasses.

Summary.

Vibrating objects create waves such as sound, light and water waves. Standing waves occur when traveling waves from two opposite directions combine on a string, for example. The wave relation is an equation involving the wave speed, wavelength and frequency of a wave. The superposition principle is a mathematical statement of how the wave functions of combining waves in a medium are added together. Superposition is also called wave interference. Waves that start in one medium encounter an interface when they reach another medium. At an interface part of the initial wave is reflected and part is transmitted. The reflected wave obeys the law of reflection while the transmitted wave obeys the law of refraction (Snell's law). An important property of a medium is its index of refraction, which appears in the law of refraction. These two laws of optics underlie all of geometric optics and therefore form the basis of our understanding of mirrors and lenses. Physical optics treats such phenomena as wave diffraction, two-slit wave interference, the dispersion of a wave and the polarization of a wave.

QUESTIONS.

1. A mass attached to a spring oscillates with a position versus time graph as shown. At point A, the mass has

(a) negative velocity and negative acceleration

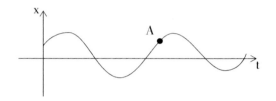

(b) positive velocity and positive acceleration

(c) negative velocity and positive acceleration

(d) positive velocity and negative acceleration

(e) cannot determine

2. At what position is the velocity of a simple harmonic oscillator maximum? zero? At what position is the acceleration maximum? zero?

3. A simple pendulum consists of a pendulum bob of mass m that is attached to a rope of length L. The period of vibration of a simple pendulum, T, is given by the expression

$$T = 2\pi\sqrt{(L/g)}.$$

A pendulum clock is taken to the Moon. How will this effect the period of the pendulum?

4. Estimate the period of oscillation of your arm approximated as a simple pendulum. For background, see the previous question on the pendulum.

5. The length of a pendulum is quadrupled (see question 3 for background). The ratio of the new period to the original period would be?

6. The energy transported by many waves is proportional to the square of the wave's amplitude. If the amplitude is tripled by how much is the energy changed?

7. Seismic waves in the earth are S or P waves. Use the Internet (e.g. Google.com) to find out about these waves (e.g. their type, their speed, etc.)

8. Consider the two waves sketched below. Which wave has the greater wavelength, amplitude, period, and frequency? Note: You are looking at y vs x at time zero.

(a)   (b)

9. Two waves have the same velocity but the first wave has twice the frequency of the second. What is the ratio of the wavelength of the second wave to that of the first?

10. Suppose acoustic (i.e. sound) waves traveled with a speed that varied appreciably with frequency. How would this change the experience of listening to an orchestra or rock concert?

11. A wave pulse on a string at a given instant is graphed below. The pulse is moving toward the right. What direction is the (a) string and (b) wave moving at the three points labeled 1, 2, 3?

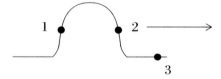

12. While at the beach a student notices that a wave arrives at the shore every 2.0 s. What is the period and frequency of the waves?

13. A student notices that a wave on a lake passes the student every 3.0 s and the wave has a speed of 15 m/s. Determine the wavelength of the lake waves.

14. A snapshot of a wave pulse on a string is shown below.

Which of the graphs below best represent a graph of the position x versus time t graph of point A on the string?

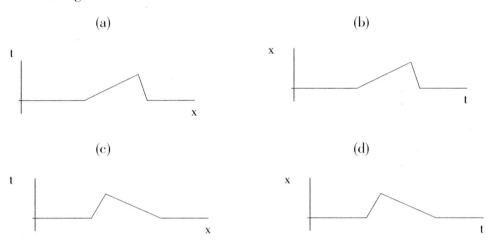

15. Two identical wave pulses travel in opposite directions on a rope. The only difference between the pulses is the second is upside down from the first (see figure below).

Which of the following statements is(are) true?

(a) There is a moment when the string is completely straight.

(b) There is a point on the rope that does not move.

(c) When the two pulses add, the energy of the pulses is momentarily zero.

(d) There are a number of points on the rope that do not move.

(e) When the pulses meet they bounce back just like particles.

16. Inhaling helium makes the frequency at which you speak increase. Why?

17. You have the flu and are very congested. Why does the pitch of your voice change?

18. A horizontal and vertical mirror are touching at their common corner. Make a ray diagram for a light ray that impinges on the horizontal mirror at an incident angle of 60°.

19. The incident ray shown below encounters an interface where "n" is the index of refraction. Which ray best represents the reflected ray?   a   b   c   d   e

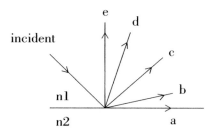

20. Which letter below best represents the location of the image of the object O?

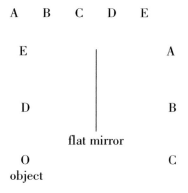

21. A ray of light moves from air into a glass block as shown below. The transmitted ray is best represented by which of the rays in the figure?   a   b   c   d   e

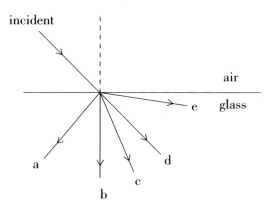

22. Two rays of light are parallel in air and encounter an interface. The interface ray 1 encounters is water (index of refraction of 1.33) while ray 2 encounters glass (index of 1.5). Which ray is bent the most?

23. A fish rests on the bottom of a clear pond as shown below. Which of the rays below best illustrate the refracted ray's path?

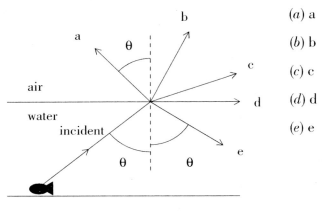

(*a*) a

(*b*) b

(*c*) c

(*d*) d

(*e*) e

fish

24. Air above the hot desert floor becomes more dense as you go up because of the heat. Generally the index of refraction varies with the density so that rays above the floor travel slower than rays near the floor of the desert. Explain, using a ray diagram with wave fronts, why these facts are relevant in understanding the cause of a mirage in the desert. Hint #1: A wave front is a set of points of the same phase and so, for example, for a set of horizontal parallel rays, the wave fronts are vertical lines. Hint #2: in a mirage a vertical tree appears, from the viewpoint of an observer, to be upside down.

PROBLEMS.

1. A 2.0-kg mass is attached to a spring with spring constant 200 N/m. The mass moves back and forth on the x-axis between −10.0 cm and +10.0 cm. Assume the phase constant of the motion is zero. Find (a) the period of vibration and (b) the position of the mass at time 5.0 seconds.

2. A frequency of great importance to an orchestra is 440.0 Hz—a note called concert A. Find the period of this note.

3. Diatomic molecules may be modeled as two particles connected by a spring. In the O_2 molecule the oxygen atoms vibrate with a period of 2.1×10^{-14} s. Find the corresponding vibration frequency.

4. The normal human can hear sounds spanning the frequency range, 20.0 to 20,000 Hz. Find the corresponding range in periods for the audible range.

5. A 5.0-gram mass is attached to a spring and vibrates with a frequency of 2.0 Hz. Find the spring constant of the spring.

6. A simple pendulum consists of a pendulum bob of mass m that is attached to a rope of length L. The rope hangs vertically from a ceiling. By applying Newton's second law to this system, one finds that the shadow of the bob on the floor vibrates as if it is attached to a spring. The period of vibration, T, is given by the expression,

$$T = 2\pi\sqrt{(L/g)}.$$

Calculate the period of a simple pendulum of length 1.0 m.

7. Jean Foucault was a French physicist who in 1851 used a simple pendulum as a way of demonstrating that the earth rotates on its axis. The plane of oscillation of the Foucault pendulum slowly rotates during a time of one day. Use the expression given in problem 6 to determine the period of Foucault's pendulum which had a length of 61.0 m.

8. The audible range of the human ear extends from 20.0 Hz up to 20,000.0 Hz. The speed of sound is 340.0 m/s. Compute the audible wavelength range corresponding to this frequency range.

9. Underwater sound travels with a speed of about 1500.0 m/s. A dolphin while under the water emits sounds of frequency 2.0×10^5 Hz. Find the wavelength emitted by the dolphin.

10. Radio waves are used in studies of the thickness of ice in the Antarctic. The speed of radio waves in ice is 1.7×10^8 m/s. A radio pulse takes 32.9×10^{-6} s to go from the top down to the bottom of the ice and reflect back. From this find the thickness of the ice.

11. If lightning and thunder emerge from the same location then by knowing the difference in time between seeing the lightning and hearing the thunder an observer may determine how far away this location is from the observer. Let d represent the distance between observer and where the lightning/thunder occur and t_S (t_L) represent the time for the thunder(lightning) to travel from the location to the observer. Finally, let $v_S(v_L)$ represent the speed of sound(light). Show that the following relation holds,

$$d = (t_S - t_L)/(1/v_S - 1/v_L).$$

12. Use the results from problem 11 to determine the distance from a storm in which the time delay between seeing the lightning and hearing the thunder is 2.4 s. The speed of sound is 340 m/s and that of light is 3.0×10^8 m/s.

13. The two identical waves graphed below at time zero are moving toward each other on a string with a speed of 10.0 m/s. Draw graphs of the resultant wave at times 0.1, 0.2, and 0.3 s. The curves are sine functions.

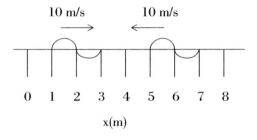

14. Repeat problem 13 for the sinusoidal graphs below.

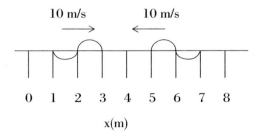

15. The fundamental frequency is 392 Hz for the 0.69 m long G-string of a banjo. Find (a) the speed of waves on this string and (b) the frequency for the second and third harmonics of the string.

16. A rubber tube is vibrated from one end at a frequency of 15.0 Hz and three bumps separated by nodes are produced. Determine the fundamental frequency and the frequencies of the second and third harmonics for this tube.

17. A hollow tube can sustain standing sound waves of certain frequencies. At an end of the tube that is open there is an anti-node while at a closed end a node appears. Find the fundamental frequency of sound waves of the 2,779 m long Brooklyn-Battery Tunnel in New York City. (Assume both ends are open and use for the speed of sound, 340 m/s.)

18. Use the information at the beginning of problem 17 to find the fundamental frequency of the outer ear of a human. The outer ear behaves as a tube of length 2.6 cm and closed at the eardrum. The speed of sound is 340 m/s.

19. The distance from one ear to the other ear of a human is about 15.0 cm. Model this as a tube of that length that is open at both ends and find the fundamental vibration frequency of a sound wave inside this "tube." (Assume the speed of sound is 340 m/s and see the beginning of problem 17 for information.)

20. Two 8.0 m long mirrors stand vertically, are parallel to each other, and are 0.4 m apart. A ray of light reflects off the bottom of the mirror on the right with an angle of reflection of 45.0° and bounces back and forth between the mirrors over the 8 m length. (a) How far did the ray travel in its route between the mirrors and (b) how long did it take to travel this distance?

21. A mirror is horizontal and abuts a vertical mirror. A ray of light is incident on the horizontal mirror with an incident angle of 65.0° and reflects off it and onto the vertical mirror. Determine (a) the angle of incidence of the light at the vertical mirror and (b) show that the reflected ray from the vertical mirror is parallel to the original ray entering the system of mirrors.

22. Make a ray diagram of a 2.0 m tall man standing in front of a vertical mirror assuming his eyes are at the top of his head. From this diagram determine what is the shortest mirror in which the man can see himself entirely?

23. Repeat problem 22 assuming the man's eyes are 4.0 cm below the top of his head.

24. The speed of light in Jell-o is 2.1×10^8 m/s. Determine the index of refraction of Jell-o.

25. Radio waves passing through ice have an index of refraction of 1.305. Assuming an Antarctic ice sheet has a thickness of 2,400 m determine the total time for a radio wave to go from the top of the sheet to the bottom and back to the top of the sheet.

26. The time for light to travel from the Sun to the Earth is 500.0 s. Find the distance from the Sun to the Earth.

27. A pulse of light in air is incident on a medium with an incident angle of 30.0°. The velocity of light in the medium is $c/2$. Find the refracted angle of the light.

28. Use Snell's law to find the index of refraction of a diamond given an incident angle of 30° for a ray of light which has a refracted angle of 18° in the diamond.

29. Use Snell's law to find the angle represented below by the question mark in the figure.

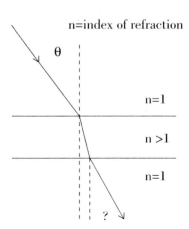

30. A ray of light in air travels into the glass that is a side of an aquarium. The index of refraction of the glass is 1.6. The ray then enters the water inside where the index of refraction is 1.33. If the incident angle is 25° at the air-glass interface then find (a) the transmitted angle of the ray inside the glass and (b) the final transmitted angle of the ray leaving the glass and entering into the water.

Hints and answers to problems.

1) 0.628 s and −0.0238 m   2) 2.27 m/s   3) 4.76 × 10¹³ Hz   4) 5 × 10⁻⁵s   5) 0.79 N/m
6) 1.99 s   7) 15.5 s   8) 17 m to 0.017 m   9) 7.5 mm   10) 2800 m   11) Hint: find $t_S − t_L$
12) 816 m   13) Hint: each 1 s it moves 1 m   14) Hint: each 1 s it moves 1 m   15) 541 m/s and
784 Hz, 1176 Hz   16) 5, 10, 15 Hz   17) 0.061 Hz   18) Hint: the open end is an antinode and
the closed a node. 3269 Hz   19) 1133 Hz   20) 11.3 m and 3.8 × 10⁻⁸s   21) Hint: the sum of
the angles of a triangle is 180 degrees.   22) 1 m   23) 1 m   24) 1.43   25) 2.088 × 10⁻⁵ s
26) 1.5 × 10¹¹ m   27) 14.5°   28) 1.62 29) ? = θ   30) 15.3° and 18.5°

⁊Section III.

ELECTRICITY.

Rubbing a rod as in the above figure can cause the rod to become charged. The rod then electrically attracts small pieces of paper.

CHAPTER VIII.
STATIONARY CHARGES.

Abstract.
The concept of charge is introduced. The fundamental force between charges is presented along with the fundamental concepts: electric field, electric potential energy, and electric potential which is also called voltage. The eighteenth-century physicist Charles Coulomb is profiled. The importance of point charges is strongly emphasized.

Definitions. charge, electrostatics, conductors, insulators, test charge, electric field, lines of force, electric potential energy and electric potential (voltage)

Principles. principle of superposition

Fundamental Equations. Coulomb's force law, electric field and potential of a point charge

Gravity was the first fundamental force of nature to be understood. The second fundamental force is the electric force. In all, there are four fundamental forces in physics but only the first two operate in classical physics. The other two forces are important in the domain of nuclear and sub-nuclear physics.

Fundamental forces in physics play a role similar to the role played by the gods for ancient peoples. Forces (and gods) remove mysteries as to why things occur in the natural world. For example, consider lightning. To moderns lightning is explained on the basis of our understanding of the electric force. But thousands of years ago people believed lightning to be caused by a storm god such as Zeus or some other deity. Some ancient persons (e.g. the Hebrews) eventually reduced the number of their gods to just one. For many decades physicists have been on a similar quest to unify all fundamental forces into just one force. Today, this quest is near completion. However, gravity has yet to be combined with the other three forces. Of course, some scientists would state that there is a god in addition to the fundamental forces of physics. The question of whether deities exist, though, is a risky question and a matter of personal faith.

Returning to the forces of physics about which there are no doubts, it has been found that there is a beautiful symmetry between the gravitational and electrical forces as we will see shortly. But not all is symmetric since these fundamental forces have perplexing and important differences.

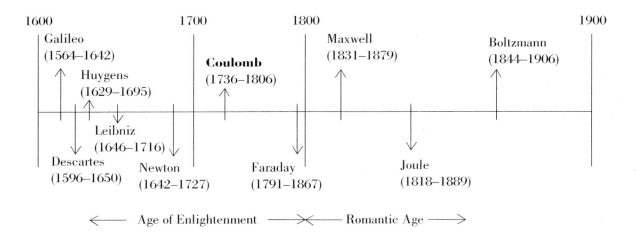

$$\longleftarrow \text{Age of Enlightenment} \longrightarrow \!\!\!\times\!\!\!\longleftarrow \text{Romantic Age} \longrightarrow$$

A. Charles Augustin Coulomb (1736–1806).

Courtesy of Réunion des Musées Nationaux/Art Resource, NY.

Although Coulomb was among the leading physicists of the eighteenth century, his contributions to physics were not on the same level of importance as the work of Newton or Galileo. For this reason, our profile of his life will be somewhat abbreviated.

Coulomb was born in France to a family of high social position. The Coulomb family moved often due to the governmental career of his father. Charles' mother wanted him to become a physician but instead he decided to study mathematics. Coulomb became a junior member of a prominent French scientific organization at an early age. Later, he chose to become a military engineer, receiving the necessary training by attending a college in Paris. Afterward, he gained additional practical scientific and engineering experience by virtue of his role in overseeing the construction of Fort Bourbon on the French Caribbean island of Martinique. In 1773 the Paris Academy announced a contest involving the construction of magnetic compasses. Coulomb entered the contest and tied for first place. Part of his work for the contest involved the study of how electric charges exert force on each other. This, his major work in physics, made use of a torsion balance that he invented (see Figure 1).

The stationary charge q_1 in the figure is attracted (or repelled) by the movable charge q_2 that is a distance r away. The movement of q_2 causes the thin fiber to twist, and Coulomb was able to use the amount of twist to ascertain how the electric force between the charges depends on their charges and their separation.

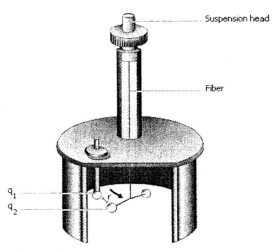

FIG. 1. COULOMB'S TORSION BALANCE. THE
SMALL BALLS ARE A DISTANCE r APART AND
HAVE CHARGE q_1 AND q_2. THE ELECTRIC
FORCE F_q BETWEEN THE CHARGES CAUSES
THE FIBER TO TWIST. FROM THE VALUES OF
THESE VARIABLES ONE IS ABLE TO CONFIRM
COULOMB'S LAW OF ELECTRICAL FORCE AND
OBTAIN A VALUE FOR THE CONSTANT, k, THAT
APPEARS IN COULOMB'S LAW.
Microsoft Encarta Encyclopedia.

Other of his interests included the strength of materials and the engineering of building designs. In 1781 Coulomb studied frictional forces, and won another academic prize based on that endeavor. Coulomb also studied and contributed toward the design of windmills and canals. He lost his position on a government commission during the French revolution but he was able to avoid the Terror (guillotine) by fleeing to his properties well outside of Paris. At an advanced age Charles turned toward plant physiology as an area of study.

On a more personal level, the aged Coulomb lived with a woman thirty years younger than he was. The couple eventually married and had a son, followed seven years later by a second son in 1797. His final governmental service was an assignment given to him by Napoleon in 1802. The assignment was to serve on a commission to redesign the French educational system. (Some things never change!) In 1806 Charles Coulomb died of a "fever."

References.

Remarkable Physicists, Ioan James (Cambridge UP, 2004).

Great Physicists, William H. Cropper (Oxford UP, 2004).

Physics, the Human Adventure, Gerald Holton and Stephen G. Brush (Rutgers University Press, 2001).

B. Electric Charges at Rest.

One of the most significant contributions of the twentieth century to physics was the confirmation of the atomic model. Nowadays, all agree that matter is made of atoms, and atoms consist of a nucleus surrounded by electrons. The atom is roughly a spherical object with a diameter on the order of 10^{-10} m ($= 1$ Å $= 1$ Angstrom $= 10$ nm). The nucleus, which is also approximately spherical in shape, is tiny by comparison to the atom. The nucleus is about 10,000 times smaller than the atom. The nucleus is made of protons and neutrons. Each of these fundamental particles have mass (see the flyleaf for the numerical values), but the proton and electron also have another important property, ***charge***. The neutron has almost the same mass as the proton but it has zero charge. The proton and electron have charges of magnitude,

$$q = e = 1.6 \times 10^{-19} \quad \text{Coulombs.}$$

The unit for charge is named after Charles Coulomb whom we just profiled above.

Ever since the time of Benjamin Franklin we have known there are two types of charge, positive and negative. For the proton, $q = e > 0$ while for the electron, $q = -e < 0$. But how do we know there are two types of charge rather than just one type? Basically, the reason is, one finds experimentally that charges may attract or repel one another while gravitational forces are always attractive. See below for further elaboration on this topic.

Charge is also an important property for objects bigger than fundamental particles. For instance, an atom is charged if the number of protons it contains differs from the number of electrons. In this case, the atom is called an *ion* and ions can be positive or negative depending on whether there are more protons than electrons or less. Everyday objects can also have charge if there isn't a balance between the total number of protons in the object and the total number of electrons. Often, everyday objects acquire charge if they are rubbed, since some electrons can be added to or subtracted from the object by rubbing. In fact, the word electron was used by the ancient Greeks to refer to amber. Amber is a resinous sap that flows from softwood trees and hardens. The Greeks found that amber attracts small pieces of lint when it is rubbed with a cloth. Early on it was found that when two amber rods were rubbed by two identical cloths, the rods would repel one another. However, when two *different* rods are rubbed, e.g. a glass rod rubbed with silk and a rubber rod rubbed with fur, the two rods may attract one another. These observations form the grounds for the familiar statement about the electric force operating between two charges,

"like sign charges repel each other; unlike sign charges attract one another."

Notice there is a fundamental difference between electric and gravity forces, to wit: the gravitational force is always attractive since there is only one kind of mass; while the electric force is either attractive or repulsive depending on the signs of the charges interacting. The electric force has this dual behavior because of the two types of charge, positive and negative, and consequently, it is somewhat more complicated than gravity. Today, we understand rubbing a rod brings about a deposition or a removal of electrons. Depositing electrons on the rod makes it have a net negative charge while removing electrons causes the rod to be positively charged.

In this chapter we will concentrate on situations where charges are not moving—a subfield of electricity called **electrostatics**. Materials that do not allow charges to move inside (or on) them are called **insulators**, such as glass, wood and plastic. Other materials are called **conductors**, such as a metal. Conductors allow the motion of charge. Some materials are neither conductors or insulators but such ("semiconducting or superconducting") materials are more complicated and will not be discussed here.

In general, there are two procedures for giving an object a charge: charging by contact and by induction. Figure 2 illustrates these two methods. In part (a) charging by contact is shown. One begins with two conducting spheres, one with a positive charge and the other that is neutral. When the positive sphere touches the neutral sphere, some of the positive charges are transferred to the neutral one, giving it also a positive charge. Why does this happen? The reason is, the positive charges repel each other and this causes the transfer to occur. In part (b) a rubber rod has been rubbed with a piece of cat fur—the rod is negatively charged due to the transfer of electrons from the fur. The rubber, which is an insulator, is brought near to a neutral conducting sphere. The presence of the rod induces a movement of some of the sphere's electrons away from the rod—we say the sphere has become polarized. In the last part of (b), a person touches the sphere with their finger, and some of the electrons are transferred to the finger leaving the sphere with a positive charge.

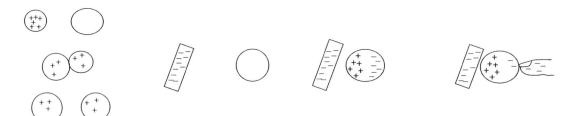

FIG. 2. (A) CHARGING BY CONTACT. THE INITIALLY CHARGED CONDUCTING BALL IS BROUGHT INTO CONTACT WITH AN IDENTICAL SECOND NEUTRAL BALL, AND WHEN THE TWO ARE FINALLY SEPARATED BOTH ARE FOUND TO HAVE THE SAME SIGN OF CHARGE ON THEM.

(B) CHARGING BY INDUCTION. THE NEGATIVELY CHARGED INSULATING ROD IS BROUGHT NEAR THE INITIALLY NEUTRAL CONDUCTING SPHERE. THIS CAUSES THE SPHERE TO BECOME POLARIZED. A PERSON TOUCHES THE POLARIZED SPHERE AND SOME OF THE NEGATIVE CHARGES ON THE SPHERE LEAVE THROUGH THE FINGER. ON SEPARATING THE ROD AND FINGER, THE SPHERE IS FINALLY FOUND TO HAVE CHARGE OF OPPOSITE SIGN TO THAT OF THE ROD.

C. Fundamental Force: Coulomb's Electric Force.

The electric force between two charges was studied in detail by Coulomb, who determined the form of this force law experimentally. *Coulomb's law* states the force between two point charges is proportional to the charges, q_1 and q_2, but inversely proportional to the square of the separation of the charges, r. This means the force becomes smaller as the charges get further away from each other but it becomes larger the greater the charges. Stated mathematically,

Coulomb's Law of Electric Force
$$F = k\,q_1\,q_2/r^2 \quad \text{and like charges repel, unlikes attract.} \tag{1}$$

The quantity k in equation (1) has been measured in the laboratory, $k = 9 \times 10^9$ N-m²/C². The form of equation (1) is known as an inverse-square law. The gravitational force is also an inverse-square law but the gravitational force has the product of the masses in the numerator while the electric force has the product of the charges. Equation (1) only gives the magnitude of the force.

Since force is a vector, the signs of the interacting charges must be considered to determine the direction of the force. Note: the force lies along the line connecting the two point charges.

Example One.—*Gravity versus electric forces at the atomic level.*

The hydrogen atom is the simplest atom. It consists of a stationary proton with a single electron at a distance of about 0.5 Angstroms away. As such, the atom is neutral. Compare the electric force on the electron by the proton to the gravitational force of attraction between the two particles.

Solution.

We are asked to find the ratio

$$F_q/F_g = [ke^2/r^2]/[Gm_em_p/r^2],$$

where m_e and m_p are the masses of the electron and proton, respectively.

The r^2 cancels out, and we find

$$F_q/F_g = ke^2/[Gm_em_p] = 9 \times 10^9(1.6 \times 10^{-19})^2/[6.67 \times 10^{-11} \times 9.11 \times 10^{-31} \times 1.67 \times 10^{-27}]$$

$$F_q/F_g = \underline{2.3 \times 10^{39}}$$

This simple example has major consequences in that it shows us that at the atomic level the electric force is enormous compared to the gravitational force. In the atomic and subatomic world the gravitational force is so feeble compared to electric forces that it can be safely ignored. Chemists rarely have to consider gravitational forces but astronomers do!

Coulomb's law strictly applies only between two *particles* of charge. When the two charged objects are extended rather than particles, the tools of integral calculus are used to compute the force.

Life is usually more complex than just two particles. Suppose we have a system of three charged particles. How can we find the force on a given charge due to the other two? The answer to this question is provided by the all important *principle of superposition,*

$$\vec{F}_{total} = \text{total force on charge one by two and by three} = \vec{F}_{on\ 1\ by\ 2} + \vec{F}_{on\ 1\ by\ 3}.$$

To find the force on one by two, simply use Coulomb's law, ignoring the presence of charge three. If a fourth charge is present then the force on 1 by 4 would have to be added to the vector sum above. Since forces are vectors, the process of adding vectors becomes relevant once again.

The importance of the electric force can not be over emphasized. Indeed, a large portion of chemistry may be understood by considering the electrical force between the molecules involved in chemical reactions. It is the electric force that gives rise to the bonds between atoms of a molecule.

As in the case of the gravitational force, the electric force does not require contact between the two particles. To circumvent "action at a distance" the concept of a field was introduced in gravitation theory. Similarly, it is convenient to introduce an electric field.

D. The Electric Field: A Field Theory.

A particle of charge, q, situated at the origin of our coordinate system will exert a force on any other charged particle that is nearby. Suppose there is another particle that has a very small positive charge, q_{test}. This other particle we will refer to as a *test charge*. Let r denote the distance between the two charges. According to Coulomb's law the test charge will experience a force by q of magnitude,

$$F_{\text{on test charge by q}} = kqq_{\text{test}}/r^2.$$

If we divide this force by the value of the test charge, the result will depend only on q and the distance from q, denoted r. The spatial region surrounding q is then viewed as a space under the influence of q. This influence is called the electric field, $\vec{E}$, due to q at a distance r, and is defined to have a magnitude,

$$\text{Electric field of a point charge}$$
$$E \equiv F_{\text{ontestcharge}}/q_{\text{test}} = E = kq/r^2 \qquad (2)$$
(electric field of point charge q a distance r away (units, N/c), of $g > 0$ $\vec{E}$ points away)

In general, the ***electric field*** at a point in space is defined as the electric force experienced by a test charge that is placed at that point of space, divided by the test charge,

$$\vec{E} \equiv \vec{F}_{\text{on test charge}}/q_{\text{test}}. \qquad (3)$$

Equation (2) is just a special case of the general definition of equation (3). Equation (3) states that the electric field is a vector and it points in the same direction as the force acting on the test charge. We can always determine the direction of an electric field at a point in space by placing a test charge at that point, and noting the direction of the force on the test charge. For example, if q is positive then a test charge would experience a force of repulsion away from q. Hence, *for a positive charge* q, *the electric field produced by* q *points **away** from* q *and the opposite holds if* q *is negative, i.e. the electric field of a negative charge points **toward** the negative charge.* These ideas are summarized in Figure 3.

The arrows in the figure are descriptive of the electric field and are called ***lines of force*** which were introduced by a pioneer of field theory, Michael Faraday. (The notation

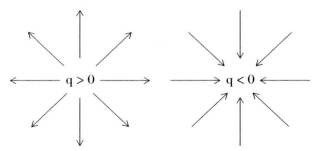

FIG. 3. DIRECTION OF ELECTRIC FIELD PRODUCED BY POSITIVE AND NEGATIVE CHARGES.

is a bit confusing since they should be called lines of "field" but the field and force are parallel, so it doesn't really matter.) The direction of the line of force at a point gives the direction of the electric field at that point. The density of the lines of force in a region give an indication of the size of the electric field in that area because the density of the lines are high near q, which must be true since the field is large there, but the field and line density are low far from q where the field is weak.

Given a collection of point charges, the superposition principle may be used to find the total electric field produced by the collection. Simply find the field by each charge using Equation (2) then add all of the electric field vectors to obtain the total field. If there are many charges the vector addition becomes time consuming. A way around having to add all these vectors is to first find a scalar property of the charges, from which the field may be determined. This scalar property that is produced by a charge q a distance r away is called the electric potential or voltage. The idea is, we find the voltage by a group of charges by adding the voltages of the individual charges—a scalar addition. Then from the total voltage one can extract the total field, as will be shown later. Before we get to voltage, however, let us first consider a couple of simple examples of how to find an electric field produced by a single point charge or just two point charges.

Example Two.—*Electric field inside the hydrogen atom.*

Find the electric field produced at the electron by the proton in a hydrogen atom. See Example one for data that is needed.

Solution.

Using equation (2) with $q = e$ and $r = 0.5 \times 10^{-10}$ m,

$$E = ke/r^2 = 9 \times 10^9 \times 1.6 \times 10^{-19}/(0.5 \times 10^{-10})^2$$

$$\vec{E} = \underline{5.76 \times 10^{11} \text{ N/C, pointing away from the proton.}}$$

Example Three.—*The electric field node between two point charges.*

Two point charges, 2 μC and 3 μC, are a distance of 50.0 cm apart. Find the distance from the 2 μC along the line connecting the two charges where the total electric field vanishes. This point of vanishing field may be called an electric field node.

Solution.

Let's place the 2 μC charge at $x = 0$ and the 3 μC at $x = d = 0.5$ m (notice we had to change this distance from cm to m in order to not "mix" CGS and MKS units). Denote by x the position of the node. At the node the 2 μC will have a field that points to the right while the other charge has a field that points to the left. These two fields will oppose each other, and at the node we demand the two fields to have the same magnitude in order to cancel each other out. Let 2 μC = q_1, 3 μC = q_2, and so,

$$kq_1/x^2 = kq_2/(d - x)^2.$$

Rearranging this and canceling the k gives,

$$(d - x)^2/x^2 = q_2/q_1.$$

Taking the square root,

$$(d - x)/x = \pm\alpha, \quad \text{where} \quad \alpha \equiv (q_2/q_1)^{1/2},$$

or

$$(d - x) = \pm\alpha x$$

$$d = x(1 \pm \alpha).$$

Finally,

$$x = d/(1 \pm \alpha).$$

Choosing the $+$ sign (why?), we get

$$x = 0.5/(1 + 1.225) = \underline{0.225 \text{ m}}$$

It makes sense that the node had to be closer to the 2 μC than the 3 μC since the 3 μC creates a larger field.

E. Electric Potential Energy and Electric Potential (Voltage).

Recall, potential energy is energy that is stored in a system because of position. There are some statements that can be made in general about potential energy and voltages. Electric potential or voltage (V) is related to electrical potential energy (U_q) but the two concepts are not the same. The *electric potential* change, ΔV, which is also called the voltage change, is defined as the increase in electric potential energy, ΔU_q ($= W_{ext}$), of a test charge q_{test}, due to its displacement by an external force, divided by q_{test}.

Electric Potential Energy and Electric Potential (Voltage)

$$\Delta U_q \equiv W_{ext} \quad \text{and} \quad \Delta V \equiv W_{ext}/q_{test} = \Delta U_q/q_{test}. \tag{4}$$

Stated more succinctly, **the difference in electric potential, ΔV, between two points in space is the external work, W_{ext}, to move a test charge between the points divided by the test charge. The external work to move the test charge is the increase in electrical potential energy, ΔU_q, of the system.** The units for ΔV are J/C or volts, i.e. 1 Volt $\equiv$ 1J/1C. This means if an external force does one Joule of work as it moves a charge of one Coulomb from one point in space to another then that corresponds to an increase of one Volt associated with the displacement.

Two important special cases are pertinent to gaining a more complete appreciation for electric potential energy and the related idea of electric potential. In the first case it is assumed the electric field is constant while in the second case the field is variable due to the presence of a point charge.

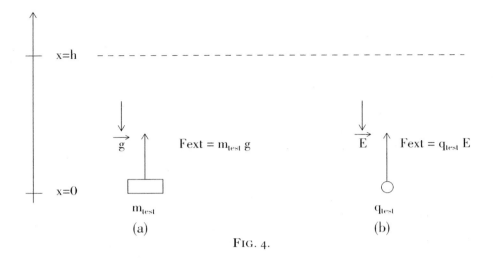

FIG. 4.

Case (i) Constant Electric Field.

Figure 4(a) reviews gravitational potential energy. A test mass m_{test} starts at the origin in the presence of a constant gravitational field, $\vec{g}$. The mass would ordinarily accelerate in the direction of $\vec{g}$ but assume a constant external force, $m_{test}g$, is applied to m_{test}, where $g = |\vec{g}|$. If the external force is made slightly larger than $m_{test}g$, then m_{test} slowly moves a distance h. The work done by the external force, W_{ext}, is $m_{test}gh$. Therefore, the system gains gravitational potential energy in the amount,

$$\Delta U_g \equiv U_g(h) - U_g(0) = W_{ext} = m_{test}gh. \quad \text{(constant } g = |\vec{g}|)$$

We arbitrarily choose $U_g(0)$ to be zero and call $x = 0$ the datum or reference location for gravitational potential energy. Therefore we recover the familiar result (where I have removed the "test" subscript from m_{test}),

$$U_g(h) = mgh \quad \text{(constant } g = |\vec{g}|)$$

In Figure 4(b) the analogous electrical situation is sketched. In this case, a positive test charge q_{test} starts at the origin in the presence of a constant *electrical* field, $\vec{E}$, pointing down in the diagram. The charge would ordinarily accelerate in the direction of $\vec{E}$ but assume a constant external force, $q_{test}E$, is applied to q_{test}, where E is $|\vec{E}|$. If the external force is made slightly larger than $q_{test}E$, then q_{test} slowly moves a distance h. The work done by the external force, W_{ext}, is $q_{test}Eh$. Therefore, the system gains electrical potential energy in the amount,

$$\Delta U_q \equiv U_q(h) - U_q(0) = W_{ext} = q_{test}Eh. \quad \text{(constant } E = |\vec{E}|)$$

We arbitrarily choose $U_q(0)$ to be zero and call $x = 0$ the datum or reference location for electrical potential energy. Therefore, on removing the "test" subscript from q_{test}, we obtain the new result that is analogous to **mgh** above, but note, *q can be positive or negative.*

Electrical Potential Energy
$$U_q(h) = qEh. \quad (\text{constant } E = |\vec{E}|) \tag{5a}$$

Equation (4) has $\Delta V \equiv W_{\text{ext}}/q_{\text{test}} = \Delta U_q/q_{\text{test}}$ and using this in equation (5a) q_{test} (i.e. q) divides out giving the simple result,

Electric Potential (Voltage)
$$V(h) = Eh \quad (\text{constant } E = |\vec{E}|) \tag{5b}$$

In equation (5b) we have chosen the datum or reference location for voltage to be $x = 0$—the same datum location as for the electrical potential energy. The place where the voltage is set to zero is called *ground.* This word is used since often in dealing with electric circuits the voltage datum is chosen to be literally the earth, or ground. In other occasions, for example in the physics of point charges, the datum is usually chosen to be a distance that is infinitely far away and then the ground is at infinity (the latter phrase sounds profound).

Example Four.—*Voltage in everyday devices: flashlight.*

A flashlight operates on a 12 volt source, a battery. Assume the electric field inside the source is constant and the battery has a length of 3.0 cm. Find the size of the electric field inside the source.

Solution.

Since the field is constant we may use equation (5b) with $V = 12$ volts and $h = 0.03$ m,

$$E = V/h = 12/0.03 = \underline{400 \text{ N/C or Volts/m}}.$$

Example Five.—*Flashlight again: speed of charge.*

Find the speed of an electron inside the flashlight battery in the previous example, assuming the only force on the electron is due to the electric field. Clearly, the electron goes from the negative terminal to the positive terminal of the battery.

Solution.

There are several ways of solving this problem and each require a review of some ideas we studied in mechanics.

First method—shortcut equation.

The (constant) positive force on the electron produces a constant acceleration,

$$a = F_{\text{net}}/m, \quad \text{Newton's second law}$$

and so,
$$a = eE/m > 0.$$

Using this in the *shortcut equation* with initial speed and initial position of zero,

$$v^2 = v_0{}^2 + 2a(x - x_o)$$

$$v^2 = 0 + 2(eE/m)(h - 0)$$

$$v = [2eEh/m]^{1/2} = [2 \cdot 1.6 \cdot 10^{-19} \cdot 400 \cdot 0.03/9.11 \cdot 10^{-31}]^{1/2}$$

$$v = \underline{2.05 \times 10^6 \text{ m/s.}}$$

This answer is far too large because in real life another force besides the electric force acts on the electron. The other force is due to the resistance of the battery and this causes v_f to be much smaller than our simple answer.

Second method—work-kinetic energy relation.

Recall the work-kinetic energy relation, $W_{net} = \Delta K$, and using $F_{net} = (-e)(-E) = eE > 0$,

$$W_{net} \equiv F_{net} \, \Delta x \bullet \cos(0) = eE(x - x_0) \bullet 1 = eE(h - 0) = eEh,$$

and
$$\Delta K = \tfrac{1}{2} \, mv^2 - 0.$$

Equating the net work to the change in kinetic energy gives,

$$eEh = \tfrac{1}{2} \, mv^2.$$

Clearly this last result will give the same value of v as was found in the first method.

Third method—conservation of energy.

We use energy conservation where the electron starts at rest at the negative terminal with an electric potential energy given by equation (5a),

$$U_{qi} = 0, \text{ since } h \text{ is zero}$$

and it arrives at the positive terminal where it has electric potential energy,

$$U_{qf} = qEh = -eEh,$$

where we have used the fact that the charge of the electron is negative. Therefore,

$$E_i = K_i + U_{qi} = 0 + 0 \quad \text{and} \quad E_f = K_f + U_{qf} = \tfrac{1}{2} \, mv^2 + -eEh.$$

Equating these,

$$E_i = E_f$$

or
$$0 = \tfrac{1}{2} \, mv^2 - eEh$$

and once again we get the same answer as before!

There is a deeper meaning to the above voltage results. **Just as a charge alters the space around it by creating an electric field (vector) at all points in the surrounding area, the charge also creates a voltage (which is a scalar) at all points nearby.** However, for a point charge the field that is created is *not* constant and so the voltage produced by a point charge is not given by equation (5b). We turn to the case of a varying electric field.

Case (ii) Variable Electric Field Due to a Point Charge.

A point charge q creates both a vector and a scalar at a distance r away. The vector is the electric field which we found earlier to be given by the expression,

$$\vec{E} = kq/r^2 \quad \text{(points away for } q > 0\text{)}.$$

Imagine a positive test charge, q_{test}, beginning at a distance infinitely far away from the positive point charge q. Because of the repulsion one must apply an external force, F_{ext}, to move q_{test} from infinity to a distance r away from q. When the separation of the two charges is r' the external force is given by Coulomb's law,

$$F_{ext}(r') = kqq_{test}/r'^2.$$

The external force does external work, W_{ext}, in moving q_{test} from infinity to position r away from q. But the external force is *not* constant so we must use the techniques of integral calculus to compute the external work—the result is,

$$W_{ext} = kqq_{test}/r.$$

By definition, the change in electric potential energy of the system equals this external work,

$$\Delta U_q = U_q(r) - U_q(\infty) = W_{ext} = kqq_{test}/r. \quad \text{(point charges)}$$

We arbitrarily choose $U_q(\infty)$ to be zero and call $r = \infty$ the datum or reference location for electrical potential energy. Let $q_{test} = q'$, and the new result analogous to equation (5a) is,

Electrical Potential Energy

$$U_q(r) = kqq'/r \text{ } (q, q' \text{ are point charges}) \tag{6a}$$

One may think of this result as a bond energy between the charges. In addition, Equation (6a) works no matter what sign q and q' happen to have.

The point charge q also creates a scalar around it, the electric potential or voltage. We use equation (4) to find the change in voltage between the initial position of the test charge (which was infinite) and the final position (which is r away from q):

$$\Delta V \equiv W_{ext}/q_{test} = \Delta U_q/q_{test}$$

or

$$V(r) - V(\infty) = (kqq_{test}/r)/q_{test} = kq/r.$$

Choosing $V(\infty) = 0$, we say the "ground is at infinity" and obtain for the voltage produced by q a distance r away.

Voltage of a point charge
$$V(r) = kq/r \quad \text{(point charge } q, r \text{ away)}. \tag{6b}$$

One of the primary reasons for introducing voltage is the relative simplicity of adding voltages (scalars) rather than adding electric fields (vectors) to find the total voltage or field at a place. Moreover, by first finding the voltage it is possible to determine the field from the voltage by using a technique from calculus called differentiation.

If instead of one charge the system under examination consists of a collection of point charges then by the superposition principle the total voltage at a place is found by using equation (6b) to find the voltage due to each charge separately and then adding up all of the voltages.

Bond energies also are found from the superposition principle. For example, suppose one has a system made of three point charges. At this juncture we know how to find the electric forces between as well as fields and voltages produced by the point charges at any place in space. Beyond this there is the remaining task of finding how much energy is stored in this system. We know energy is stored because in order to assemble the three charges, external work had to be performed. Why? Suppose the charges are all positive, then we know they repel one another. To bring the charges together, starting from when they are very far apart, a force must be applied to overcome their mutual repulsion. The force does external work and once again we have an increase in potential (stored) energy,

$$\Delta U_q = W_{\text{ext}}.$$

One might give this external work to assemble the system of charges the exalted title of creation energy. No matter the name that is chosen, the definition assumes the charges are moved slowly by the external force and so they acquire negligible kinetic energy in the process. Using integral calculus, the amount of work may be determined exactly and it is found the total potential energy of the system of three charges is given by

Potential energy of point charges
$$U_q = kq_1q_2/r_{12} + kq_1q_3/r_{13} + kq_2q_3/r_{23}, \tag{7}$$

where r_{12} denotes the distance between point charges one and two, etc. Equation (7) takes infinity as the datum (baseline) for potential energy where the charges are infinitely far apart and the potential energy is zero. There are three terms in equation (7), each having the form of Equation (6a). One can think of the three terms as "bond energies" connecting the particles. This is another instance where the physics of electricity is relevant to the chemistry of atoms and molecules. If there are more than three charges then more bonds will need to be added to equation (7).

Example Six.—*The voltage node between two charges.*

Two point charges, $q_1 = 2$ μC at $x = 0$ and $q_2 = -3$ μC at position $x = d = 50.0$ cm. Find the distance, x, from the 2 μC along the line connecting the two charges where the total voltage vanishes. This point of vanishing voltage may be called a voltage node.

Solution.

Superposition gives $0 = V_{total} = kq_1/x + kq_2/(d - x)$.

Rearranging, $(d - x)/x = -q_2/q_1 = 3/2$ Note: the q's have a sign.

$$x = d/(1 + 3/2) = 0.5/[1 + 3/2]$$

$$x = \underline{0.2\ m}$$

Example Seven.—*The hydrogen atom revisited and equipotential surfaces.*

Find (a) the voltage produced at the electron by the proton in a hydrogen atom, (b) the bond energy of the atom, and (c) the shape of an *equipotential surface,* which is defined to be a surface with all points on the surface having the same potential.

Solution.

(a) Using the point charge formula for voltage, equation (6b), with $q = e = 1.6 \times 10^{-19}$ C and $r = $ ½ Angstrom (which must be converted to meters),

$$V = kq/r = ke/r = 9 \times 10^9(1.6 \times 10^{-19})/0.5 \times 10^{-10}$$

$$V = \underline{28.8\ Volts}$$

(b) The bond energy is the stored potential energy given in equation (7) but with only two charges present rather than three, therefore, there is only one bond contributing,

$$U_q = kq_1q_2/r_{12}.$$

Using $q_1 = e$ (the proton), $q_2 = -e$ (the electron), and $r_{12} = $ ½ Angstrom (in meters), we find

$$U_q = -ke^2/r_{12} = -9 \times 10^9(1.6 \times 10^{-19})^2/(0.5 \times 10^{-10}) = \underline{-4.61 \times 10^{-18}\ J}.$$

It is often convenient in atomic and molecular physics to express energies in units of *electron volts* instead of Joules. One *eV* is the energy acquired by an electron when it moves through a potential difference of one volt. Therefore,

$$1\ eV = 1.6 \times 10^{-19}\ C \times 1\ V = 1.6 \times 10^{-19}\ J.$$

The above bond energy is then (neglecting signs)

$$4.61 \times 10^{-18}\ J \times (1\ eV/1.6 \times 10^{-19}\ J) = \underline{28.8\ eVs}$$

(c) The voltage is the same at all points a distance r away from the proton. A surface that is the same distance from a point is the familiar sphere. At all points on such a sphere, with the proton at the center, the voltage is the same value and so the sphere is an equipotential surface. For more complicated charge distributions the equipotential surfaces are different from spherical shapes.

Example Eight.—*NaCl bond energy.*

Ordinary table salt consists of sodium (Na) and chlorine (Cl) atoms in a regular array called a crystal. In salt the Na atoms are positive ions each with charge $+e$ while the chlorine atoms have charge $-e$. The Coulomb force between the Na and Cl ions is what holds the crystal together— the bond is called ionic. The distance between a Na and a nearby Cl ion in salt is 4.88 Angstroms. Find the bond energy of one Na-Cl bond in units of eV's. Ignore the presence of the other Na and Cl ions in the crystal.

Solution.

This example is identical to part (b) of the previous example but with one modification, replace 0.5×10^{-10} m with 4.88×10^{-10} m,

$$U_q = -ke^2/r_{12} = -9 \times 10^9 (1.6 \times 10^{-19})^2/(4.88 \times 10^{-10}) = \underline{-4.72 \times 10^{-19} \text{ J}}.$$

Converting to eV's and neglecting the negative sign,

$$4.72 \times 10^{-19} \text{ J} \times (1 \ eV/1.6 \times 10^{-19} \text{ J}) = \underline{2.95 \ eVs}$$

Comparing the bond energy of NaCl (2.95 eV) to that of the hydrogen atom (28.8 eV) one can draw the important conclusion that it would be easier to break the ionic bond between NaCl than to break the "electronic" bond between the proton and electron of the hydrogen atom. It is well known that, generally, the bonds holding the electrons to a nucleus are larger in energy than the molecular bonds between atoms in a molecule.

In this chapter, in addition to charge, a presentation of four fundamental electrical concepts has been given: force, field, potential energy and potential (voltage). Each of these have different units and pertain to systems with one or more charges. The formulas for these quantities contain charge to the first or second power and distance to the first or second power. Table 1 is a brief summary of these results and is intended to help you keep these four concepts distinct in your mind.

TABLE 1. SIMPLEST SYSTEMS TABLE

	Force	Field	Potential Energy	Potential (Voltage)
Two charges q_1 and q_2 r apart	kq_1q_2/r^2	$\vec{E}_1 + \vec{E}_2$	$U = kq_1q_2/r$	$V_1 + V_2$
One charge q, r away	NA	$E = kq/r^2$	NA	$V = kq/r$

F. Applications: Static Charges.

In this last section no new fundamental principles are presented. Instead, additional applications are given to round out the topic.

Example Nine.—*Electric force.*

Two identical small spheres are 20.0 cm apart and have the same charge q. (a) If the force one sphere exerts on the other is 1.0 N, then what is the value of q? (b) How many protons would it take to equal q? (c) Do the spheres attract or repel each other?

Solution.

(a) According to Coulomb's law, $F = kq^2/r^2$.

Solving this for q, $q = r(F/k)^{1/2}$.

Substituting in the numbers, $q = 0.2(1/9 \times 10^9)^{1/2} = \underline{2.1 \times 10^{-6}\ \text{C}}$.

Clearly, it only takes a small amount of charge in Coulomb's to create a non-negligible force.

(b) Since each proton has charge e, the number of protons, N, would equal

$$N = q/e = 2.1 \times 10^{-6}/1.6 \times 10^{-19} = \underline{1.3 \times 10^{13}}.$$

So it takes *many* protons to obtain 2.1×10^{-6} C of charge!

(c) Because both spheres have the same charge, they repel each other.

Example Ten.—*Electric field of a Van de Graaf generator.*

A Van de Graaf generator is a device that deposits charge on a sphere. Assume the sphere has a radius of 20.0 cm and that the electric field at the surface of the generator has the value, 3×10^6 V/m. (At this value of an electric field, called the breakdown field, sparks between the Van de Graaf can occur when you place your finger near to the surface—ouch.) (a) Find the amount of charge on the surface of the sphere. Note: you may assume all of the charge is actually at the center of the sphere and behaves as a point charge. (b) How many protons would this be?

Solution.

(a) The field produced by a point charge q at a distance r away is,

$$E = kq/r^2.$$

Solving this for q and substituting in the numbers we find,

$$q = Er^2/k = 3 \times 10^6\ (0.2)^2/9 \times 10^9 = \underline{1.33 \times 10^{-5}\ \text{C}}.$$

(b) Similar to the previous example, $N = q/e = \underline{8.3 \times 10^{13}}$.

Example Eleven.—*Voltage at the Van de Graaf surface.*

Find the value of the voltage at the surface of the Van de Graaf generator in the previous example.

Solution.

Once again with the charge q at the center we may use the point charge formula for voltage,

$$V = kq/r.$$

Substituting in the numbers, $V = 9 \times 10^9 (1.33 \times 10^{-5})/0.2 = \underline{599,000\ Volts}$!

This is a large voltage! Van de Graaf generators are used by physicists to accelerate subatomic particles. Some Van de Graaf's operate at 20 million volts.

Example Twelve.—*Potential energy stored in three charges.*

Three charges are situated on the vertices of an equilateral triangle of side 10.0 cm. The charges are q, q, and $-q$. (a) Assuming $q = 10^{-6}$ C, determine the energy stored in this charge configuration. (b) Is this charge configuration stable?

Solution.

(a) There are three bonds, and so $\quad U = kq^2/r - kq^2/r - kq^2/r = -kq^2/r.$

Substituting in the numbers, $\quad U = -9 \times 10^9(10^{-6})^2/0.1 = \underline{-0.09\ J}.$

(b) Clearly, the net force on any one of the charges does not equal zero, and as a result the charges would have to be held in place by some outside agent. Therefore, the charge configuration is not stable.

Summary.

Four fundamental concepts are stressed in this chapter in addition to that of charge: electric force, electric field, electric potential energy and electric potential (voltage). All matter is broadly classified as either an electrical insulator or a conductor. Point charges are the basic building blocks of electricity. Point charges at rest is the subject of the field known as electrostatics. Electric forces, fields, and voltages obey the principle of superposition. The potential energy of a charge distribution is relevant to chemical bond energies. Voltage is especially useful because it is a scalar property; it is easier to add voltages than forces or fields which are vectors. Loosely, voltage is to electricity as pressure is to plumbing.

QUESTIONS.

1. Two identical small spheres a distance r apart are initially electrically neutral. A charge q is taken from one of the sphere's and placed on the other sphere. In terms of these variables, express the force one of the spheres exerts on the other. Is the force repulsive or attractive?

2. Given your understanding of a conservation law, how would you accurately express the conservation of charge?

3. If a charge q is placed below a very large sheet of paper, will an equal charge q above the sheet experience an electric force due to the charge below the sheet?

4. Shown in the figure below is a common laboratory device called an electroscope. This device stores charge. Explain why when charge is placed on the top conducting ball, the metallic leaves inside the jar repel each other as indicated.

5. Which of the statements below are false? The electric force

(a) decreases with the inverse square of distance between two charges

(b) between an atomic nucleus and an electron is much stronger than the gravitational force acting between them

(c) between two electrons a distance r apart is larger than the electric force between two protons a distance r apart.

(d) may be either repulsive or attractive.

6. A material that allows charge to move inside of it is called

(a) an insulator

(b) a conductor

(c) a capacitor

(d) an inductor

7. When the electric charge of each charged particle is doubled, the electric force acting between the two charges is

(*a*) doubled

(*b*) quadrupled

(*c*) the same

(*d*) none of the above

8. Which of the statements below is false?

(*a*) electric fields obey the law of superposition

(*b*) the lines of force give the direction of the electric field

(*c*) the greater the number of lines of force in a region, the greater the size of the electric field in that region

(*d*) electric field lines point away from negative charges and toward positive charges.

9. A point charge $q > 0$ is a distance r from the origin, while a point charge of $2q$ is a distance $2r$ from the origin on the x-axis. At the origin there is a point charge $Q > 0$. The total voltage at point x, where $r < x < 2r$, is given by

(*a*) $k\{Q/x + q/(r - x) + 2q/(2r - x)\}$

(*b*) $k\{Q/r + q/x + 2q/(2r - x)\}$

(*c*) $k\{Q/x + q/(x - r) + 2q/(2r - x)\}$

(*d*) none of the above

10. The total electric potential energy of the system of charges in question 9 is

(*a*) $k\{Qq/r + Q2q/2r + q2q/r\}$

(*b*) $k\{Qq/r + Qq/2r + q2q/r\}$

(*c*) $k\{Qq/r + Q2q/2r + qq/r\}$

(*d*) none of the above

11. Three small balls are charged. We find that balls 1 and 2 repel each other while balls 2 and 3 also repel each other. From this we know

(*a*) balls 1 and 3 have charges of the same sign

(*b*) balls 1 and 3 have charges of opposite signs

(*c*) all three balls have the same sign of charge

(*d*) one of the balls is neutral

(*e*) no way to answer this question given the above information.

12. Two small balls are electrically charged with ball 2 having three times the charge on it compared to ball 1. Which force diagram best illustrates this situation?

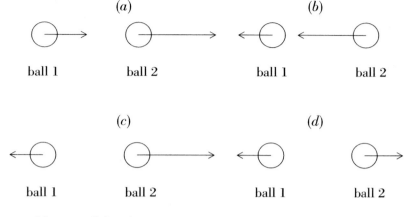

(a)

ball 1   ball 2

(b)

ball 1   ball 2

(c)

ball 1   ball 2

(d)

ball 1   ball 2

(e) none of the above

13. A charge Q resides at the origin. The voltage at $2r$ divided by the voltage at r is

(a) 1/3

(b) 1/4

(c) 1/5

(d) 2

(e) none of the above

14. Consider two separate situations involving point charges Q and q.

A: $Q > 0$ is at the origin, and $q > 0$ is r away   B: $Q > 0$ is at the origin, and $q < 0$ is r away

For which situation is the electrical potential energy smaller?

(a) A (b) B (c) the same (d) cannot answer without further information.

15. Two charges each having a charge $q > 0$ are a distance D apart. Is it possible to place a third charge q' somewhere so that all three charges experience zero net force? If so, where do you place q' and what is the value of q'? If not, why not?

16. A charge $q > 0$ moves in the direction of a constant electric field. Does the system's potential energy increase, stay the same, or decrease?

17. If the voltage at some point is zero, does that mean there are no charges near that point? Explain.

18. A positive point charge q of known mass m starts with a speed v very far from a positive point charge Q that is fixed in space. As q approaches Q it loses kinetic energy because of the repulsive force acing on it. At a distance r from Q, q momentarily stops and turns around. Find an expression for r in terms of q, m, v, and Q. Use the conservation of energy.

PROBLEMS.

1. One mole of anything consists of Avogadro's number of that thing, $N_A = 6.02 \times 10^{23}$. What is the value of the charge in Coulombs of N_A positive hydrogen ions that have lost their electron?

2. Given one mole of NaCl "molecules" and the fact that the Na has one more proton compared to its number of electrons, find the total charge of the Na ions. (See the previous problem for the definition of Avogadro's number.)

3. In the helium atom there are two protons separated by a distance of 2.0×10^{-15} m. Find the force of repulsion of the protons.

4. In the helium atom there are two electrons that are separated by a distance of 1.5×10^{-10} m. Find the force of repulsion of the electrons.

5. Three equal charges of 1 μC are separated by a distance of 10.0 cm and are at the vertices of an equilateral triangle. Find the force vector on the top charge due to the other two charges (see figure below).

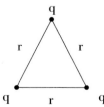

6. Four 100.0 μC charges reside on the vertices of a square of side 2.0 m. Determine the total force vector on the charge at the top right corner due to the other three charges.

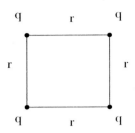

7. Find the electric field vector produced by a Uranium nucleus at a distance of 10.0 Angstroms. The Uranium nucleus has an **atomic number**, Z, equal to 92 protons.

8. Find the electric field vector produced by a Carbon nucleus at a distance of 5.0 Angstroms. The Carbon nucleus has an **atomic number**, Z, equal to 6 protons.

9. Two opposite charges separated by a distance is called an **electric dipole**. A geologist puts two terminals of a voltage supply in the ground 500.0 m apart. The left electrode has a charge of -2.0×10^{-4} C and the right electrode 2.0×10^{-4} C on it. Find the total electric field midway between the two point charges along a line connecting the charges.

10. The water molecule (H_2O) is an electric dipole (see previous problem) with the geometry sketched below.

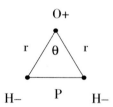

Assume the oxygen has a charge $+e$, and the hydrogen atoms each have a charge $-e$; this is an approximation since the bonds are actually polar covalent. The angle θ is about $105°$ and the bond length r equals 0.99 Angstroms. Find the total electric field vector at point P—midway between the two hydrogen ions and directly below the oxygen.

11. Find the electric field, assumed constant, inside a 12.0 V battery that has terminals a distance of 5.00 cm apart. Assume the battery is a cylinder with one terminal on the top end and the other at the bottom end.

12. Assume an electric eel is a cylinder of length 20.0 cm with one end being positive and the other negative. If the voltage difference across the eel is 5,000 volts, find the (constant) electric field inside the eel.

13. In a television set the electron gun has a potential difference of about 22,000 volts across it. Determine the speed of an electron exiting the gun using energy conservation.

14. Answer problem 13 using the work-kinetic energy relation.

15. A nerve cell membrane has a voltage across it of 0.085 volts and the thickness of the membrane is 7.0 nm. Find the electric field inside the membrane, assuming the field is constant.

16. A parallel plate capacitor is a common electronic element used in circuits. The voltage across the plates is 12.0 V and the distance between the plates is 2.00 mm. Find the (constant) electric field between the parallel plates.

17. Determine the electrical potential produced a distance of 5.00 cm away from a marble of negligible radius that has a net charge of 6.00 μC on it.

18. A ping pong ball of negligible radius has a charge of 5.00 μC. Find the voltage produced a distance of 2.00 cm away.

19. During a lightning flash 15.0 C of charge pass through a voltage difference of 80 million volts. What is the change in electric potential energy of these charges?

20. Terrible Tom scuffs across the carpeted floor and acquires a charge. He brings his 20,000.0-volt finger near your nose and a spark flies. The charges experience a change in potential energy of 3.0×10^{-7} J as they jump from his finger to your nose. (a) How much charge is this and (b) how many electrons are in that charge?

21. Determine the work done by a 12.0 volt battery that causes a 5 mC charge to move through the circuit the battery is in series with.

22. The electrical potential difference between two locations differs by 50.0 volts. How much work is done as a 10 nC charge is moved between these two locations?

23. An electron is at each of the corners of a square that has sides of length 20 Angstroms. How much bond energy in electron volts is present? Note: $1\ eV = 1.6 \times 10^{-19}$ J.

24. Three electrons are placed on the x-axis at: $x = -10.0$ Angstroms, $x = 0$, and $x = +10.0$ Angstroms. How much bond energy in electron volts is present? Note: $1\ eV = 1.6 \times 10^{-19}$ J.

Hints and answers to problems.

1) 96,300 C   2) 96,300 C   3) 58 N   4) 1.02×10^{-8} N   5) 1.56 N up   6) 30.5 N, 30.5 N
7) 1.33×10^{11} N/C   8) 3.46×10^{10} N/C   9) 57.6 N/C to left   10) 3.96×10^{11} N/C down
11) 240 N/C   12) 25,000 N/C   13) Hint: see example five, 8.79×10^{7} m/s   14) 8.79×10^{7} m/s
15) 1.21×10^{7} N/C   16) 6,000 N/C   17) 1.1 MV   18) 2.3 MV   19) 1.2×10^{9} J. Hint: see
equation (4)   20) 1.5×10^{-11} C, 9.38×10^{7}. Hint: see equation (4)   21) 0.06 J   22) 5×10^{-7} J
23) 3.9 eV 24) 3.6 eV

CHAPTER IX.
MOVING CHARGES.

Abstract.
The movement of electric charge in several simple circuits is examined. Ohm's law for conductors is reviewed and average power delivered by a battery and average power loss due to a resistance is considered.

Definitions. battery, DC and AC current, fuse, open and short circuits, ammeters and voltmeters, series and parallel circuits

Principles. none

Fundamental Equations. Ohm's law, power in electricity, equivalent resistance of series and parallel resistors

A. Electric Current and Ohm's Law.

A *current* consists of stuff in motion. This stuff can be water, birds, cars, or anything. Whether an object is in motion depends on your point of view, though. If I stand on a street corner and cars pass by in front of me, then I observe a car current. More precisely, the number of cars that pass in front of me per second is the car current. The road in front of me can be a one lane or a multilane road. In the latter case, I count the total number of cars per second passing by me in all of the lanes. But suppose I am instead inside one of the cars. Under these conditions no cars pass me and there is no car current. (I am assuming all of the cars, including mine, are moving with the same velocity relative to the street.) So a current is a relative quantity that depends on the observer (me or you). Unless otherwise stated, we will assume all currents are relative to the street or the physics laboratory room.

The situation is similar for electric currents where the stuff that is moving is electric charge. The electric current in a wire is the amount of charge that passes through a cross-section of the wire per second. In all situations we will encounter, the moving charges are electrons. The only reason electric current is more abstract than a car current is we can directly see cars but not electrons.

Let us place this discussion into the language of mathematics. If during a time interval, Δt, an amount of electric charge, Δq, passes a cross-section of the wire, then an electric current, I, exists in the wire, which is defined,

$$\textit{Electric Current}$$
$$I \equiv \Delta q / \Delta t. \tag{1}$$

From equation (1) the units of electric current are those of charge divided by time, or Coulombs per second. A current of one Coulomb passing a cross-section of the wire during a time interval of one second is called one Ampere of current, abbreviated,

$$1 \text{ Ampere} \equiv 1 \text{ C/s}.$$

Ampere was a nineteenth century French physicist who pioneered the study of electrical currents. One Ampere is a relatively sizable current that is typical of currents found in home circuits. Modern electronic equipment carry currents that are usually in the milliamp (1 mA = 0.001 A) range.

Another metaphor is sometimes used to describe a current. Think of water moving in a pipe. In this case the stuff making up the current is moving water. Typically water current is expressed by the number of kilograms of water passing a cross-section of a pipe per second or the number of liters of water per second. The analogy of water in a pipe is a useful way of thinking of electrical currents and will be explored later in this chapter.

Example One.—*Currents in everyday electronic devices.*

Modern electrical equipment typically carry currents in the mA range. Find how many electrons pass a cross-section of a wire per second if the wire has a current of 1.0 mA.

Solution.

Each electron has a charge of magnitude, e. Let N denote the number of electrons passing through the cross section during time interval, Δt. Then,

$$I = \Delta q/\Delta t = Ne/\Delta t.$$

Using $I = 0.001$ Amp and $\Delta t = 1$ s and solving for N,

$$N = I\Delta t/e = (0.001\text{A})(1\text{s})/(1.6 \times 10^{-19}\text{C}) = \underline{6.25 \times 10^{15}}.$$

Often cars are at rest, water in a pipe stands stagnant, and electric currents are not present in a wire. So we ask, what causes a current to appear in a wire? In the case of water in a pipe, there must be a difference in pressure between the two ends of the pipe to produce the flow of the water. What plays the role of a pressure difference in a wire that must be present for an electric current to appear?

To answer this question, even though it must be pointed out that all of the above metaphors we have used to describe electric currents are limited, we introduce yet another metaphor. Think of charges moving in a wire as analogous to a swarm of bees. In a swarm the individual bees are moving every which way with different speeds but assume the swarm as a whole is at rest. Then, if a breeze appears, the swarm is pushed down the street and this creates a bee *drift* current. The adjective *drift* is introduced to distinguish the speed of the swarm as a whole from the much larger speeds of the individual bees. In the case of charges, the individual charges are moving every which way with varying speeds. The collection of charges can acquire a drift current and move as a group with the much slower drift speed. That which is loosely analogous to the pressure difference in a water pipe or the breeze pushing the bees is a *voltage difference across the ends of the wire. The voltage difference results from the presence of a constant applied electric field within the wire. A* **battery** *produces the electric field and resulting voltage difference when it is connected to the wire.*

The first battery was invented by Count Volta in the early eighteen hundreds. Volta began with a single voltaic cell consisting of a pair of different metals separated by cardboard that had been soaked in salt water. The metals acquire opposite charges and therefore a voltage difference between the metals is maintained. By stacking voltaic cells on top of each other a "Voltaic pile" is created where the difference in voltage between the first metal and the last metal is the number of cells times the voltage across one cell.

A battery has two terminals, one has a voltage of zero and is called ground while the other terminal has a voltage *V*. It is customary to choose the negative terminal as ground. A chemical reaction takes place inside the battery which maintains the voltage difference across the terminals. If a conducting wire is attached to one of the terminals and the other end of the wire is attached to the other terminal, the battery creates a potential difference across the ends of the wire by producing an electric field inside. A portion of the electrons in the wire are free to move. These free electrons respond to the electric force due to the field. But the free electrons also experience a frictional force due to their collisions with the atoms of the wire. The net result is, the electrons move with a constant drift speed along the wire and the wire has an electric current inside. Different wires present different amounts of frictional force. Wires with large friction are said to have a large resistance to the current. It has been found in the laboratory that for conducting wires the current, *I*, produced in the wire (the effect) is proportional to the voltage, *V*, across the ends of the wire (the cause).

$$I \approx V.$$

Introducing a proportionality constant denoted $1/R$, where *R* is the resistance of the wire, this becomes an important relation known as Ohm's law,

$$I = V/R. \tag{2}$$

Equation (2) implies the bigger the voltage, the greater the current produced but for a given value of *V*, the bigger the resistance, the smaller the current produced. Ohm's law is not universal—it applies to conductors but not all electronic devices. Rearranging equation (2) gives, $R = V/I$. If one volt produces one amp the resistance is called one Ohm, where the symbol for Ohm is the last letter of the Greek alphabet, Ω.

$$1\ \Omega \equiv 1\ \text{Volt}/1\ \text{Amp}.$$

Example Two.—*Electric chair: not for the squeamish.*

The first person executed by an electric chair was the New York axe murderer William Kemmler in 1890. Of course, execution by electrocution continues to be a controversial topic even though it has been conjectured that death by the electric chair is painless. Presumably, the body's nerve signals pass to the brain after the brain has already been paralyzed by the electric current due to the chair. The twitching that is observed is an involuntary muscular reaction of an unconscious human according to this hypothesis. It is likely that not all agree with this conjecture.

In this grisly act, one electrode is attached to the victim's shaved scalp whilst the other is connected to his or her shaved left calf. Although in actual cases the high voltage is applied over several closely spaced time intervals, for our purposes let's approximate the event by assuming a single voltage of 2,000 V is applied. This voltage is an accurate figure according to our sources. Assuming dry skin, we estimate the resistance from the brain to the leg as about 400 Ω. The resistance is lower if the skin is wet. The current passing through the brain to the leg is given by Ohm's law,

$$I = V/R = 2000/400 = 5 \text{ A}.$$

It is known that a current of only 0.1 Amp passing through the heart for an extended period of time (say a few seconds) is normally lethal. Apparently, the electrocutioners are not taking any chances that a victim will survive the 2000 Volts.

For those desiring further gruesome details of this procedure, consult our source for all things bizzarre: *Encyclopedia of Crime*, pp. 11–12, 120, 228, 416. For the resistance of the human body we consulted, *Physics, A General Introduction*, Alan Van Huevelen (Little Brown, 1982), pg. 487.

B. DC Circuits.

A battery's terminals must be attached at both ends of a conductor in order for an electric current to be established in the conductor. There must be a closed path for the charges to move through. For example, if you attach a wire to a battery you will notice the wire heating up due to the current. (Warning: it is not a good idea to do this since it quickly ruins the battery and can burn your fingers.) While the current is present, if the wire is cut the current will cease. Cutting the wire creates an ***open circuit***.

Another phenomenon occurs that can be dangerous. Shown in Figure 1(a) is a sketch of a battery, wires connecting the battery's terminals to a conducting device (a resistor). The resistor could be a light bulb, a toaster or some other conducting electrical appliance. The electric circuit forms a closed conducting path for the charges to move through. Shown in Figure 1(b) is a *schematic* of the circuit in (a), which is a symbolic representation of the actual circuit. If a wire is placed between points P and Q as shown in Figure 1(b) then a *short circuit* is created. This may be dangerous because the short circuit path generally has a much lower resistance than the path containing the resistor. With the wire from P to Q present the current no longer is in R but instead passes entirely through the very low resistance short since current takes the path of least resistance.

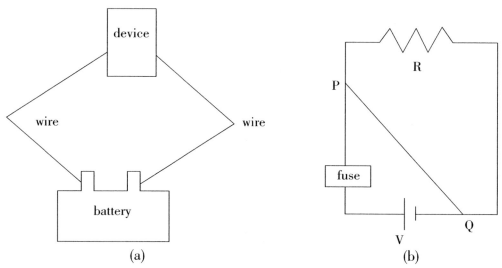

FIG. 1. (A) BATTERY IS ATTACHED TO A DEVICE USING TWO WIRES. (B) SCHEMATIC OF CIRCUIT IN (A). AN EXTRA WIRE IS SHOWN CONNECTING POINTS P AND Q. THE WIRE CAUSES A SHORT CIRCUIT.

Moreover, with the short circuit present, the current in the circuit dramatically increases. Large currents can create high temperatures in the circuit and can thus be a potential cause of a fire. For this reason, fuses are placed in a circuit as shown in Figure 1(b). A *fuse* is a resistor placed in the circuit that will burn out if the current becomes too large. When the fuse burns out, an open circuit is created and the current falls to zero eliminating the danger of a fire being created.

The above simple circuit is an example of a ***direct current*** (DC) circuit. In a DC circuit the charges move only in one direction, namely the direction of the electric field produced by the battery. For example, in Figure 1 the charges move from one terminal of the battery, around the closed path and back to the other terminal of the battery. We will only consider DC circuits in this book. ***Alternating current*** (AC) circuits are more complicated since the charges vibrate and therefore move back and forth. This motion arises because the electric field changes direction and size in AC circuits. In AC circuits a generator is used to provide the voltage source rather than a simple battery.

In general there are two kinds of simple DC circuits: a ***series*** and a ***parallel circuit***. Figure 2 shows schematics of series and parallel circuits where in each case there is one battery and two resistors.

In a series circuit the charges have no choice about which path they will take through the circuit because there is only one conducting path: through the two resistors. The current is the same through R_1 and R_2. As the current passes through R_1 there is a drop in voltage across R_1 since

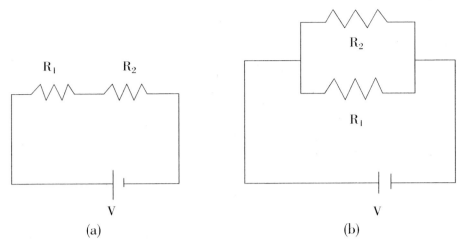

FIG. 2. (A) RESISTORS CONNECTED IN SERIES. (B) RESISTORS CONNECTED
IN PARALLEL.

Ohm's law holds. Denote the voltage across R_1, $V_1 = IR_1$. Likewise there is a voltage drop across R_2 of size V_2. The sum of these voltage drops must equal the voltage across the battery, V:

$$V = V_1 + V_2.$$

Using Ohm's law for V_1 and V_2 gives,

$$V = IR_1 + IR_2 = I(R_1 + R_2) \equiv I\,R_{eq},$$

where

$$R_{eq} = R_1 + R_2. \quad \text{(series)} \tag{3}$$

The *equivalent resistance*, R_{eq}, has the same current through it as the original resistors in the circuit and the same total voltage across it as the sum of the voltages across the original resistors. In other words, we could replace the two resistors by R_{eq} and the current in the circuit would not change.

The case of the parallel circuit is slightly more obtuse. In this case the voltage across both of the resistors is the same as that across the battery, V. However, part of the charges that make up the total current through the battery pass through R_1 while the remaining current passes through R_2. Denote the current through R_1 as $I_1 = V/R_1$ (invoking Ohm's law once again) and similarly, $I_2 = V/R_2$. The current through the battery, I, splits into two parts at the resistors and since we don't lose any current,

$$I = I_1 + I_2.$$

Applying Ohm's law for I_1 and I_2 gives,

$$I = V/R_1 + V/R_2 = V(1/R_1 + 1/R_2) \equiv V/R_{eq},$$

where

$$1/R_{eq} = 1/R_1 + 1/R_2. \quad \text{(parallel)} \tag{4}$$

For the case of two resistors, algebraic manipulation of equation (4) gives for the equivalent resistance "the product over the sum,"

$$R_{eq} = R_1 R_2/(R_1 + R_2). \quad \text{(parallel)} \tag{5}$$

The *equivalent resistance*, R_{eq}, has the same voltage across it as the original resistors in the circuit and the same *total* current through it as the sum of the currents through the original resistors. In other words, we could replace the two resistors by R_{eq} and the current through the battery would not change.

Example Three.—*Series circuit: A typical home circuit.*

A set of three resistors are attached in series to a 120 Volt battery. The three items are a toaster (resistance of 20 Ω), a light bulb (240 Ω), and a crock pot (80 Ω) in addition to a fuse of negligible resistance. Determine (a) the equivalent resistance of this circuit and the (b) the current present. Note: For simplicity, in this example we are neglecting the fact that home circuits are AC instead of DC.

Solution.

(a) Using equation (3) but with one more term for R_3,

$$R_{eq} = R_1 + R_2 + R_3 = 20 + 240 + 80 = \underline{340\ \Omega}$$

(b) Applying Ohm's law,

$$I = V/R_{eq} = 120/340 = \underline{0.35\ \text{Amps}}.$$

If this amount of current passed through a human heart it would kill the person.

Example Four.—*Parallel circuit: typical home circuit (again).*

Suppose the resistors in the circuit in example three were instead placed in parallel with each other. Find the (a) equivalent resistance and (b) current in this case.

Solution.

(a) Using equation (4) with one more term, we find

$$1/R_{eq} = 1/R_1 + 1/R_2 + 1/R_3 = 1/20 + 1/240 + 1/80 = 0.0666.$$

Inverting gives $\quad R_{eq} = \underline{15\ \Omega}$.

(b) Applying Ohm's law,

$$I = V/R_{eq} = 120/15 = \underline{8\ \text{Amps}}.$$

This example demonstrates two important features of circuits. First, the same resistors attached in parallel have a much lower equivalent resistance than when placed in series. And secondly, the parallel arrangement therefore draws a much larger current than the series combination of the same resistors. The parallel combination is much more dangerous. Finally, one finds that in a parallel combination, more of the current will pass through the lower resistance than the higher resistance: "currents take the path of least resistance."

We have not exhausted the number of circuit elements used in modern electronic circuitry. Circuits often contain capacitors, inductors, diodes and transistors. But many of the ideas discussed for batteries and resistors carry over to these more elaborate circuit elements. Of course, there are also other applications such as the use of a transistor as a switch or an amplifier. The latest computer cpu contains tens of millions of transistors.

Another area where it is important to know the difference between series and parallel circuits is the area of electrical measurements. Electrical meters have two terminals just like a battery. Electric currents are measured by ammeters while voltages are measured by voltmeters. To measure the current at a particular location in a circuit it is necessary to place an ammeter in series at that point. To do this, the circuit must be opened up in order to attach the terminals of the meter. In contrast, voltage is always associated with two points in a circuit. For example, to measure the voltage drop across a resistor in a circuit, the voltmeter must be attached in parallel with the resistor.

Meter:	Ammeters (I)	Voltmeters (V)
Attach in:	series	parallel

C. Ohm's Law and Electric Power.

To this point in our presentation no mention has been made of energy transmission in electric circuits. Batteries convert stored chemical energy into electrical energy. In turn, electric currents cause circuit elements, such as resistors, to heat up. Often a circuit is designed to produce heat, as in a toaster or oven. Other times the circuit element is useful as a source of light as in a light bulb. In the next chapter we will see how electronics may be used to do work in other devices such as DC motors. Work is required to produce voltages as in a generator. We will find that motors and generators are basically the same device, the difference is in a motor the desired output is work while in a generator the output is a voltage. For all these reasons it is important to understand how energy transfer happens inside circuits.

Consider a battery. In some ways a battery is like a small town airport that has just two terminals. Airplanes arrive at one terminal and depart from the other. Similarly, in a battery charges leave one terminal, travel through the battery, exit through the other terminal and then travel through the circuit that is attached to the battery. Suppose a charge Δq starts at the negative terminal of a battery where the voltage is zero. The battery expends chemical energy to do work in moving the charge to the positive terminal where the voltage has a value, V. The amount of work, ΔW, done by the battery is,

$$\Delta W = V\Delta q. \tag{6}$$

Equation (6) is simply a rearrangement of the definition of V. (Recall V is the work done per charge.) Assuming it takes a time interval Δt for the charge to move between the terminals then the average power, P_{ave}, delivered to the charge by the battery is,

$$P_{ave} = \Delta W/\Delta t = (V \, \Delta q)/\Delta t$$

or
$$P_{ave} = IV. \tag{7}$$

Equation (7) is a general statement of the average power delivered by any source of voltage. The units work out as required since we know power has units of Watts,

$$\text{Amps} \times \text{Volts} = (\text{C/s}) \times (\text{J/C}) = \text{J/s} = \text{Watts}.$$

What happens to the energy delivered by the battery in establishing the current? From experience we know that a resistor gets warm when it carries a current. (Think of jumper cables for your car.) This thermal energy came from the energy supplied by the battery. If we attach a resistor to the terminals of a battery then there will be a current produced in the resistor and the current is given by Ohm's law,

$$V = IR.$$

Assuming all of the batteries power that is supplied to the circuit appears as heat loss in the resistor then the average rate of heat loss in the resistor is,

$$P_{ave}{}^{loss} = IV = I^2R = V^2/R. \tag{8}$$

Equation (8) is called the Joule heat loss relation. It is a restatement of the most fundamental idea in all of physics, the conservation of energy.

Example Five.—*Electric chair: revisited.*

Using the numbers from example two, find (a) the average power delivered by the electric chair and (b) the average power loss through the victim.

Solution.

(a) Using equation (7), the average power of the chair is its voltage times the current it produces,

$$P_{ave} = IV = 5 \times 2000 = \underline{10,000 \text{ W.}}$$

(b) Equation (8) gives for the rate of heat generation,

$$P_{ave}{}^{loss} = I^2R = (5)^2 \, 400 = \underline{10,000 \text{ W.}}$$

Compare these wattages to the typical hair dryer.

Example Six.—*A typical home circuit again.*

The home circuit in examples three and four deliver power to the resistors. Find (a) the average power by the 120 Volt source in the series and parallel circuits and (b) whether or not the 40 W fuse blows out in either case.

Solution.

(a) The average power is

$$P_{ave} = IV = I\,120.$$

For the series circuit the current was 0.35 Amps while that for the parallel circuit was 8 Amps. Using these above gives,

$$P_{ave} = 0.35 \times 120 = \underline{42\ W.}\ \text{(series)}$$

$$P_{ave} = 8 \times 120 = \underline{960\ W.}\ \text{(parallel)}$$

(b) In both cases the fuse blows. However, the situation is a little more involved in real home wiring since the current is AC and not DC.

Example Seven.—*Power loss in simple circuits.*

For the circuits shown in Figure 2, find the current present and the average power loss to heat, given the values $V = 12$ Volts, $R_1 = 100\ \Omega$, and $R_2 = 200\ \Omega$.

Solution.

For the series circuit (Fig. 2a) we have from Ohm's law and the equivalent resistance relation,

$$I = V/(R_1 + R_2) = 12/(300) = \underline{0.04\ Amps.}$$

And for the power loss to heat,

$$P_{ave}{}^{loss} = I^2(R_1 + R_2) = (0.04)^2(300) = \underline{0.48\ W.}$$

For the parallel circuit (Fig. 2b) this becomes,

$$I = V(R_1 + R_2)/(R_1 R_2) = 12(300)/20000 = \underline{0.18\ Amps.}$$

and

$$P_{ave}{}^{loss} = I^2 R_1 R_2/(R_1 + R_2) = (0.18)^2\,20000/(300) = \underline{2.16\ W.}$$

Again the parallel circuit draws the larger current and expends more energy to heat.

Summary.

Electric current is the amount of charge passing through a cross-section of a wire per second. The voltage across the ends of a wire, the ensuing current in the wire and the resistance of the wire are related to each other through Ohm's law. At least this relation holds for some circuit devices.

Current that moves in one direction is direct current while alternating currents move back and forth. If one applies a voltage to a circuit consisting of resistors and a current is produced then one can replace the resistors by a single equivalent resistance without changing the applied voltage or total current present. Resistors in series and in parallel have simple equivalent resistance expressions. Finally, the power delivered by a battery and the power loss through a resistor are expressed in terms of the applied voltage, the current and the resistance of the resistor.

QUESTIONS.

1. Electrons travel with a relatively small velocity in a home circuit due the presence of resistance in the wires. However, when you turn on the light switch at the wall, you notice the light goes on immediately. Why is this so? Hint: is it the electrons near the switch that produces the light by the bulb or the electrons in the bulb?

2. Explain why if you attach a conducting wire to only the positive terminal of a battery no current is present even though if you attach a water hose to a faucet and turn on the faucet, water comes out.

3. If you touch the positive terminal of a battery, why do you not experience an electric current?

4. Why do electricians who work around high voltage devices keep one hand in their pocket and work with only the other hand?

5. In a circuit the voltage is doubled. What happens to the current?

6. In a circuit the resistance is doubled. What happens to the current?

7. Two resistors are connected in series. The current in the second resistor compared to the current in the first resistor is

    (*a*) larger

    (*b*) the same

    (*c*) smaller

    (*d*) dependent on the resistances

8. When two resistors are placed in parallel the equivalent resistance is the product of the resistances divided by the sum. Is this true for three resistors placed in parallel? Justify your answer.

9. As you add more resistors in parallel to a parallel combination of resistors the equivalent resistance

(*a*) increases

(*b*) decreases

(*c*) stays the same

(*d*) depends on the values of the resistors

10. A current exists in a light bulb. Suppose a highly conducting wire is connected across the bulb as shown below. What happens? What if the wire is an insulator?

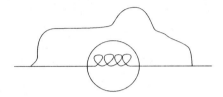

(*a*) half the current stays in the bulb, the other half goes into the wire

(*b*) all the current stays in the bulb

(*c*) the bulb goes out

(*d*) none of the above

11. Two identical light bulbs have equal brightness in the circuit below. The brightness is determined by the power loss in the bulb. When the Switch is closed, the brightness of bulb *B*

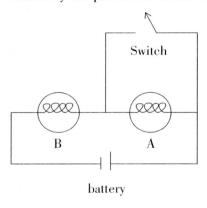

(*a*) stays the same

(*b*) decreases

(*c*) increases

12. The light bulbs in the circuits below are identical. Which circuit creates the most light?

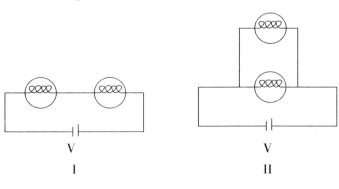

(*a*) I

(*b*) II

(*c*) equal brightness

13. The two bulbs below are identical and initially have equal brightness. Then a highly conducting wire is placed as shown. Bulb B

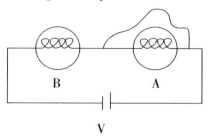

(*a*) becomes brighter

(*b*) becomes dimmer

(*c*) stays the same brightness

(*d*) completely goes out

14. Three identical bulbs are connected as shown. The sum of the brightness of bulb *B* and *C* together compared to the brightness of bulb *A* is

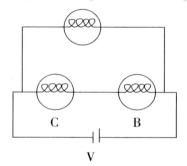

(*a*) half as much

(*b*) twice as much

(*c*) the same

15. How would you wire a battery and two identical light bulbs to produce light for the longest time?

16. Which light bulb has the higher resistance, a 60 Watt bulb or a 100 Watt bulb? Which bulb has the higher current in it?

17. Circle the right answer(s).

When resistors are in parallel, the (current, potential difference, power) is/are the same for each.

When resistors are in series, the (current, potential difference, power) is/are the same for each.

18. Consider the circuit below where all the bulbs have the same resistance R and the battery has a voltage V. (a) Determine the current in each one of the bulbs. (b) Assume bulb B has been unscrewed and determine the current in each of the bulbs. Place your answers in the table. Note: all currents will be some fraction times V/R.

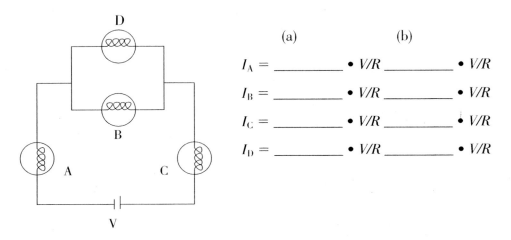

(a) $\qquad\qquad$ (b)

$I_A =$ _____ • V/R _____ • V/R

$I_B =$ _____ • V/R _____ • V/R

$I_C =$ _____ • V/R _____ • V/R

$I_D =$ _____ • V/R _____ • V/R

PROBLEMS.

1. A flock of 30 birds fly in formation in single file with each bird having a speed of 5.0 m/s. The length of the file is 5.00 m. Find the number of birds passing a given point per second, the bird current.

2. A school of 20 fish swim in formation in single file with each fish having a speed of 3.0 m/s. The length of the file is 3.00 m. Find the number of fish passing a given point per second, the fish current.

3. A flashlight battery will operate for 3.00 hours carrying a 0.5 A current before it dies. Determine the total number of electrons that flow through a cross section of the flashlight circuit during the 3.00 hours.

4. The starter motor of a car operates with a current of 100.0 A. Find the number of electrons per second that pass through a cross section of the starter circuit.

5. If each second Avogadro's number of electrons flow pass a cross section of a wire then how many amps of current is this?

6. At a Krispy Kreme donut store over a period of 60 seconds 300 donuts pass a point beside the conveyor belt. What is the corresponding donut current in donuts per second?

7. A car engine has a starter motor that operates at 12.0 V. The resistance of the motor is 0.10 Ω. Find the current inside the motor using Ohm's law.

8. The leg of a human has a resistance of 200.0 Ω. If a 120-volt power supply is attached to the leg then how much current passes through the leg? Use Ohm's law to answer this.

9. (a) Determine the resistance of a toaster given it draws a current of 10.0 A when there is a voltage of 120.0 volts across the toaster. (b) Find the current in a 3.00 volt flashlight battery that has a resistance of 0.35 Ω.

10. A woman grabs a 120.0 volt power line with one hand while using the other hand to touch the ground wire which is at 0 volts. Find the current through her body when (a) her body is dry and the resistance is 100,000 Ω and (b) her body is wet and the resistance is 5,000 Ω. Do you think she will survive?

11. In the lab you measure the current through a device and the voltage across the ends of the device, obtaining: (I,V) = (0,0), (0.112,1.0), (0.337,3.0), (0.675,6.1). Make a graph of this data and from the graph explain why this device obeys Ohm's law. What is the resistance of the device?

12. A wire in a home carries a current of 15.0 A. The voltage drop across the wire is 1.00 volt. What is the resistance of the wire?

13. What is the equivalent resistance in the circuit shown below?

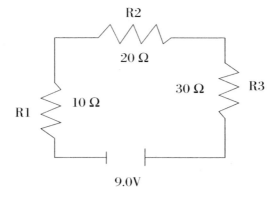

14. Find the current in each of the resistors in the circuit of problem 13.

15. Find the power input and the power loss through each of the resistors in the circuit in problem 13.

16. Find the equivalent resistance of the home circuit shown below. Assume the resistances: crockpot = 80 Ω, toaster = 20 Ω, and light bulb = 240 Ω.

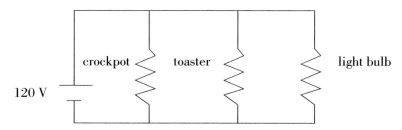

17. Find the current in each of the resistors in the circuit of problem 16.

18. Find the power input and the power loss through each of the resistors in the circuit in problem 16.

19. What is the equivalent resistance in the circuit shown below?

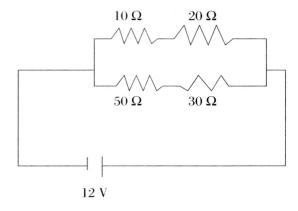

20. Find the current in each of the resistors in the circuit of problem 19.

21. Find the power input and the power loss through each of the resistors in the circuit in problem 19.

22. A 1,200-W hair dryer operates with a voltage of 120 volts for ten minutes. (a) How many Joules of energy are used? (b) What is the resistance of the heater?

23. A 12.0-volt car battery powers a car radio that draws a current of 0.20 amps. (a) How much energy is provided by the battery to the radio in one hour? (b) What is the resistance of the radio?

24. A refrigerator runs for an hour while connected to a 120 volt source. The refrigerator draws a current of 3.0 A. Find how much energy is used by the refrigerator.

25. Lightning transfers 6.00 C of charge in 1 ms across a potential difference of 10 MV. Determine the average power of the lightning.

26. Your car has a dead battery. To recharge it you run a current through the battery in the opposite direction for one hour using a battery charger. The circuit is shown below.

dead

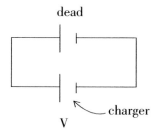

V   charger

If you run 5 amps while placing the battery charger as shown (where $V = 12$ volts) then how much energy does it take to recharge your battery?

Hints and answers to problems.

1) 30 birds/s   2) 20 fish/s   3) 3.4×10^{22} 4) 6.3×10^{20} 5) 96,300 A   6) 5 donuts/s
7) 120 A   8) 0.6 A   9) 12 Ω, 8.6 A   10) 1.2×10^{-3} A, 0.024 A   11) ≈ 8.6 Ω 12) 0.07 Ω
13) 60 Ω 14) 0.15 A   15) 1.35 W, 0.225, 0.45, 0.675 W   16) 15 Ω 17) 1.5, 6, 0.5 A
18) 960 W, 180,720,60 W   19) 21.8 Ω 20) 0.4 and 0.15 A   21) 6.6 W, 4.8, 1.8 W
22) 720,000 J, 12 Ω 23) 8640 J, 60 Ω 24) 1.3 MJ   25) 6×10^{10} W   26) 216 kJ

Section IV.

MAGNETISM.

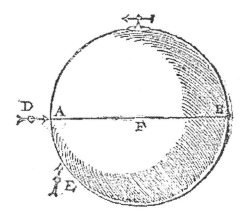

CHAPTER X.
MAGNETIC FORCES ON MOVING CHARGES.

Abstract.

A short overview of the history of magnetism is given. Then the topic of magnetic forces is addressed with particular attention given to the magnetic force on charged particles and current-carrying wires placed in a magnetic field. Oersted's discovery of the magnetic field produced by a current is touched on after which certain applications of magnetism are discussed. The special importance and basic physics of the DC motor is presented. The new mathematics in this chapter is the multiplicative operation known as the cross product between two vectors. This operation yields a vector. Two right-hand rules are given in the chapter.

Definitions. magnetic monopoles and dipoles, magnetic field, right-handed screw rule, and the Tesla

Principles. Oersted's law, magnetic force law, right-handed rule #1 for the field direction produced by a current-carrying wire, right-handed rule #2 for magnetic forces on charges and current-carrying wires placed in a magnetic field

Fundamental Equations. magnetic force by a magnetic field on a moving charged particle and a current-carrying wire

A. Magnets in Antiquity.

Once again we are in debt to the ancient Greeks this time for their investigations of the magnetic properties of the mysterious mineral known as lodestone or magnetite. The ancient ones found lodestone attracts certain metallic objects made of, e.g. iron, but many other metals were not attracted. The Greeks, and even earlier the Chinese, further found lodestone, when it is free to rotate, tends to rotate to one particular North-South alignment. This was the first step toward the later development of the magnetic compass in 1600 by the English physician William Gilbert. Gilbert spent years studying the magnetism in lodestone and the electrical properties of amber concluding his work with the groundbreaking book, *De Magnete,* in which his results were presented. By studying the attractive and repulsive forces between two magnets that were near each other, Gilbert surmised that the magnetic compass works because the Earth itself is a giant magnet. In Gilbert's day the Earth's magnetic field was thought to be due to the presence of iron inside the Earth. Today we believe the source of Earth's field is more complicated than simply saying it is due to iron. Although it was a later investigator, the Englishman Michael Faraday, who first proposed the concept of a field, Gilbert came very close to this idea over two hundred years before Faraday.

The magnetic field in a region of space may be described in a manner analogous to how we described the electric field in a region by introducing *field lines* or equivalently, *lines of force*. The greater the density of lines in a region of space, the greater the size of the field there. Since magnetic fields are vectors the direction of the field must also be specified. The direction of the lines give the direction of the field. The fundamental source of magnetism is the magnetic **dipole**, which consists of two poles, North and South. Notice, this is one occasion where magnetism and electricity differ from one another since the fundamental source of electricity is an electric **monopole** but the most basic source of magnetism is a *dipole*. Bringing two magnets near each other, it is straightforward to discover that *likes poles repel one another while unlike poles attract*. By convention the magnetic field points away from the North pole and toward the South pole. Further, the greater the separation of the poles of two magnets from one another, the smaller their magnetic force of interaction. In fact, just as in Coulomb's law of electricity, the force between two magnets decreases as the inverse square of the distance between the poles.

A remaining question is, why are some materials magnetic while most materials are not? Said another way, what is the ultimate source of a magnetic field? Could there be more than one ultimate source? Clearly one source of magnetic fields is magnetic materials like lodestone. But what is it that makes lodestone magnetic and are there other sources? The first hints to the answer to these questions was found in 1820 by the Danish physicist Hans Christian Oersted.

B. The Magnetic Field: A Field Theory.

Throughout the history of physics there have been incidents where an individual made an important initial discovery by chance. Oersted's discoveries occurred during the period of 1819 to 1820 and provide an example of such an accidental discovery although his continuing investigations were motivated by a deep philosophical desire to unify the forces of physics. Indeed, Oersted's unification quest was influenced by Schelling who was a German nature philosopher. Reportedly, it was during a classroom demonstration that Oersted found a magnetic compass needle was deflected when placed near a current-carrying wire. (Oersted later denied that the discovery was accidental.) He inferred from this incident what is now called Oersted's law: **magnetic fields** *arise due to the motion of electric charges*. Shortly thereafter the French physicist Andre Marie Ampere, in addition to performing fundamental experiments on how wires carrying electric current exert magnetic forces on each other, proposed that the *only* source of a magnetic field is the motion of an electric charge. It was left to another giant of physics, James Clerk Maxwell, to later point out another source of a magnetic field. Maxwell's discovery involved a subtle connection between electric and magnetic fields and will be reviewed in the next chapter. In any case, we see that magnetism arises out of electricity (electric currents). For further insight into the history of magnetism see, *Physics, the Human Adventure*, Gerald Holton and Stephen G. Brush (Rutgers University Press, 2001).

But, you object, what about permanent magnets such as lodestone where there is no obvious presence of electric current and still the mineral produces a magnetic field? It was not until the twentieth century that this objection was conclusively answered by the development of the modern theory of magnetic materials. At present we know that even in lodestone (and other magnetic materials) the magnetic field also is produced by the motion of charge. In magnetic materials the field is produced by the movement of electrons inside the atoms of the material. The electrons orbit the atomic nucleus and spin on their own axis. Both of these motions produce a magnetic field. The situation for the electrons is much like the Earth that both revolves around the sun while spinning on its axis. The theory of magnetic materials was not fully understood until the advent of quantum mechanics, though. Magnetism remains an active area of physics research to this day. These quantum effects have led us far from classical physics. So let us return to Oersted's discovery.

Shown in Figure 1 are the two situations where a magnetic field is produced. In Figure 1(a) a bar magnet produces the dipole field while in Figure 1(b) a side view of a wire carrying a current is shown. In Figure 1(b) the field arises because of the presence of the electric current in the wire. The circle with a cross is a common symbol that is used in magnetic studies. The cross symbol indicates the field is pointing into the page while the circle with a dot inside indicates the field is pointing out of the page. Here is a mnemonic: think of an arrow. If the arrow points toward you, you see its tip (the dot) while if it points away from you, you see its tail feathers (the cross). In Figure 1(c) a front view of the wire in Figure 1(b) is shown. The dot there indicates the current is coming out of the page. Notice the magnetic field lines circling the wire in Figure 1(c). The lines form concentric circles which are circles that all have the same center.

The direction of the field produced by the wire shown in 1(c) is given by *right-hand rule #1*. Imagine grasping the wire using your right hand with your thumb pointing in the direction of the current. Your fingers curl in the direction of the magnetic field lines.

In both situations illustrated in Figure 1 the field is a dipole field because both north and south poles are present. We repeat, by convention the field leaves the north pole and enters at the south pole. The field becomes weaker the further one goes from the source. We will leave to the

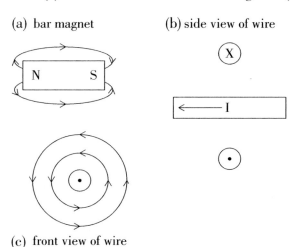

(a) bar magnet   (b) side view of wire

(c) front view of wire

FIG. 1. (A) MAGNETIC FIELD PRODUCED BY A BAR MAGNET. (B) MAGNETIC FIELD PRODUCED BY A CURRENT *I* IN A WIRE. (C) MAGNETIC FIELD PRODUCED BY A CURRENT COMING OUT OF THIS PAGE.

next chapter the question as to why a dipole is the fundamental magnetic field source rather than the simpler monopole. This is one of the great remaining mysteries in physics.

For those going on to take additional physics coursework, here is a preview. In electricity a common past time for physicists is to determine the electric field due to a configuration of charges using a principle called Gauss' law. This calculation can be a considerable challenge involving some complicated calculus derivations. In an analogous manner, physicists often devote themselves to determining the magnetic field produced by a configuration of electric currents using a principle called Ampere's law. Because of the mathematical complexities of such calculations we will not pursue this topic further, although these two laws are two of Maxwell's equations that will be discussed in the next chapter.

Therefore, leaving aside the question of precisely how currents produce a magnetic field, let us turn to how a given magnetic field exerts a force on charges. One situation is where two bar magnets are brought near to one another. As alluded to earlier, the magnetic force between two bar magnets is an inverse-square force law. However, it turns out that this situation is not something that arises often in applications of magnetism and so we will not give it further attention.

A more common situation lies at the heart of this chapter, i.e. how are magnetic forces involved in the operation of a DC electric motor. We will approach this problem in two steps. First, we will see how a magnetic field can produce a force on an individual charge and second, how the field can exert a force on a current in a wire. The former is relevant to the operation of charge accelerators used in high energy particle experiments, such as, the work performed at the Fermi National Accelerator Laboratory in Chicago or CERN in Switzerland. The latter is of interest because of its relevance to the enormously important DC electric motor. Let's learn more about how magnetic forces operate.

C. Fundamental Force: Magnetic Force on a Moving Charge.

The magnetic force is like no other force we have encountered so far. It is both more complicated than electric and gravitational forces and more strange. Suppose a magnetic field penetrates the plane of this page, and is pointing out of the page with a constant magnitude and direction. Recall, to represent this we use a circle with a dot at its center. (The magnetic field is a vector so we must specify both its magnitude and direction.) If an electric point charge q is brought into the region where the magnetic field exists, experimentally it is found that no magnetic force will be exerted on q if the charge is at rest. This is the first oddity of magnetic forces: *the charge must have a velocity to experience a magnetic force.* Clearly, magnetic forces are much different than electric forces since electric forces do not require movement. Furthermore, experience shows the magnetic force on q vanishes if q moves parallel to the field, $\vec{B}$. Shown in Figure 2 is precisely how the magnetic field exerts a force on q when it has a velocity $\vec{v}$. But before we unravel this mysterious figure in detail there is a short detour into the magical world of pure mathematics.

A Mathematical Aside.

Previously we learned how to add and subtract vectors. Earlier in the book we examined the work concept where we found nature requires us to know how to multiply vectors. Recall, work was defined in terms of the scalar or dot product according to which two vectors are multiplied and the result of this operation was a <u>scalar</u>. At this point nature impels us to define a new way of multiplying vectors where the outcome is a <u>vector</u>. The new operation is called the ***cross*** or ***vector product***, written in the following fashion,

$$\vec{A} \times \vec{B} = \vec{C}. \tag{1}$$

This procedure will be unambiguous once we know how $\vec{C}$ is determined in terms of the vectors $\vec{A}$ and $\vec{B}$. Since $\vec{C}$ is a vector, we must precisely specify how $\vec{A}$ and $\vec{B}$ give $\vec{C}$'s magnitude and direction. The magnitude is straightforward,

$$|\vec{C}| \equiv |\vec{A} \times \vec{B}| = |\vec{A}|\,|\vec{B}|\sin\theta, \text{ where } \theta \text{ is the } \textit{smallest} \text{ angle between the vectors } \vec{A} \text{ and } \vec{B}. \tag{2}$$

Notice, $\vec{C}$ will be zero if the angle between the vectors is either $\theta = 0°$ or $180°$ because $\sin(0) = \sin(180) = 0$ but $|\vec{C}|$ will have its maximum value when $\theta = 90°$ since $\sin(90) = 1$. Recall the dot or scalar product was just like equation (2) except $\cos\theta$ was present rather than $\sin\theta$.

The direction of $\vec{C}$ in equation (1) takes a bit of explaining. First, consider the two vectors $\vec{A}$ and $\vec{B}$. Geometrically $\vec{A}$ and $\vec{B}$ are line segments. These two vectors therefore define a plane. The direction of $\vec{C}$ is defined to be perpendicular to the plane formed by $\vec{A}$ and $\vec{B}$. For example, if both $\vec{A}$ and $\vec{B}$ lie in the plane of this page then $\vec{C}$ is perpendicular to this page. But wait, there is an ambiguity. $\vec{C}$ could point out of the page or into the page. This ambiguity is resolved by something known as the right-handed screw rule. A right-handed screw has the property that if it is rotated counterclockwise it comes toward you but a clockwise rotation makes the screw move away from

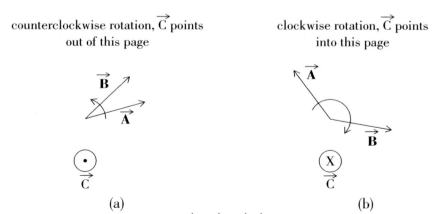

counterclockwise rotation, $\vec{C}$ points out of this page

clockwise rotation, $\vec{C}$ points into this page

(a)   (b)

FIG. 2. (A) CROSS PRODUCT $\vec{A} \times \vec{B} = \vec{C}$, $\vec{C}$ COMES OUT OF THIS PAGE. (B) SAME CROSS PRODUCT BUT $\vec{C}$ GOES INTO PAGE.

you. (There exists left-handed screws that do just the opposite but in the USA we usually use right-handed screws!) The right-handed screw rule we will call *right-hand rule #2* and it says:

Starting with the tail of $\vec{A}$ coinciding with the tail of $\vec{B}$, rotate $\vec{A}$ toward $\vec{B}$ through the angle θ and $\vec{C}$ points in the direction that a right-handed screw would move under such a rotation.

This rule is summarized in Figure 2. In (a) rotating $\vec{A}$ toward $\vec{B}$ sets up a counterclockwise rotation, and the screw (and $\vec{C}$) would come out of the page as indicated by the circle with the enclosed dot. On the other hand, in (b) the rotation is clockwise, $\vec{C}$ points into the page and this is represented by the circle with a cross inside.

This completes the mathematical aside. Let us return to the physics of magnetic forces.

Going back to the magnetic force on a charge *q*, the force $\vec{F}$ by the field $\vec{B}$ on the charge moving with velocity $\vec{v}$ is expressed succinctly in terms of the cross product between the velocity and the field,

$$\vec{F} = q\,\vec{v} \times \vec{B}. \tag{3}$$

Equation (3) is the fundamental magnetic force law and it captures all of the properties of magnetic forces we mentioned previously. It contains a great deal of information. For example, if $q = 0$, the charge experiences no magnetic force. This would be the case for a neutron, for instance. Further, if the charge is at rest, $v = 0$ and there is no force. Notice also that *q* can be positive or negative, so the force on an electron by the field is opposite the force on a proton (in the same field) even if the two have equal velocities. Due to the nature of the cross product, the force is zero if the velocity is parallel to the field.

We won't prove the next statement. Based on the character of the magnetic force, *moving charges generally move in a circle with a constant speed when placed in a constant magnetic field*. In such a case, there follows from equation (3) the result,

$$F = qvB = ma = mv^2/r \ (\vec{v} \perp \vec{B}), \tag{4}$$

where I have used Newton's second law and the formula for centripetal acceleration.

What about the units of B? Equation (3) provides a convenient way of expressing the units for a magnetic field. If 1 Coulomb of charge moves at 1 m/s and it experiences a magnetic force of 1 N, then this defines the MKSA unit for magnetic field,

$$1 \text{ Tesla} \equiv 1 \text{ N}/(1\text{C} - 1\text{m/s}). \tag{5}$$

A field of one ***Tesla*** is a very large magnetic field. For example, the Earth's magnetic field is about 5×10^{-5} T and a common refrigerator magnet produces a field of around 0.3 T. Another common unit for magnetic field is the Gauss, where

$$1 \text{ Tesla} \equiv 10^4 \text{ Gauss}.$$

The field of the Earth is then about 0.5 Gauss. *In working problems using MKSA units it is essential that you always express the magnetic field in Tesla not Gauss.*

Example One.—*An electron in the Earth's magnetic field inside a television.*

An electron in a television cathode ray tube (the picture tube) is accelerated across a voltage of about 20,000 Volts. Find (a) the speed acquired by the electron. Next, imagine this electron enters a region of constant magnetic field of magnitude the same as that of the Earth's field and pointing out of this page. (b) Determine the radius of the electron's circular orbit.

Solution.

(a) This is a review question. Recall from the chapter where voltage was introduced, $W = eV > 0$, where W is the positive work by the electric field inside the TV. But also from our study of mechanics we derived the work-kinetic energy relation,

$$W = \Delta K = \tfrac{1}{2} mv^2,$$

where I have assumed the electron started from rest. Equating the two results for W and solving for v gives,

$$eV = \tfrac{1}{2} mv^2 \text{ or } v = (2eV/m)^{1/2}.$$

Putting in numbers for the charge and mass of the electron,

$$v = (2 \times 1.6 \times 10^{-19} \cdot 20{,}000/9.11 \times 10^{-31})^{1/2} = \underline{8.38 \times 10^7 \text{ m/s}}.$$

This is about the speed of electrons inside your television's picture tube. The speed is nearly 1/3 the speed of light! We have neglected relativistic effects.

(b) Applying the magnetic force law, equation (4), to the moving electron,

$$F = evB = ma = mv^2/r,$$

where I have assumed the field is perpendicular to the velocity of the electron. Solving for the radius r gives

$$r = mv/eB.$$

This result is quite useful. It implies the radius of the orbit is larger the bigger the speed of the charge, while it is smaller the greater the charge and field become. Placing numbers into this expression, where B is that of the Earth, we find

$$r = 9.11 \times 10^{-31} \times 8.38 \times 10^7/(1.6 \times 10^{-19} \times 5 \times 10^{-5}) = \underline{9.54 \text{ m}}.$$

One practical consequence of this result is, television designers do not have to worry much about the Earth's magnetic field when designing their sets since it does not deflect the electron appreciably.

Example Two.—*Measuring the mass of atoms and molecules: the mass spectrometer.*

In a mass spectrometer, a common instrument used by chemists, an atom or molecule is first ionized then accelerated across a voltage difference and finally the ion passes into a region where there exists a constant magnetic field. Knowing the charge of the ion and the value of the voltage, it is possible to find the speed of the ion as we did in the previous example. Inside the spectrometer there is a detector that measures the radius of the ion's circular orbit inside the field B. (a) Find the mass of the ion in terms of the above variables and (b) use the following numbers to evaluate the mass of a Li^+ ion: $B = 0.35$ T, $q = e$, $r = 0.17$ m, and $v = 8 \times 10^5$ m/s. Make sure your answer in (b) is in the ballpark by looking up the constituents of Li.

Solution.

(a) As in the previous example we use, $r = mv/eB$, which can be rearranged to solve for m,

$$m = reB/v.$$

This is the fundamental equation for mass spectrometers.

(b) Plugging the given data into the equation in (a),

$$m = 0.17 \times 1.6 \times 10^{-19} \times 0.35/8 \times 10^5 = \underline{1.19 \times 10^{-26} \text{ kg.}}$$

Does this result make any sense? Recall, Li is the third element in the periodic chart. It consists of three protons and four neutrons but these are nearly of the same mass. The atom contains electrons but the electron's mass is not very significant so we will ignore it. Using for the mass of a proton, 1.67×10^{-27} kg, therefore,

$$m \approx 7 \times 1.67 \times 10^{-27} = \underline{1.17 \times 10^{-26} \text{ kg.}}$$

The answers in (a) and (b) are very close. We have successfully "weighed" the mass of an atom!

D. Fundamental Force: Magnetic Force on a Current-Carrying Wire.

Normally a wire will experience no force if it is placed inside a magnetic field. But if there exists an electric current in the wire, then generally there will be a magnetic force exerted on it by the magnetic field. The reason for this is simple. The current consists of drifting charges and so each of the moving charges experiences a force given by equation (3). Suppose the portion of the current-carrying wire that is inside the magnetic field has a length $\vec{L}$ where this new vector points in the same direction as the current I and has a magnitude equaling the length of the wire. If the total amount of drifting charge contained in the length L is denoted Δq and this charge takes a time interval Δt to move the length L, then the velocity of the charges contained in L is, $\vec{v} = \vec{L}/\Delta t$ and the total current is $I = \Delta q/\Delta t$. Putting these into equation (3) gives the total magnetic force on the length L of wire,

$$\vec{F} = \Delta q \, \vec{v} \times \vec{B} = \Delta q \, (\vec{L}/\Delta t) \times \vec{B},$$

or
$$\vec{F} = I\vec{L} \times \vec{B}. \tag{6}$$

Equation (6) only holds under certain conditions: the field must be constant and the wire must be straight. These restrictions are not that serious since in most applications both conditions are met.

The statements made about a single charge moving in a magnetic field apply also to a current-carrying wire in a field. For example, if the wire is oriented parallel to the field then there is no magnetic force on the wire.

Example Three.—*Utility wire in the Earth's magnetic field.*

Time for a Fermi question. Do electric wires in a power line experience significant forces due to the Earth's magnetic field? Assume the line carries a current of 100.0 Amps.

Solution.

Consider one meter of the wire and assume the current is perpendicular to the Earth's field. Using equation (6),

$$F = ILB\sin 90° = ILB = 100 \times 1 \times 5 \times 10^{-5} = \underline{0.005 \text{ N.}}$$

The wire might have a weight about that of an apple, 1 N. Clearly, the magnetic force is negligible compared to the force of gravity acting on the wire.

Example Four.—*Magnetic force on a square loop of current-carrying wire.*

You are given a wire that forms a square loop that lies in the plane of this page and that carries a current of 5.00 Amps. If there is a constant magnetic field of 7.0 Tesla pointing out of this page then what is the total magnetic force on the loop? Assume the current is counterclockwise.

Solution.

We will find the force on each segment of the loop and then add the four force vectors to get the total force. In each case we use equation (6).

Left side	Right side	Top side	Bottom side
$\vec{F} = ILB$ (left)	$\vec{F} = ILB$ (right)	$\vec{F} = ILB$ (top)	$\vec{F} = ILB$ (bottom),

where left means the force points toward the left side of this page, etc.

The total force adds up to <u>zero</u> and so the magnetic field will not cause the loop to accelerate but we will shortly see there is an important effect of the field on the loop.

E. Application: Magnetic Forces and Electric Motors.

Figure 3 is a crude rendition of a simple DC motor. A piece of wire is bent into the shape shown, and placed in the external constant magnetic field of the permanent magnet whose poles are shown. A DC current is introduced in the wire and as a result the magnetic field exerts a force on each segment of the wire that is inside the field. Let use calculate the magnetic force on the wire. Notice in the skewed view shown in Figure 3(a) the bent portion of the wire that is inside the magnetic field region has three line segments: a front (closest to us), top and back piece. In the side view shown in Figure 3(b) only the front piece of the wire is visible and it makes an angle θ with the horizontal direction which is the direction of the magnetic field.

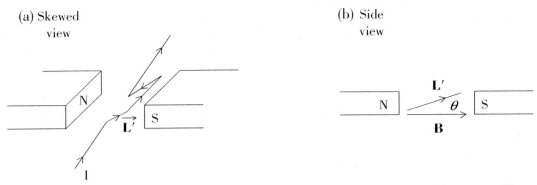

FIG. 3. THE WIRE CARRIES A CURRENT *I* IN THE PRESENCE OF THE MAGNETIC FIELD. THE FIELD EXERTS A TWISTING FORCE ON THE WIRE, MAKING IT ROTATE. THIS IS THE BASIC PHYSICS UNDERLYING THE ELECTRIC MOTOR.

Let the front and back pieces have a length L' while the length of the top piece call *L*. Using equation (6) we find the force on each segment in 3(b),

Front Segment
$\vec{F} = IL'B\sin\theta$ (into this page)

Back Segment
$\vec{F} = IL'B\sin\theta$ (out of this page)

Top Segment
$\vec{F} = ILB$ (down)

The forces on front and back segments cancel each other out. However, the force on the top segment of the bent wire points toward the bottom of Figure 3(b). This force makes the wire rotate in the magnetic field. This crude model illustrates the basic physics of the DC motor, i.e. a current-carrying loop of wire when placed inside a magnetic field will rotate. The rotation may be used to do useful work.

Of course, real motors are more complicated than our simple motor. Real motors consist of many loops of wire, known as an armature, that are placed between the poles of a permanent magnet. Moreover, a device known as a commutator is required. The commutator looks like the ring with the gap down the middle seen in Figure 4(a). The role of the commutator is to reverse the direction of motion of the current every half rotation of the armature. This reversal is needed so that the magnetic force on the loops always makes the loop rotate in the same direction. Without the commutator the loops would not make a full rotation. There are brushes (i.e. electrical contacts) that are connected to the commutator and the brushes are attached to wires that supply the current to the motor. A real motor is shown in Figure 4 (b).

DC motors and magnets are present throughout modern automobiles. Other applications and phenomena involving magnets include: maglev trains, biomagnetic effects in pigeons that are important in helping the pigeon navigate, the Earth's magnetism, cyclotron accelerators, the Aurora Borealis (the Northern lights), magnetic recording, and magnetic imaging used in modern medicine. The list could be greatly extended.

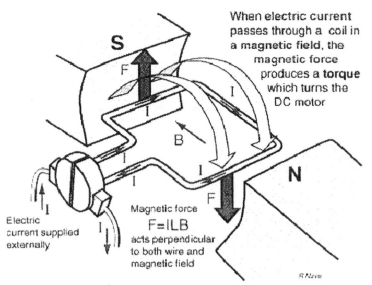

When electric current passes through a coil in a magnetic field, the magnetic force produces a **torque** which turns the DC motor

S

F

I

B

I

N

I

I

Electric current supplied externally

Magnetic force

$F = ILB$

acts perpendicular to both wire and magnetic field

R Nave

FIG. 4. (A) DC MOTOR: SCHEMATIC. THE MAGNETIC FIELD EXERTS A TWISTING FORCE (I.E. A TORQUE) THAT CAUSES THE CURRENT-CARRYING LOOP OF WIRE TO ROTATE. THE CURRENT IS INJECTED INTO THE LOOP AT THE COMMUTATOR VIA BRUSHES.

Carl Rod Nave, Georgia State University, Department of Physics & Astronomy.

(B) A REAL ELECTRIC MOTOR. Reprinted from *Industrial Electronics*, Second Edition, Prentice Hall (2006), Prentice-Hall, Inc.

Summary.

Oersted discovered that an electric current is a source of a magnetic field. The magnetic force is a rather complicated expression that involves the mathematical multiplication of vectors called the cross product. Two expressions for the magnetic force are given, one for the force on a moving point charge and the other for the force on a current-carrying wire placed in a magnetic field. Both expressions contain the cross product. Charges generally move in circles when placed in a uniform magnetic field. The DC electric motor consists of a current-carrying loop of wire placed inside a magnetic field. The way the motor works is based on the magnetic force on the loop of wire.

QUESTIONS.

Q

I

R (•) P

S

1. Current in a wire is perpendicular to this page, as indicated in the diagram. What is the direction of the current, out or into this page? State the direction of the magnetic field produced by the wire at points *P, Q, R,* and *S.*

2. Two vectors when crossed have zero cross product. What must be true of the vectors?

3. A particle is inside a region where there exists a magnetic field but it does not experience a magnetic force. What are the three possible reasons for this to happen?

4. If the magnetic force on a moving charge is out of this page then what is the direction of the force if the velocity of the charge is reversed?

5. The magnetic force on a charge does not depend on the position of the charge inside the uniform magnetic field. Is this the only case of a force that does not depend on position?

6. Is it possible to cause a stationary charged particle to accelerate using a magnetic field? Explain why or why not.

7. A charged particle is found to move in a straight line. Therefore, there is no magnetic field in the region of space. True or False? Explain.

8. A uniform magnetic field points out of this page. An electron and a proton enter the field with the same velocity in the plane of this page and to the right parallel to the bottom side of this page. What is the direction of the magnetic force on the two? Which charge experiences the greater force?

9. The ancient Greeks believed in a mythical island in the Mediterranean Sea made entirely out of lodestone (magnetite) which is the material some common bar magnets are made of. From this they argued that ships should not be made with iron nails. Explain why.

10. A positive charge moves along a line near a bar magnet that produced the magnetic field shown in the figure below. What is the direction of the magnetic force on the charge?

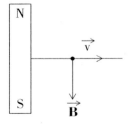

11. A charged particle moves into the region of a mass spectrometer where the magnetic field is perpendicular to the velocity vector of the charge. The particle subsequently moves in a path that is (a) a straight line (b) parabolic (c) a point since it stops (d) circular.

12. Cosmic rays are charged particles coming toward the Earth from all directions. Given the magnetic field of the Earth is a dipole field (see figure) that can deflect the rays, where would you expect the cosmic rays to be most prevalent near the ground?

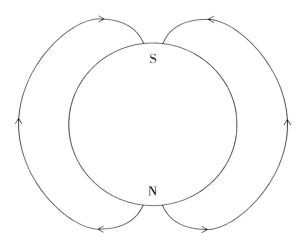

13. Why is the speed of a charged particle that moves in a uniform magnetic field constant?

14. A wire is bent into the shape shown in the diagram below. The current in the wire is as shown and there is a constant magnetic field.

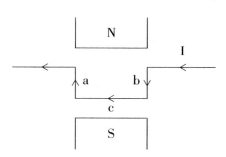

What is the direction of the magnetic force produced by the permanent magnetic in the figure? Why is the magnetic force zero on segments labeled *a* and *b*? What is the direction of the magnetic force on the segment labeled *c* in the figure?

15. Two long parallel wires carry the same current *I*. What is the direction of the force by the lower wire acting on the upper wire in (a) and (b) below?

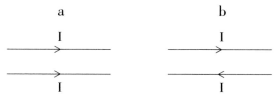

16. For a bar magnet, magnetic field vectors point away from the North Pole and toward the South Pole. True or False?

17. Recall magnetic field lines or lines of force describe a magnetic field. Why is it impossible for two magnetic lines of force to cross?

18. The igneous rock called lodestone is more properly called magnetite and is found in nature to be magnetized. When an object is magnetized the atomic magnetic dipoles all point in the same direction. How do you suppose this came about?

19. Given that the Earth acts as a giant bar magnet, it has been found that the geographic North Pole of the Earth is actually the magnetic South Pole. Therefore, explain how a compass works.

PROBLEMS.

1. A vector $\vec{A}$ of length 12 lies along the x-axis and a second vector $\vec{B}$ of length 20 lies along the y-axis. Assume the x-y plane is this sheet of paper. Determine the (a) magnitude and (b) the direction of $\vec{C} = \vec{A} \times \vec{B}$.

2. A vector $\vec{A}$ of length 10 lies along the x-axis and a second vector $\vec{B}$ of length 20 lies along the y-axis. Assume the x-y plane is this sheet of paper. Determine the (a) magnitude and (b) the direction of $\vec{C} = \vec{B} \times \vec{A}$.

3. Consider the two vectors below that reside in the plane of this page. Let $|\vec{A}| = 12$ and $|\vec{B}| = 10$. Find $\vec{A} \times \vec{B}$, both its magnitude and its direction.

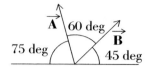

4. Consider the two vectors below that reside in the plane of this page. Let $|\vec{A}| = 12$ and $|\vec{B}| = 14$. Find $\vec{B} \times \vec{A}$, both its magnitude and its direction.

5. A car travels with a speed of 30.0 m/s along the x-axis. Due to its motion the car acquires a positive charge of 2.0×10^{-5} C. The Earth's magnetic field has a magnitude of 5×10^{-5} Tesla and points along the y-axis. Determine the magnetic force vector on the car—treating the car as a point charge.

6. An electron moves with a speed of 1.0×10^7 m/s inside a television set's picture tube in the presence of a uniform magnetic field $\vec{B}$. See the figure below where $\vec{g}$ represents the gravitational field of the Earth. (a) What is the direction of the magnetic force on the electron in the figure? (b) How large must the magnetic field be such that the magnitude of the magnetic force on the electron equals the electron's weight?

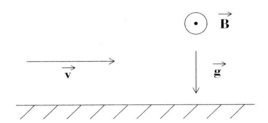

7. An electron moves between two parallel charged plates that create a uniform electric field $\vec{E}$ that has a magnitude of 500.0 V/m (see the figure below). There is also a uniform magnetic field between the plates $\vec{B}$ of magnitude 0.12 Tesla. (a) What is the direction of the magnetic force on the electron? the electric force? (b) At what speed must the electron be moving such that the magnitudes of the electric and magnetic forces are equal. This device is known as a velocity selector since only electrons of one speed pass between the plates without being deflected.

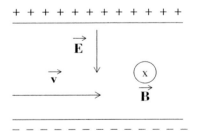

8. An electron is accelerated starting from rest through a potential difference of 22,000 Volts in a certain television picture tube. (a) Determine the speed acquired by the electron. (b) The electron then enters a region with a constant magnetic field of magnitude 4.0×10^{-5} T and that is perpendicular to the velocity of the electron. Inside the magnetic field the electron moves in a circle of radius r. Compute the value of r.

9. A carbon ion consists of 6 protons and 6 neutrons with one of its usual electrons missing. The mass of the ion is 1.99×10^{-26} kg. (a) What is the charge of the ion? (b) The ion moves with a speed of 1.5×10^5 m/s as it enters a mass spectrometer that has a uniform magnetic field of 0.90 T that is perpendicular to the ion's velocity. Determine the radius of the ion's circular motion inside the spectrometer.

10. In 1932 at the University of California the particle accelerator called the cyclotron was invented by E. Lawrence. Inside the accelerator a proton moves in a circle of radius 0.14 m in a uniform magnetic field of 1.1 T that is perpendicular to the velocity of the proton. Find the speed of the proton.

11. A 200.0 m long power line of mass 150.0 kg carries a current of I and runs parallel to the ground. The uniform magnetic field of the Earth has a magnitude of 5.00×10^{-5} T and is perpendicular to the wire (see diagram below).

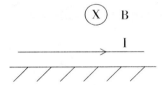

(a) Using $g = 10$ m/s² find the weight of the power line and (b) what must be the current in the power line so that the weight is balanced by the magnetic force on the power line?

12. If the current in the power line in problem 11 was in the opposite direction from what is shown in the figure, and the current is 100 A, find the magnetic force vector on the power line.

13. A square loop of wire of side 10.0 cm resides in the plane of this page. A 7.00 T magnetic field points out of this page. Find the magnetic force vector on each side of the loop assuming a current of 5.00 A runs clockwise around the loop.

14. A wire carrying 10.0 A of current consists of three segments, a 10 m, 7 m, and 14 m piece. There is a 1.0 T magnetic field as shown below. The 7 m long segment makes the angle θ with the horizontal segments. Find the magnetic force on each segment of the wire.

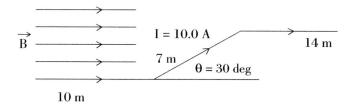

15. One of the famous experiments of Ampere during the early nineteenth century involved two long wires that carry a current. Suppose the wires in the diagram below carry the same current of 5.00 A and each have the same length of 10.00 m. Assuming that the wire at the bottom creates a uniform magnetic field at the location of the top wire of 2.0 T that points out of the page, determine the force vector on the top wire due to the magnetic field created by the bottom wire. See answers below for a hint.

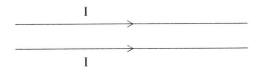

16. Work problem 15 on the assumption the top wire's current is directly opposite from that shown in the figure.

17. A square loop of wire with sides of length 10.0 cm has a total resistance of 5.00 Ω. The loop is in series with a 12.0 volt battery and is attached to a table using hinges as shown below. There is a uniform magnetic field of 1.2 T that is parallel to the plane of the table top. Find the magnetic force on each of the sides of the loop except for the side that lies on top of the table where the hinges are. Let θ = 30°.

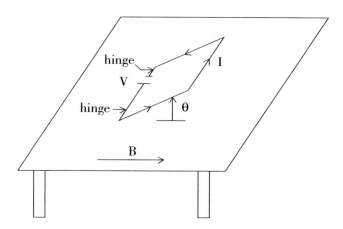

18. A wire points out of this page with a current of 3.0 A and resides between the poles of a magnet that produces a magnetic field of 2.0 T as shown below. Determine the force vector acting on the 1.2 m long wire.

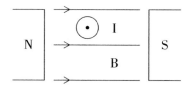

Hints and answers to the problems.

1) 240, out of page   2) 200, into page   3) 104 into page   4) 165 into page   5) 3×10^{-8} N out of page   6) up, 5.7×10^{-18} T   7) down, up 4,200 m/s   8) 8.8×10^7 m/s, 12.5 m 9) e, 0.0207 m   10) 1.48×10^7 m/s   11) 1,500 N, 1.5×10^5 A   12) 1 N down   13) <u>top side</u> down 3.5 N, <u>right side</u> left 3.5 N, <u>bottom side</u> up 3.5 N, <u>left side</u> right 3.5 N   14) 10 m: 0, 7 m: 35 N into page, 14 m: 0   15) 100 N attractive   16) 100 N repulsive   17) front: 0.144 N into page, side: 0.288 N down, back: 0.144 N out of page   18) 7.2 N up

SECTION V.

ELECTROMAGNETISM.

What does light have to do with electricity and magnetism?

CHAPTER XI.
ACCELERATED CHARGES
AND ELECTROMAGNETIC FIELDS.

Abstract.

Two highly significant nineteenth century physicists are profiled, Michael Faraday and James Clerk Maxwell. The new concept of magnetic flux is defined and used in the statement of Faraday's law of electromagnetic induction. The fundamental laws of electricity and magnetism—-Maxwell's equations, are presented without an inordinate emphasis on the mathematical complexities of the equations. Maxwell's fundamental contributions include a new term called the displacement current and the conception of light as an electromagnetic field wave. Applications in this chapter include the electric generator, transformer and the electromagnetic spectrum.

Definitions. magnetic flux, induced voltage, motional emf, electric flux, and displacement current

Principles. electromagnetic induction

Fundamental Equations. generator equation, transformer equation, Maxwell's equations, the wave relation

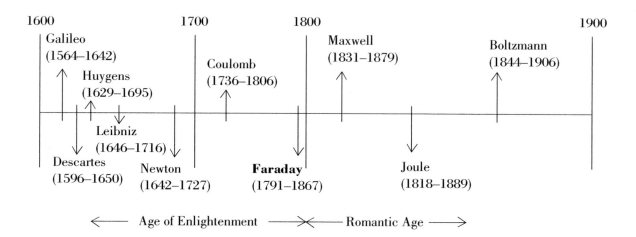

Courtesy of Private Collection/The Stapleton Collection/The Bridgeman Art Library.

A. Michael Faraday.

Michael Faraday (1791–1867) was an English scientist who was one of the leading experimentalists during the nineteenth century. He made fundamental contributions to both physics and chemistry. Michael came from a poor, working-class family who lived in a slum on the outskirts of London. His parents were strict, intelligent and religious. Faraday's father died when Michael was young, leaving the impoverished widow to raise the children. Not surprisingly, the mother was to have a lasting influence on Michael's life.

Faraday received very little formal education—he was to eventually become an apprentice to a book binder. At the age of twenty-nine Michael became a member of a rather unusual and rigorous Protestant sect known as the Sandemanians. This very small (less than a few hundred souls), persecuted group originated in Scotland as a break away society from the well established Presbyterian Church of Scotland. Faraday maintained his membership in this organization throughout his life, even on occasion serving as an Elder in the sect. In the tradition of Descartes, Faraday kept his religion and science as largely separate compartments from one another.

Faraday was first attracted to science by reading an article on electricity in the Encyclopedia Britannica. He began his scientific career at the Royal Institution of London working under the mentorship of the great English chemist Sir Humphrey Davy. Faraday spent his entire professional life at the Royal Institution. Davy was to have a tremendous impact on the scientific development of young Faraday. During these early days, Faraday made many important contributions to chemistry, especially in the general area of electrochemistry. Noteworthy of his successes during this period was his discovery of the compound benzene. Further, in 1832 he developed the electrochemical process known as electrolysis. Michael's greatest contributions to physics was his concept of a field and his 1831 discovery of the law of electromagnetic induction which is now known as Faraday's law. Although not an outstanding mathematician, Michael had a keen sense of visualization which he used to unravel properties of the electric and magnetic fields. His geometric insights extended to interests outside of science to an attraction to the visual arts.

Michael Faraday's scientific work built largely on the foundations set in place by Oersted, who you will recall had made the serendipitous discovery that an electric current creates a magnetic field. A younger contemporary, James Clerk Maxwell, about whom we will learn more later in this chapter, made extensive use of Faraday's experimental findings. Many lay persons often do not realize the extent to which scientists must rely on the earlier work of their colleagues. Progress in science is an evolutionary process that involves essential communication among the workers in the field. This is why such great importance is placed on publishing scientific research results in journals. Even science is a social endeavor.

Unfortunately, the social side of science can give rise to less than positive events. For example, Faraday and Davy eventually had a falling out. For reasons history seems to be unaware of, in 1840 Faraday had a nervous breakdown from which he never fully recovered.

On a more positive note, by all accounts Faraday was an excellent popular lecturer. He became famous because of his Friday evening lectures intended for lay audiences. These lectures began in 1826 and were known to attract a number of wealthy persons. On other occasions Michael delivered a different kind of lecture known as his Christmas lectures. These were for children, although adults also attended. The most famous of the Christmas lectures was his lecture on the candle where he spoke at length on the chemical and physical properties of an ordinary candle. The lectures were given at the Royal Institution.

Toward the end of his life Faraday conducted experiments on the effects of magnets on light. Shortly before his death he became interested in seeing if somehow the gravitational and electric forces were different manifestations of the same underlying force of nature. This has been a topic of longstanding interest to physicists, and continues even to this day. For example, Einstein spent the last decades of his life trying to unify gravity and electricity by developing a "unified field theory." Even Einstein was unsuccessful and the complete unification of fundamental forces continues to be one of the great unsolved problems in physics today.

Let us end this short profile of Faraday's work and life with a couple of personal observations. Faraday's wife exerted a profound influence on his life. The couple married in 1821 but were never able to have children. Michael Faraday lived to the age of 75, which was a very long life for people living during the nineteenth century.

References.

Remarkable Physicists, Ioan James (Cambridge UP, 2004). Chapter 4.

Great Physicists, William H. Cropper (Oxford UP, 2001). Chapter 11.

B. Magnetic Flux.

Magnetic fields are vector fields produced by electric currents. Suppose there is a constant magnetic field passing through this sheet of paper pointing out from the page. Shown in Figure 1(a) are the magnetic field lines passing through the page as seen from an edge view. The magnetic field intersects the plane of the page at a right angle and since the field is constant the field lines are equally-spaced. The vector $\vec{A}$ in the figure is called the area vector of the page. It is defined to have a length proportional to the area of the page and a direction perpendicular to the plane of the page. In Figure 1(b) the page has been rotated by ninety degrees. Notice the magnetic field lines no longer pass through the page but are now parallel to the plane of the page. The situations in

Figure 1(a) and Figure 1(b) are extremes since in Figure 1(a) the maximum number of lines of $\vec{B}$ pass through the page while in 1(b) no lines of $\vec{B}$ pass through the page.

Qualitatively, the *magnetic **flux*** (flux is Latin for flow), Φ, passing through an area, A, is defined to be proportional to the number of lines of magnetic field $\vec{B}$ passing through the surface.

Accordingly, in Figure 1(a) Φ is a maximum (nine lines—count 'em) while in Figure 1(b) it is zero. In Figure 1(c) the page has been rotated through an angle θ and notice now the number of field lines passing through the page is only five. The magnetic flux in Figure 1(c) is intermediate between that in 1(a) and 1(b).

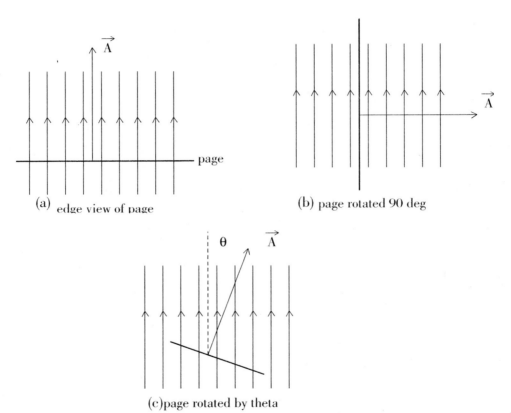

(a) edge view of page

(b) page rotated 90 deg

(c) page rotated by theta

FIG. 1. (A) MAGNETIC VECTORS PASS THROUGH THE PAGE PARALLEL TO THE NORMAL VECTOR, $\vec{A}$. THE MAGNETIC FLUX IS MAXIMUM (NINE LINES). (B) THE PAGE HAS BEEN ROTATED SUCH THAT $\vec{A}$ IS PERPENDICULAR TO $\vec{B}$ AND NO LINES OF FORCE PASS THROUGH $\vec{A}$. THE FLUX IS ZERO. (C) THE PAGE HAS BEEN ROTATED THROUGH AN ANGLE OF θ, AND SOME LINES (FIVE LINES) OF FORCE PASS THROUGH $\vec{A}$. THE FLUX IS INTERMEDIATE.

But we need to be more quantitative about this. Mathematically, we say there is a *magnetic flux*, Φ, penetrating the sheet in 1 (a) that is given by,

$$\Phi \equiv BA \quad (\text{constant } \vec{B} \parallel \vec{A}).$$

The qualitative and quantitative definitions for flux are in agreement. For example, increasing $\vec{B}$ or $\vec{A}$ causes the number of field lines penetrating $\vec{A}$ to increase, thereby making the flux larger. The above expression for flux, BA, implies the same thing. This expression is not the most general mathematical definition of flux, however. A more general definition allows for the case where the *constant* magnetic field vectors make an angle θ with the area vector $\vec{A}$, as depicted in Figure 1(c). In this case, the magnetic flux definition is written in terms of the dot product as,

$$\Phi \equiv \vec{B} \cdot \vec{A} = BA\cos\theta. \tag{1}$$
$$(\vec{B} \text{ constant})$$

Equation (1) is also consistent with our qualitative discussion of flux. For instance, in Figure 1(a) we use $\theta = 0$ to obtain $\Phi \equiv BA$ as before, while in 1(b) $\theta = 90°$ and $\Phi = 0$. In this we have used: $\cos(0) = 1$ and $\cos(90°) = 0$, respectively. In Figure 1(c), equation (1) is used with a non-zero value for θ and the flux is in between the values of 0 and BA.

And yet, equation (1) is not the most general situation that is encountered since in (1) we assumed the field to be constant. If the field is not constant, calculus is required to properly compute flux but this case will not be considered further.

Equation (1) gives the proper (MKSA) units for magnetic flux, Tesla-meter^2. Always convert to these units in handling flux.

Example One.—*Magnetic flux passing through the lens of wire-rim glasses.*

Estimate the magnetic flux of the Earth's field through one lens of a person's wire-rim glasses.

Solution.

Recall the magnetic field due to the Earth has a value of approximately $B = 5 \times 10^{-5}$ Tesla. Assume the wire-rim is a circle of radius 2.0 cm and the magnetic field penetrates the area enclosed by the rim at right angles, i.e. $\theta = 0$. Therefore, using these in equation (1) along with the formula for the area of a circle, πr^2,

$$\Phi = BA\cos\theta = 5 \times 10^{-5} \quad \pi(0.02)^2\cos(0) = \underline{6.3 \times 10^{-8} \text{ T-m}^2.}$$

Example Two.—*Magnetic flux dependence on angle.*

Suppose the field passing through a rectangular loop of sides 5.0 cm by 10.0 cm has a constant value of 7.0 Tesla (a large field). For each value of θ below, determine the flux through the loop.

(a) $\theta = 30°$
(b) $\theta = 45°$
(c) $\theta = 60°$

Solution.

In each case we use equation (1), $\Phi = BA\cos\theta$.

$$\Phi = 7.0 \times (0.05) \times (0.10) \cos\theta = 0.035 \cos\theta,$$

which leads to,
(a) $\Phi(30°) = \underline{0.0303 \text{ T-m}^2}$.
(b) $\Phi(45°) = \underline{0.0247 \text{ T-m}^2}$.
(c) $\Phi(60°) = \underline{0.0175 \text{ T-m}^2}$.

Situations where the magnetic flux passing through a surface is changing with time are relevant to the remainder of this chapter. Therefore, consider the next example.

Example Three.—*Changing flux through wire-rim glasses.*

Returning to Example one, imagine the person rotates her head through an angle of 90° during a time interval of 0.5 s. Estimate (a) the change in magnetic flux through one lens of her wire-rim glasses and (b) the *average rate of change in flux* in (a).

Solution.

(a) Assume she starts out with the magnetic field lines meeting the plane of the lens at an angle of 90° with $\theta = 0°$. The initial flux will be given by the answer to Example one,

$$\Phi_i = 6.3 \times 10^{-8} \text{ T-m}^2.$$

On rotating her head, the angle between $\vec{A}$ and $\vec{B}$ becomes $\theta = 90°$ and the final flux vanishes since $\cos(90°) = 0$.

$$\Phi_f = 0.$$

The change in flux is

$$\Delta\Phi = \Phi_f - \Phi_i = -6.3 \times 10^{-8} \text{ T-m}^2.$$

(b) The average rate of change of a quantity is by definition the change in the quantity divided by the time interval during which the change occurs. Thus,

$$\Delta\Phi/\Delta t = -6.3 \times 10^{-8}/1/2 = \underline{-1.26 \times 10^{-7} \text{ T-m}^2/\text{s}}.$$

It is essential to understand the concept of magnetic flux since this quantity is fundamental to our next topic, Faraday's law of induction.

C. Faraday's Law of Electromagnetic Induction.

In example three above the average rate of change in magnetic flux was introduced. We return to this idea because it lies at the heart of the topic of this section. Through painstaking experimental observations over a long period of time Michael Faraday arrived at his *law of electromagnetic induction*, which states:

For any surface in which the magnetic flux passing through the surface is varying with time, there is induced an average voltage around the boundary of the surface, that is,

Faraday's Law of Induction
$$V_{\text{ave induced}} = \Delta\Phi/\Delta t. \tag{2}$$

The key to using this law is to understand how magnetic flux through a surface can change with time. Below are some specific cases:

Case (i) A time-varying magnetic field

Case (ii) A time-varying area of the surface through which the field passes

Case (iii) Moving the surface so that it goes from a field-free region to a region of field; in this case the induced voltage is called a *motional emf*

Case (iv) Rotating a surface in a constant magnetic field; in this case the device is called an *electric generator* (see Section D below)

The above list covers most of the common applications of equation (2). Before examining specific examples of each of these situations, a few comments are in order. Apparently, equation (2) gives 1 T-m²/s = 1 Volt. Besides the mundane issue of units there is a more technical point to be made. Technically, there should be a negative sign on the right hand side of equation (2). This is needed in order to comply with Lenz's law, which has to do with how the polarity of the induced voltage is determined. For example, suppose the area in question is the area enclosed by a circular loop of wire. If, for whatever reason, the magnetic flux through the circle is increasing then there will be an induced voltage in the wire. The situation is the same as if a battery with a voltage equaling the induced voltage had been placed in series with the wire with no magnetic flux present. However, there are two ways in which the induced voltage could appear in the wire. In one way the induced voltage in the loop would cause the charges to move clockwise and in another the charges would move counter-clockwise around the wire. Lenz's law shows which way the charges will move. In the future, let's agree not to worry about the results of Lenz's law in this book. For those who will be taking future physics courses Lenz's law can not be ignored.

Example Four.—*Case (i) A time-varying magnetic field.*

A spatially constant magnetic field has a value at time zero of 7.0 Tesla and passes through a rectangular sheet (dimensions 10.0 cm by 20.0 cm). Assume the field makes an angle of 30° with the plane of the rectangle. (a) Find the initial magnetic flux through the sheet. (b) Next, assume over a time interval of 3.00 s the magnitude of the field falls to zero, and find the average induced voltage produced over the interval.

Solution.

(a) Using equation (1) with B = 7 T, A = 0.1 × 0.2 m², and θ = 60° (for the attentive student: why this rather than 30°?) we find,

$$\Phi(0) = 7 \times 0.02 \times \cos 60° = \underline{0.07 \text{ T-m}^2}.$$

(b) Applying equation (2) with $\Delta\Phi = 0 - 0.07$ and $\Delta t = 3$, gives

$$V_{\text{ave induced}} = \Delta\Phi/\Delta t = 0.07/3 = \underline{23.3 \text{ mVolts.}}$$

Notice we have ignored the minus sign since we are not going to fret over the sign of the induced voltage.

Example Five.—*Case (ii) A time-varying area of the surface through which the field passes.*

The radius of a circle increases with time, according to

$$r(t) = 1.00 \text{ cm} + (2.00 \text{ cm/s}) \, t.$$

A constant magnetic field of 0.3 Tesla (a refrigerator magnet) passes perpendicularly through the circle at all times. Find the average induced voltage around the circumference of the circle over the time interval 0 to 5.00 s.

Solution.

Faraday's law states $V_{\text{ave induced}} = \Delta\Phi/\Delta t$ where in this example Δt is 5 s. The magnetic flux change is determined once we recall the area of a circle, πr^2.

$$\Delta\Phi = \Phi_f - \Phi_i = BA_f - BA_i = B\pi \, (r_f{}^2 - r_i{}^2) = 0.3\pi[r^2(t = 5) - r^2(t = 0)],$$

$$\Delta\Phi = 0.3\pi[(0.01 + 0.02 \times 5)^2 - (0.01)^2] = 0.0113 \text{ T-m}^2.$$

$$V_{\text{ave induced}} = 0.0113/5 = \underline{2.26 \text{ mV}}.$$

Example Six.—*Case (iii) Moving the surface so that it goes from a field-free region to a region of constant field, in this case the induced voltage is called a motional emf.*

In Figure 2, (a) shows a rectangular loop of sides L by W that is moving with a constant speed of v. For $x < 0$ no magnetic field is present, while for $x > 0$ a constant field points into the page. Assume at time zero the right edge of the loop coincides with $x = 0$, and at time t shown in (b) the loop has moved a distance vt into the region where the field is present. Determine the average induced voltage in the loop at all times.

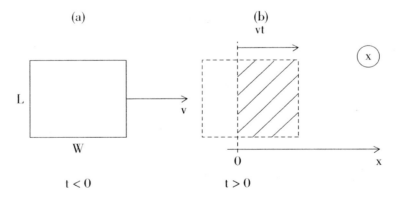

FIG. 2. (A) A RECTANGULAR LOOP ($L \times W$) IS TRANSLATING
WITH SPEED v. (B) THE LOOP ENTERS A UNIFORM
MAGNETIC FIELD REGION ($x > 0$) WHERE THE FIELD
POINTS INTO THE PAGE.

Solution.

Our mission is to find how the magnetic flux through the loop varies with time. Clearly, for $t < 0$ there is zero flux. On the other hand, at $t = W/v$ the loop will have fully entered into the region where the field exists, and so for times beginning at $t = W/v$ the flux is BLW and is no longer changing. At the time shown in (b) the amount of flux passing through the loop equals the field B times the area of that portion of the loop that is crossed out. The crossed out rectangular area has a value of Lvt. Hence,

$$\Phi(t) = 0, \qquad t < 0$$
$$BLvt, \qquad 0 < t < W/v$$
$$BLW, \qquad t > W/v.$$

There will only exist an (average) induced voltage during the middle time interval above, and during that time span, $\Delta\Phi = BLv\,\Delta t$, which means $V_{\text{ave ind}} = \Delta\Phi/\Delta t = BLv$. In summary,

$$V_{\text{ave ind}} = 0, \qquad t < 0$$
$$BLv, \qquad 0 < t < W/v$$
$$0, \qquad t > W/v.$$

The average induced voltage in this situation is called a *motional emf.* Emf is a synonym for induced voltage. The adjective "motional" is indicating the induced voltage arises from the motion of the loop into the region of the magnetic field.

D. Applications: Generators and Transformers.

A fourth case was mentioned in the last section. In this case a magnetic flux is made to vary, causing the production of an induced voltage in the following manner.

Case (iv) Rotating a surface in a constant magnetic field produces a variable flux and induced voltage. Such a device is called an electric generator. The example below gives the simplest version of an AC electric generator.

Example Seven.—*AC electric generator.*

Shown in Figure 3 is the simplest version of the generator. A rectangular loop of wire of sides L and W (therefore, A = area of loop = LW) is placed in between the poles of a magnet. Wires are attached to the

(a) Skewed view

(b) Side view

FIG. 3. VIEWS OF A LOOP OF WIRE THAT IS PLACED BETWEEN THE POLES OF A PERMANENT MAGNET AND ROTATED. THE VARYING MAGNETIC FLUX THROUGH THE LOOP INDUCES A VOLTAGE IN THE LOOP CREATING AN ELECTRIC GENERATOR.

loop thus forming a closed circuit. A handle is attached so that the loop may be rotated in the (constant) magnetic field. Assume the hand crank rotates with a constant angular velocity, $\omega = 2\pi/T$, where T is the period of the circular motion (the time for the loop to rotate once). Obtain an expression for the induced voltage as a function of time, t, in terms of L, W, B, and ω.

Solution.

In (b) of the sketch is shown the field, $\vec{B}$, the area vector of the loop, $\vec{A}$, and the angle between these vectors, θ, at time, t. The flux through the loop is given by equation (1),

$$\Phi \equiv \vec{B} \cdot \vec{A} = BA\cos\theta,$$

where for constant ω we write, $\theta = \omega t = 2\pi t/T$. The latter equation assumes at time zero, $\theta = 0$. The magnetic flux at time t becomes,

$$\Phi(t) = BWL \cos\omega t.$$

At this point we want to determine the average induced voltage using equation (2). Consider the situation at a time Δt later than time t. The magnetic flux at time $t + \Delta t$ is

$$\Phi(t + \Delta t) = BWL \cos[\omega(t + \Delta t)] = BWL\cos[\omega t + \omega\Delta t].$$

The last result may be simplified using the trigonometry identity,

$$\cos(\theta + \phi) = \cos\theta \cos\phi - \sin\theta \sin\phi,$$

and we get

$$\Phi(t + \Delta t) = BWL[\cos\omega t \ \cos\omega\Delta t - \sin\omega t \ \sin\omega\Delta t].$$

So,

$$V_{\text{ave induced}} = \Delta\Phi/\Delta t =$$

$$\{BWL[\cos\omega t \ \cos\omega\Delta t - \sin\omega t \ \sin\omega\Delta t] - BWL \cos\omega t\}/\Delta t.$$

This result is exact but it is a big mess!

Suppose Δt is an extremely small quantity—something mathematicians call an infinitesimal. Then in radians, $\cos\omega t \rightarrow 1$ and $\sin\omega\Delta t \rightarrow \omega\Delta t$. If you are skeptical of this last statement, good! Use your calculator in radian mode to prove the cosine of a very small angle is about 1 while the sine is about equal to its (small) argument. Under these assumptions we have,

$$V_{\text{ave induced}} = \{BWL[\cos\omega t - \omega\Delta t \sin\omega t] - BWL \cos\omega t\}/\Delta t,$$

which simplifies to our final result, the AC *generator equation*:

$$V_{\text{induced}} = -\omega BA \sin\omega t. \tag{3}$$

In the last step you will notice the "ave" was stripped off. The reason is the average over Δt, when Δt is an infinitesimal, does not require the "ave" in front. Said another way, this last result gives you the exact or instantaneous induced voltage at the time t.

(For students who know calculus, you can take the derivative with respect to time of the magnetic flux, $\Phi(t)$ above, and use the chain rule as a shortcut to get Equation (3). If you haven't studied calculus before, just ignore the last sentence.)

The sign of the voltage alternates, and therefore, the generator causes alternating currents as illustrated in Figure 4.

FIG. 4. INDUCED VOLTAGE OUTPUT OF THE GENERATOR VERSUS TIME. NOTICE THE VARIATION IN THE SIGN OF THE VOLTAGE — WHICH CAUSES THE CURRENT TO ALTERNATE ITS DIRECTION OF MOTION.

Example Eight.—*Electrical generator: a numerical example.*

Use the generator equation from the previous example to estimate the magnetic field needed to generate the maximum output voltage from a home outlet.

Solution.

For a home circuit the frequency, $f = \omega/2\pi$ is 60 Hz and the maximum voltage is 120 Volts. Assuming one rotates a rectangular loop of dimensions $W = 21$ cm by $L = 21$ cm, then we begin with (ignoring the minus sign and using $A = WL$),

$$V_{\text{max induced}} = \omega BWL.$$

Solving this for B,

$$B = V_{\text{max induced}}/WL\omega = V_{\text{max induced}}/WL2\pi f.$$

And putting in the numbers,

$$B = 120/(0.21 \times 0.21 \times 2\pi \times 60) = \underline{7.22 \text{ Tesla.}}$$

This is a considerable magnetic field. In practice, instead of there being one loop of wire inside the generator there are thousands of loops. Therefore, the required magnetic field needed to generate the same maximum voltage is much smaller than 7 Tesla.

It turns out, an electric generator and an electric motor are actually the same device. In a motor, current is supplied to a loop of wire that is inside a magnetic field, and the field does work on the loop causing it to rotate. One uses the rotating loop to do mechanical work. Just the opposite holds for the generator. In the generator mechanical work is done to rotate a loop of wire that is inside a magnetic field. The rotating loop generates a voltage by the law of induction, and the induced voltage produces a current. So a motor is a generator operating backward and vice versa. To summarize:

	Electric Motor	Electric Generator
Input	current	work
Output	work	current

Another device that makes use of Faraday's induction law is the electrical transformer. A transformer consists of two coils of wire, the primary coil which has N_p loops of wire, and the secondary coil, which has N_s loops. A time-dependent voltage is supplied to the primary coil, V_p. The voltage produces a time-dependent current in the primary coil, and this current creates a time-dependent magnetic field according to Oersted's law. The device is designed in such a way that the magnetic field of the current in the primary coil passes through the coils in the secondary. This causes the magnetic flux inside the secondary coils to change with time since the primary voltage is changing with time. By Faraday's law of induction, a voltage is induced in the secondary, V_s. The logic is straightforward:

$$V_p(t) \rightarrow i_p(t) \rightarrow B(t) \rightarrow \Phi(t) \rightarrow V_s$$

These variables are related according to the *transformer equation*, but I won't prove this equation,

$$V_s / V_p = N_s / N_p. \tag{4}$$

If the secondary has more loops or turns than the primary ($N_s > N_p$) then the transformer is called a step-up transformer since then the secondary voltage is larger than that of the primary ($V_s > V_p$) in accordance with equation (4). Just the opposite holds for a step-down transformer.

Transformers are useful because they increase or decrease voltages in circuits. It is essential for utility companies to use step-up and step-down transformers. For example, transformers are ubiquitous in a city—just look at the number of transformers found on "telephone" poles. In this application one wants the voltage supplied to a home to be much smaller than the voltage produced at the generating plant and this means step-down transformers are needed.

The transformer plays no role if the primary current is DC since then no voltage would appear across the secondary. Why? Because the flux in the secondary would not change with time if the primary current is DC and by Faraday's law therefore, no induced voltage would be created in the secondary. One reason AC currents are used in homes instead of DC is because the power loss is less with AC than DC. The transformer plays an invaluable role in accomplishing these energy savings.

Example Nine.—*Transformers in home applications.*

A 120-volt AC outlet at home is connected to the primary coil of a toy electric train's transformer. The primary coil has 800 turns. (a) If it is desired for the output voltage of the transformer to be 12 Volts, then how many turns must there be in the secondary coil of the transformer? (b) Is the train transformer a step-up or step-down transformer?

Solution.

(a) We identify the following variables, $V_p = 120$ Volts, $V_s = 12$ Volts, $N_p = 800$, and desire to know, N_s. Solving equation (4) for the unknown and using these numbers gives,

$$N_s = N_p V_s / V_p = 800 \times 12/120 = \underline{80 \text{ turns}}.$$

(b) This is a step-down transformer because the secondary voltage has been stepped-down compared to that of the primary. Stated another way, since the number of turns in the secondary is smaller than those in the primary, this is a step-down transformer.

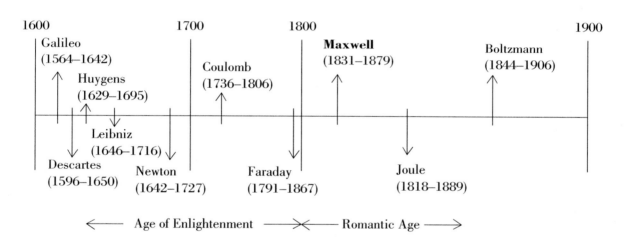

← Age of Enlightenment —✕— Romantic Age →

Courtesy of HIP/Art Resource, NY.

E. James Clerk Maxwell.

"All things excellent are as difficult as they are rare."
—Spinoza

James Clerk (pronounced "Clark") Maxwell (1831–1879) was the leading theoretical physicist of the nineteenth century. Most physicists today would agree that the three most influential physicists of all time have been, in chronological order, Newton, Maxwell and Einstein. Newton's most important work was in mechanics while Einstein contributed to the development of relativity and early quantum theory.

Maxwell's primary work was in the electromagnetic theory he extended and put in final form. James had an extraordinary scientific imagination bordering on magical. He often used analogies to uncover fundamental truths. Maxwell's accomplishments are even more startling given that he lived such a short time, having died at the young age of only forty-eight. His small frame—he was only five feet four inches tall—contrasts with his gigantic accomplishments in mathematical physics.

Maxwell was born, raised and spent much of his life in Scotland with his wealthy family. The father, an attorney, was well educated and had a keen interest in the sciences. Undoubtedly the father's scientific curiosity, as evidenced by his attendance (with young James) at the meetings of the Royal Society in Edinburgh, had a lasting impact on his son. Additional scientific mentors included the great Michael Faraday and William Thomson. The family holdings included a country estate in Scotland that they called Glenlair. A younger sister of James died in infancy, leaving him to be raised as an only child. Bright and of an inquisitive nature, young Maxwell's personality has been described as eccentric. He was not a child prodigy, however. His first schooling was provided by a private tutor who was on occasion rather abusive. The tutor seems to have had a lasting impression on Maxwell perhaps even adding to his life-long problem of stuttering when he spoke. Later, he attended the Edinburgh Academy where emphasis was placed on mathematics, physics and classical languages. The nickname given to him by his classmates at the Academy was "dafty" which means odd or weird. In spite of the persecution, Maxwell was at the top of his class at the Academy where he was especially drawn to the subjects of mathematics and classical literature. After the Academy he attended the University of Edinburgh for three years, majoring in natural philosophy (a phrase that is today the equivalent of physics). In 1850 at the age of nineteen, James began his studies at the prestigious Cambridge University in England. During this period he wrote his first research publication involving the field of electricity and magnetism and he developed a life-long interest in the theory of gases. Maxwell was an excellent student by all accounts. In fact, one professor felt that he had a nearly perfect physics intuition, saying it was "impossible for Maxwell to think incorrectly on physics subjects." He was a fast reader with an excellent memory and a very strong gift of concentration. On a more personal level, it was during his time at Cambridge when he began to stray from his Scottish Calvinistic background—his father was an Episcopalian and his mother a Presbyterian. Showing a rebellious streak, he joined a group of Christian Socialists at the University.

Maxwell's first significant job started in 1857 when he became the chair of the department of natural philosophy of Aberdeen University in Scotland. Part of his assignment included giving fifteen lectures a week—a strenuous teaching schedule indeed. In 1858 he married Katherine Dewar who was the daughter of another professor. Katherine was seven years older than James. She was ill most of her life both physically and mentally. In 1860 James moved his family to London where he took the position of professor of natural philosophy at King's College. His five years at Kings was his most productive period of physics research. Maxwell produced what are now called the four Maxwell equations (see next section) in addition to his important work on the statistical properties of ideal gases. Einstein believed the Maxwell equations to be enormously important because they unified three previously disparate areas: electricity, magnetism and light or optics. These equations also led Maxwell to infer the fundamental idea that light is an electromagnetic wave. Another interest of his was the field of color vision. While at Kings he took the world's first color photograph. During the period when Maxwell lived in London he met and became good friends with Michael Faraday.

In 1865 James left London to return to Scotland and the family estate. Because of his wealth he did not need to be employed. By this time Maxwell conducted physics research at home without the distraction of teaching. In 1870 he wrote a book in which he introduced Maxwell's demon. More will be said about the demon in the next chapter. However, James' most important book was written in 1873, *A Treatise on Electricity and Magnetism*. This massive publication was Maxwell's magnum opus. The work gave an up-to-date and authoritative account of the state of knowledge in the field of electromagnetism. At that time physicists believed the universe to be permeated by an invisible fluid called the ether. Maxwell thought light was an electromagnetic vibration of the ether. It was only a few decades after his death that the ether notion was laid to rest once and for all by the experiments of two American physicists.

Although Maxwell was a first-rate researcher, he was not a very good teacher. For example, his classes often drew only two or three students. Yet, his writing was excellent.

Let us conclude with a few notes pertaining to Maxwell's life outside of his physics interests. Besides the aforementioned areas of physics research, James was also very much attracted by the history of science, theology and theoretical mechanics. He was an exceptionally unselfish person who later in life once again became a faithful member of the Scottish Presbyterian Church. For Maxwell religion was always a private matter.

In 1879 Maxwell's life was cut short at the same age as that of his mother when she died, and for the same ailment, stomach cancer. Maxwell left no descendants.

References.

Same as those for Faraday.

F. Maxwell's Equations for the Electromagnetic Field.

The Maxwell equations are expressed in terms of some of the most complicated mathematics used by physicists, partial differential equations. This mathematics lies far beyond the level used in our textbook. In spite of these constraints, however, one may gain some appreciation for Maxwell's equations provided the mathematics is translated into ordinary language. Let us begin.

MAXWELL'S LAW ONE: Gauss' Law of Electricity.

Previously in this chapter the concept of magnetic flux passing through a surface A was defined. Recall, the magnetic flux through a surface is proportional to the number of magnetic lines of force passing through the surface. Just as for magnetism, so in electricity, the concept of *electric flux* passing through a surface A may be defined. We simply replace equation (1) by,

$$\Phi \equiv \vec{E} \cdot \vec{A} = EA\cos\theta. \quad (\vec{E} \text{ constant}) \tag{5}$$

In equation (5), $\vec{E}$ is the constant electric field at the surface represented by $\vec{A}$ and θ is the angle between the electric field and the vector $\vec{A}$. Recall, $\vec{A}$ is a vector that is perpendicular to the surface and of magnitude equal to the area of the surface. Once again, if the field is not constant then the flux is found using integral calculus.

One more item before we can state Maxwell's first law. A *closed surface* is a surface that has no holes in it, or stated another way, it is a surface that completely surrounds a region of space. Think, for example, of the surface of a baseball, basketball or football. None of these has holes—if they did the air would rush out. We now have all the background needed to understand Maxwell's first law—a relation first proven in 1839 by the German mathematician and physicist, Carl Friedrich Gauss:

The electric flux passing through a closed surface equals the net charge enclosed by the surface, or, written in symbols,

$$\Phi_{\text{closed surface}}(\text{of } \vec{E}) = q_{\text{net}}/\varepsilon_0. \tag{6}$$

Don't worry about the universal constant ε_0 that appears in equation (6) since it is simply a number that comes from experimental measurements. By net charge (q_{net}) we mean, add up all the positive and negative charges enclosed by the closed surface A_{closed}, where the positive charges have positive signs and the negative charges have negative signs. Equation (6) implies the more net charge inside, the greater the number of lines of electric field passing through the surface.

MAXWELL'S LAW TWO: Gauss' Law of Magnetism.

The second law is like unto the first, only it deals with the magnetic field and is simpler.

The magnetic flux passing through a closed surface equals zero, or, written in symbols,

$$\Phi_{\text{closed surface}}(\text{of } \vec{B}) = 0. \tag{7}$$

Equations (6) and (7) are the source of one of the remaining great mysteries of physics. For example, if I put a proton inside a basketball then by equation (6) there will be an electric flux passing through the surface of the ball. Consider doing the analogous thing with magnetism. Take a bar magnet and cut it in half and I get a north pole and a south pole as sketched in Figure 5(a) below. Next, throw away the south pole, and place the north pole inside the basketball. By analogy with the proton, the north pole should produce a magnetic flux passing through the surface of the ball. However, that violates equation (7) which states emphatically that the magnetic flux should be zero. The only logical way out of this dilemma is to say one cannot cut a magnet in half and thereby separate the north pole from the south pole. But I hear an objection since anyone can obtain a bar magnet and a hacksaw and cut the magnet in half! But it is found when this happens what is left is not a north pole and a separate south pole, but two new bar magnets are created, as illustrated Figure 5(c):

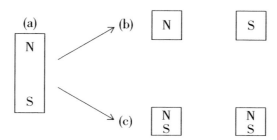

FIG. 5. (A) A BAR MAGNET. (B) THE BAR MAGNET IS CUT IN HALF.
(C) TWO NEW BAR MAGNETS ARE CREATED.

Therefore, one can never find a north pole by itself. A single pole is called a monopole. An equivalent statement of Maxwell's second law is the following statement:

It is impossible to find an isolated magnetic monopole in nature.

MAXWELL'S LAW THREE: Faraday's Law of Electromagnetic Induction.

The third law has been the primary topic of this chapter and needs very little further elucidation other than a slight restatement. The law of induction we have studied so far states that a changing magnetic flux produces an induced voltage. Another way of expressing this law is in terms of magnetic and electric fields. The magnetic flux obviously involves the magnetic field. The induced voltage arises from an induced electric field. The field theory statement of law three is:

A time-dependent magnetic field produces an induced electric field.

MAXWELL'S LAW FOUR: Ampere's Law as Modified by Maxwell.

The first three laws were well understood before Maxwell performed his work. Maxwell's first contribution to these laws was to modify Ampere's law. Maxwell was familiar with the work of both Ampere and Oersted. Here is a way of expressing Ampere's law in non-mathematical language:

Ampere's law is an equation that may be used to mathematically calculate the magnetic field produced by an electric current.

Maxwell thought about this statement and Faraday's law and he came up with a remarkable idea based on symmetrical thinking. Maxwell reasoned, if a time-dependent magnetic field produces an induced electric field (Faraday's law), then why can't a time-dependent electric field produce an induced magnetic field? The term containing the time-dependent electric field was named a ***displacement current*** by Maxwell. This reasoning was both insightful, and more importantly, confirmed by experiments. The non-mathematical statement of the fourth law follows:

A magnetic field arises from an electric current (Oersted-Ampere) and from a time-dependent electric field (Maxwell's displacement current).

Example Ten.—*Parallel-plates and a coil as sources of uniform E(t) and B(t).*

Qualitatively discuss the fields present between parallel charged plates and inside a current-carrying coil.

Solution.

Consider two large plates (see below) that are parallel and have final charges q and $-q$. It is found that there is a constant electric field between the plates. If the amount of charge gradually goes from zero to the final values of q and $-q$ then the electric field will go from zero to its final value. As the electric field increases (a "displacement current") an induced magnetic field appears. The lines of magnetic field form concentric circles inside the region between the plates.

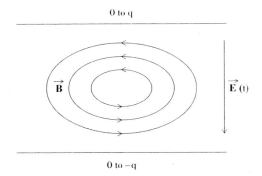

A coil that carries an electric current I produces a uniform magnetic field inside the coil. A cross-sectional view of the coil is shown below. As the current goes from zero to the final value I, the magnetic field will go from zero to its final value. As the magnetic field increases an induced electric field appears. The lines of electric field form concentric circles inside the coil.

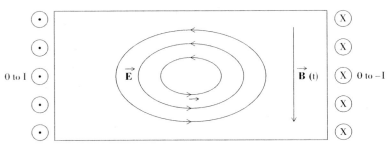

These are the famous Maxwell equations. At first sight one might wonder why they are named after Maxwell? Other than modify Ampere's law with the introduction of a displacement current, what did Maxwell accomplish that was so significant? His second contribution and most important one was to work with these four equations and from them mathematically prove that light is an electromagnetic wave having certain properties. What the properties are is the subject of the next section.

G. Application: The Anatomy, Spectrum, and Creation of Light.

Based on his four equations of the previous section, Maxwell demonstrated that both the electric and magnetic fields obey a well-known fundamental equation of physics, the wave equation. All wave phenomena may be related to an underlying wave equation. Moreover, our hero deduced that the speed of the electric and magnetic waves is that of light. This led him to assert that light is a wave consisting of vibrating electric and magnetic fields. The changing electric field produces the magnetic field, while the changing magnetic field produces the electric field. His equations further elucidate the structure of light: the fields making up the light, $\vec{E}$ and $\vec{B}$, must be perpendicular to each other and both are perpendicular to the direction of motion of the wave. The anatomy of light Maxwell uncovered is illustrated in Figure 6 where c is the symbol for the speed of light and specifies the direction of motion of the wave. Both fields vary according to a sine function.

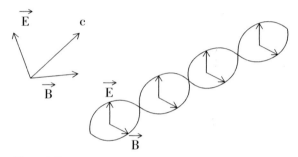

FIG. 6. LIGHT CONSISTS OF AN ELECTRIC FIELD THAT IS PERPENDICULAR TO A MAGNETIC FIELD WITH BOTH MOVING WITH THE SPEED OF LIGHT c IN A DIRECTION PERPENDICULAR TO THE FIELDS.

As in all wave phenomena, the wave speed, c, the frequency, f, and the wavelength, λ, are related by the wave relation,

$$c = f\lambda. \tag{8}$$

In equation (8), the speed of light (in vacuum) was found experimentally to have the numerical value,

$$c = 3 \times 10^8 \text{ m/s}, \tag{9}$$

a truly astronomical speed. The work of Maxwell provided the crowning achievement for the wave theory of light. Several decades later physicists' understanding of light became more murky due to certain unsettling experiments which seemed to imply that a light ray is a collection of particles called photons. But that story is for a different time.

Returning to the wave theory of light, Equation (8) allows us to spread before our eyes the electromagnetic spectrum shown in Figure 7.

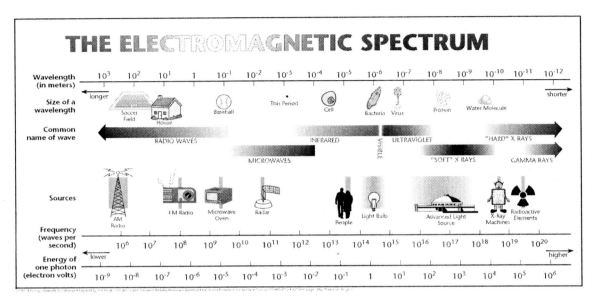

FIG. 7. THE ELECTROMAGNET SPECTRUM.
Courtesy of the Advanced Light Source, Lawrence Berkely National Lab. http://www.lbl.gov/MicroWorlds/ALSTool/EMSpec/EMSpec2.html.

All of these electromagnetic waves move with the same speed, c. The waves are all identical but for their wavelength and frequency. But the waves have much different interactions with matter. By way of summary, consider a few comments about the waves from each portion of the spectrum. Of course, the boundaries separating the various regions of the spectrum are artificial. We begin our journey through the spectrum starting with short wavelengths and continue to the longest wavelengths.

Gamma Rays: These are produced by nuclear reactions and have wavelengths that are about 300 times the size of an atomic nucleus (300×10^{-15} m). Gamma rays are often an important product of the decay of nuclei—they are a harmful component of radioactivity. Stay away from them if you can, although they are used in medicine for radiation treatment of cancer patients since they can destroy tumors.

X-Rays: These are produced by electronic transitions inside an atom and have wavelengths that are about 30 times the size of atoms (30×10^{-10} m). Everyone who has visited a dentist knows how x-rays are used. X-rays may also be formed when a charged particle is rapidly accelerated.

Ultraviolet: These are a major component of sunlight. The wavelength is about 30 nm. The motion of electrons inside an atom produce uv waves. For most people, other than your author who only burns, UV causes the skin to tan. Harmful UV light is partially adsorbed by the ozone layer.

Visible: This is everyone's favorite region since we have built-in detectors for these rays— our eyes. Blue light has a wavelength of about 300 nm while at the other end of the rainbow red light has a wavelength of 700 nm. Sometimes the word "light" means specifically visible light but other times "light" stands for the entire electromagnetic spectrum. The sense in which the word is being used is guessed from the context. Visible light is produced by the motion of electrons inside atoms—for example, when an electron moves between quantum energy levels of the atom.

Infrared: IR is sometimes called heat or thermal radiation since it arises due to the vibration of atoms and molecules inside hot objects like a stove. Their wavelength is about 30 μm. The military has some neat equipment that allows one to see at night because the equipment detects IR light.

Microwaves
and Radar: Microwaves and radar have wavelengths of a few cm. An example given below gives more information about how microwave ovens work. You are probably already familiar with one use of radar from your last speeding ticket.

Radio and TV: The wavelength for radio and TV waves ranges from a few meters to a few thousand meters. There are various subintervals or regions that separate AM, FM and TV waves that are called bands. Radio waves are produced by vibrating charges in an antenna. Unless you are an alien or have lived your whole life in a cave, you can take a wild guess as to how these waves are used. (AM is a wasteland, FM has all the best music.)

Example Eleven.—*Frequency of the various kinds of EMR.*

Use the information provided in our just completed journey and equation (8) to find the typical frequency associated with the various waves of the electromagnetic spectrum.

Solution.

Rearranging equation (8) we get the inverse-proportionality between frequency and wavelength,

$$f = c/\lambda = 3 \times 10^8/\lambda.$$

Plugging in the appropriate wavelengths mentioned in the journey through the spectrum gives:

EMR	Typical Wavelength(m)	Frequency(Hz)
Gamma	300×10^{-15}	10^{21}
X-ray	30×10^{-10}	10^{17}
UV	30×10^{-9}	10^{16}
VIS	Blue 300×10^{-9}	10^{15}
IR	30×10^{-6}	10^{13}
Microwave/radar	0.03	10^{10}
Radio to TV	3000 to 3	10^5 to 10^8

Example Twelve.—*Microwave ovens.*

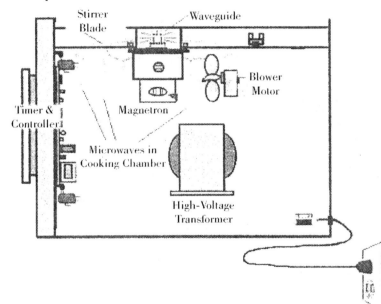

Courtesy John C. Gallawa, The Complete Microwave Oven Service Handbook on CD-ROM, Copyright © 1996–2007.

Microwave ovens illustrate many of the main ideas of this and previous chapters. The microwaves generated inside the oven cook food from the inside out because the power they deliver is absorbed by the water inside the food. This absorption works because of the electric dipole moment of the water molecules. Just as a compass needle (a magnetic dipole) rotates to line up with a magnetic field, a water molecule (like an electric "compass") lines up with the electric field of the microwaves. But the electric field oscillates, and therefore, so do the water molecules as they rock back and forth. The rotating molecules collide with their neighbors thereby giving the neighbor energy. This is what causes the food to get hot.

On the other hand, any object that does not contain water (or other polar molecules) will not be heated by the oven. For example, because of the free charges inside a metal, microwaves are reflected by a metal surface rather than absorbed. The walls of the oven are metallic in order to reflect the microwaves. A standing wave pattern is formed inside the oven. A problem with placing a metallic object inside arises if the object has any sharp points. In such a case, sparks tend to be created at the sharp points. This occurs because the metallic free charges easily respond to the electric field of the microwaves and consequently, there is a tendency for the charges to move toward the sharp points of the metallic surface. If too many charges accumulate at a sharp point then the charges create a large electric field at that point and a spark is produced as these charges discharge. Even placing a smooth piece of metal in the oven may be dangerous if the metal has a large resistance since then the current created in the metal by the microwaves causes the metal to heat up significantly as described by the relation, $P = I^2R$.

The microwave oven consists of the following key parts: high-voltage power supply, magnetron, waveguide, fan, and the outer encasement. The voltage source powers the magnetron. The magnetron is a vacuum tube which consists of two types of circuit elements, a capacitor and an inductor, which together is called a tank circuit. The field of the voltage source causes charges to vibrate inside the magnetron much like a mass on a spring and this creates the microwaves. The magnetron uses about 700 W of power to produce the microwaves. Once the waves are produced they are directed to their desired location by a waveguide, which is basically a metal pipe. The frequency of the typical microwave in a microwave oven is $f =$ 2.45 GHz.

(a) Find the wavelength of the microwaves in the oven.

(b) From the above narrative try to account for the fact that often objects placed inside the oven are cooked unevenly.

Solution.

(a) Solving equation (8) for the wavelength we have,

$$\lambda = c/f = 3 \times 10^8 / 2.45 \times 10^9 = \underline{12.2 \text{ cm.}}$$

(b) The key to why there might be uneven heating is two-fold. First, the microwaves form standing wave patterns inside the oven. With standing waves there are points called nodes where the electric field of the waves cancels out. Any food situated at a node would not heat up. This is why in real ovens the food is made to rotate inside. Secondly, if the food is partially frozen then the regions where ice is present inside the food do not absorb the microwaves as well as liquid regions. The reason for this is, the ice molecules are not as free to rotate as the liquid state water molecules.

For more details, see *How Things Work, The Physics of Everyday Life*, Louis A. Bloomfield, (Wiley, 1997), Section 14.3.

One final comment. In the first book of the Bible, Genesis, we read in chapter 1 verse 3 how the first thing God created was light, "And God said let there be light; and there was light." After the creation of light, matter was created. In physics this order is reversed: to create light one has to accelerate an electric charge (matter). Now you know how light is made!

Summary.

Michael Faraday and James Clerk Maxwell contributed significantly to the theory of electromagnetism. Magnetic flux and induced voltage are the key ideas underlying Faraday's law of electromagnetic induction. Two applications of this law are to electric generators and transformers. The four Maxwell equations are the foundation of electromagnetic theory. Maxwell added the displacement current term to Ampere's law and deduced the structure and nature of light based on his four mathematical equations and the wave equation that follows from these four. The electromagnetic spectrum is divided into regions that extend from the lowest wavelength (gamma) all the way to long wavelength radio waves.

QUESTIONS.

1. Given a bar magnet and a loop of wire. List the ways you may cause the magnetic flux passing through the loop to change with time.

2. The smaller circle in the diagram below has a magnetic field (out of the page) passing through it. The lights are connected by a conducting wire (the outer circle). Why are the lights on even though no battery is present?

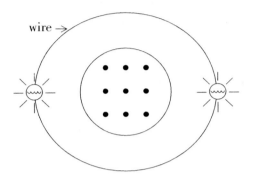

3. A highly conducting wire is placed between points P and Q in the previous question. See diagram below. What happens?

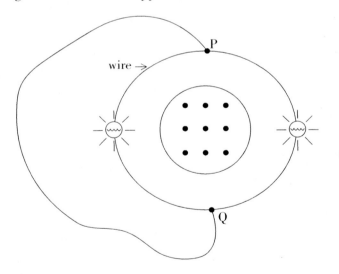

(a) The bulb on the left goes out

(b) The bulb on the right goes out

(c) Both bulbs go out

(d) Both bulbs stay on

(e) Need more information to answer the question

4. In the circuit below the switch is closed. The potential difference across the resistor R becomes (*a*) VN_p/N_s, (*b*) VN_s/N_p, (*c*) V, (*d*) zero, (*e*) not enough information

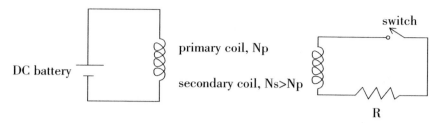

5. In the circuit below immediately after the switch is closed, in the secondary coil appears (*a*) zero current, (*b*) a finite current for a short time, (*c*) a steady current, (*d*) an alternating current

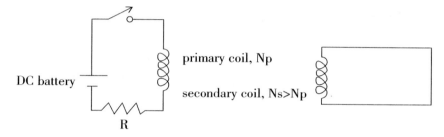

6. Faraday's law of induction has numerous everyday applications. Use the internet to find applications of this law in the operation of (i) pick up coils of an electric guitar (ii) a speaker and a microphone (iii) a credit card strip and (iv) tape recorder

7. Injecting the north pole of a magnet into a loop of wire causes current to appear in the wire. Name two ways you could cause the current to appear but moving in the opposite direction.

8. A car battery is a 12 V source. The voltage needed to create a spark inside the car's spark plugs requires thousands of volts. How can this be?

9. A loop of wire is rotated in a constant magnetic field. What happens to the maximum induced voltage if the frequency of rotation is tripled?

10. One of the early controversies in the commercialization of electricity involved a dispute over whether AC or DC is better. Why do you suppose AC won the dispute? Hint: can you use DC with a transformer?

11. If you rotate the shaft of an electric motor what happens inside the coils of wire?

12. Find the book *The Mysterious Island* by Jules Verne and describe the electric generator the castaways built in the book.

13. Why is a generator coil harder to rotate when the generator produces a current in a closed circuit than when nothing is attached to the generator?

14. Look up on the internet about how electric cars generate their voltages. Do they only use batteries or do they also use other kinds of electric generators?

15. As white light passes through air, blue light is scattered more than red light. Show how this explains why the sky near the horizon is red near sunset while the sky is blue overhead.

16. Compare the wavelength of the middle of the FM band to that of the AM band.

17. Why was sound not listed as part of the electromagnetic spectrum?

18. What is the source of radio waves that are emitted by a radio transmission antenna?

19. When the radio announcer says this is "FM 89.9" what frequency is that?

20. Use the internet to learn how AM and FM differ.

21. What evidence can you cite that proves electromagnetic waves travel through a vacuum?

22. Galileo tried to measure the speed of light using two lanterns. He had a lantern and on a nearby mountain his friend had a lantern. They started with both lanterns covered. Galileo uncovered his lantern and then when his friend noticed this he uncovered his lantern. Galileo tried measuring the time for the light to go from his location, to his friend and back to himself. Why do you suppose this did not work even though in principle it should?

PROBLEMS.

1. A sheet of paper has dimensions of 21.0 cm by 30.0 cm and is placed in a constant magnetic field of 1.50 Tesla. A side view is shown below. The vector $\vec{A}$ is the area vector. Determine the magnetic flux passing through the sheet assuming the angle θ in the figure is 35°.

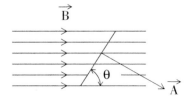

2. A sheet of paper resides in the plane of this page and has the shape of an equilateral triangle of side 10.0 cm. It is placed in a magnetic field of 2.00 Tesla out of this page. Find the magnetic flux through the triangle.

3. The Earth's magnetic field has a magnitude of 5.0×10^{-5} Tesla and makes an angle of 20° with the plane of a car window. The area of the window is 600.0 cm². Find the magnetic flux through the window.

4. A magnetic field of 7.00 Tesla makes an angle of 30° with the plane of a circular loop of wire of radius 15.0 cm. Determine the magnetic flux through the loop.

5. Imagine a dime rotates in the magnetic field of the Earth (5.0×10^{-5} Tesla) with a period of 0.5 s. Use Faraday's law of induction to determine the maximum induced voltage in the dime.

6. A circular loop of wire begins with its plane parallel to the Earth's magnetic field (5.0×10^{-5} Tesla). During a time interval of 0.50 s the loop is rotated 90° so that its plane is perpendicular to the field. Determine the radius of the loop such that the average induced voltage is 12.0 volts.

7. A circular loop of wire has a radius of 10.0 cm and begins with its plane parallel to a magnetic field of 7.00 Tesla. During a time interval of 0.50 s the loop is rotated 90° so that its plane is perpendicular to the field. Determine the average induced voltage.

8. A magnetic field varies with time, according to

$$B(t) = 1.20 + 0.1\ t,\ \text{where } t \text{ is in seconds and } B \text{ in Tesla.}$$

This field passes through a square of sides 0.13 cm. Find the average induced voltage from time 0.50 s to 1.20 s.

9. A 1.20 m long wire is attached to rails and moves toward the right with a constant speed of 2.00 cm/s as shown. There is a uniform 3.00 Tesla magnetic field pointing out of the page. Find the average induced voltage.

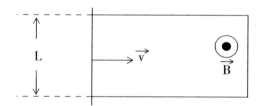

10. A square of sides 15.0 cm resides in the plane of this paper and moves toward the right with a speed of 10.0 cm/s. The square encounters a region of uniform magnetic field of 2.00 Tesla pointing out of this page. As the square enters the region where the field is present, determine the average induced voltage in the square.

11. An electric generator uses a magnetic field of 3.00 Tesla and a square loop of side 20.0 cm that has a period of rotation of 0.25 s. Find the maximum induced voltage in the loop.

12. An electric generator uses a magnetic field of 3.00 Tesla and a square loop of side 20.0 cm. Find the period of rotation in order to have a maximum induced voltage in the loop of 120.0 V.

13. A transformer steps up the voltage from 120 V to 12,000 V. What is the ratio of secondary turns to primary turns?

14. A transformer has 100 turns in its primary coil and a primary voltage of 120.0 V. Determine the number of turns needed in the secondary coil for the secondary voltage to be that needed for a toy train, 12.0 V.

15. Use Gauss' Law for Electricity (Maxwell's First Law) to answer this question. An electric dipole is placed inside a basketball of radius 10.0 cm. Calculate the electric flux through the ball's surface.

16. Use Gauss' Law for Magnetism (Maxwell's Second Law) to answer this question. A magnetic dipole is placed inside a basketball of radius 10.0 cm. Calculate the magnetic flux through the ball's surface.

17. A He-Ne laser operates with light of wavelength 621 nm. Find the frequency of the laser.

18. The human eye is most sensitive to light of wavelength of about 5,500 Angstroms. Determine the frequency of such light.

19. During a medical procedure x-rays of wavelength 2.5×10^{-11} m are used. Determine the frequency of the x-rays.

20. A particular AM radio station uses radio waves of frequency 54 kHz. What is the wavelength of the radio waves?

21. What is the wavelength of the radiation produced by a 60.0 Hz wall outlet?

22. How much time would it take for an electromagnetic signal to go to the moon and back?

23. Cobalt-60 is a radioactive isotope often used in nuclear medicine. It emits a gamma ray of wavelength 1.06×10^{-12} m. Find the frequency of this ray.

24. The UV rays that cause suntan(burn) have a wavelength of 300 nm. Find the frequency.

Hints and answers to problems.

1) 0.0542 T-m² Hint: what is the angle between $\vec{B}$ and $\vec{A}$ in the figure? It isn't θ in the figure!
2) 0.00866 T-m²   3) 1.03 × 10⁻⁶ T-m²   4) 0.247 T-m²   5) Hint: see equation (3) 4.9 × 10⁻⁸ V
6) 195 m   7) 0.44 V   8) 1.69 × 10⁻⁷ V   9) Hint: this is a *motional emf*, see example six. 0.072 V
10) 0.03 V   11) 3.02 V   12) 0.0063 s   13) 100   14) 10   15) 0   16) 0   17) 4.83 × 10¹⁴ Hz
18) 5.45 × 10¹⁴ Hz   19) 1.2 × 10¹⁹ Hz   20) 5,600 m   21) 5 million m   22) 2.56 s
23) 2.83 × 10²⁰ Hz   24) 10¹⁵ Hz

SECTION VI.

HEAT.

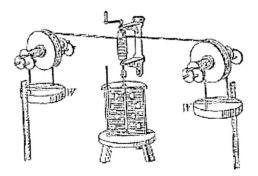

Joule's first experiment on the mechanical equivalent of heat.

CHAPTER XII.

INTERNAL RANDOM MOTIONS IN COMPLEX SYSTEMS.

Abstract.
We begin with some background centering on the influence of mechanics on society at large and how mechanics had to be broadened to model complex systems. The internal energy of a system is defined in terms of internal potential energies of its interacting particles and the random kinetic energy of the particles. Temperature is introduced along with temperature scales and this leads to the definition of heat. The central model of the theory of heat (thermodynamics) is that of the ideal gas. For isolated systems, law one of the theory of heat is an expression of energy conservation while law two is a statement of entropy increase. The life and work of two nineteenth century physicists is reviewed, Joule and Boltzmann. The chapter concludes by examining two mysteries, the reversal paradox and the recurrence paradox.

Definitions. internal energy, temperature, operational definition, temperature scales, heat, thermodynamics, superconductor, specific heat, linear thermal expansion, entropy, reversible and irreversible processes, heat conduction

Principles. first and second laws of thermodynamics

Fundamental Equations. ideal gas law, thermodynamic and statistical entropy

"The ultimate aim of physical science must be to find the movements which are the real causes of all other phenomena and to determine the motive forces upon which these movements depend. In other words, its aim is to reduce all phenomena to mechanics."

—*Hermann von Helmholtz (a 19th-century physicist)*

The physics of Isaac Newton had ramifications far outside the narrow pursuit of modeling simple physical systems. Indeed, some have noted that his work was one of the primary forces behind the development of the period in the 1700s known as the Enlightenment. Enlightenment thought centers on the belief that the world is fully rational and well ordered. Abstractness and universal principles were emphasized. Symmetry in nature and art was also important to this period. But above all else, reason was the watchword of the day, as is evident by another phrase used to denote this period of history, the Age of Reason. These enthusiastic optimists argued reason would lead the world onward and upward toward a utopian society.

In eighteenth century physics the concept of force was the watchword since force seemed to explain everything. This abstract and universalistic concept was in perfect harmony with enlightenment ideals. Not surprisingly, Newtonian physics was a major influence on the thought of enlightenment philosophers such as John Locke. The writings of Locke were especially important because they were influential in helping to mold the views of many of the founders of the United States. But as in so many cases, things began to be taken to extremes. The most prominent example of rationalist extremism is that of the violent radicals of the late eighteenth century French Revolution who displaced their King by enthroning the goddess of reason. In short, people were taking reason very seriously by the end of the eighteenth century, perhaps too seriously.

By the early 1800s the pendulum of public opinion was beginning to shift toward a new mood which stood in contrast and as a challenge to the extremes of Enlightenment rationality. This mood looked upon the Age of Reason and the parallel technological developments of the industrial revolution as being too mechanistic, too law abiding, simplistic, sterile and virtually lifeless. The critics pointed out that the enlightenment proponents gave too little thought to such things as beauty, emotion, intuition, imagination, evil, and the concreteness of everyday lives. In contrast to the Enlightenment, the new Romantic Age placed more emphasis precisely on those things neglected by the rationalists. Things like disorder, creativity, complexity, consciousness, individuality, independence, and freedom came to dominance in romantic circles. In the area of religion the romantics placed greater stress on the immanence of God in contrast with the enlightenment thinkers who stressed God's transcendence. The more extreme rationalists became deists who basically believed God created the world and then took an extended vacation, leaving the world to operate according to natural laws. In the fields of literature and music, during the first half of the 1800s, romantic poets and German "nature-philosophers" such as Goethe and Schiller exerted considerable influence.

Even scientific thought was not immune to these romantic spirits. The Newtonian mechanistic worldview had to also compete with new theories emerging in eighteenth century physics—theories that were more in tune with the romantic currents swirling about. The concepts of energy and entropy were developed and placed in their final form during the romantic period. More than force, energy and entropy were well suited to the predilections and style of the romantics. Instead of modeling the world as a machine, such as a clock, the romantics favored the thought that the world is more akin to a giant organism. Along these lines, man is more than simply cold particles in motion.

Even the "dismal" field of economics was not immune to these competing world views. We offer as evidence a passage on page 100 of *New Ideas From Dead Economists* by Todd G. Buchholz (Plume, 2007):

Just as (John Stuart) Mill floundered in the intellectual tide called rationalism, he was saved by an undertow called romanticism. In his *Birth of Tragedy*, Nietzsche depicted two powerful forces clashing in the human psyche: Apollonian and Dionysian. Apollo is the spirit of reason, order, and Mozart symphonies. Dionysius is the spirit of caprice, emotion, and Puccini operas. When eighteenth century rationalism drove Mill to despair, he turned to the poetry of Wordsworth and even Coleridge.

As romanticism gained ground it eventually influenced all of the arts and sciences. Moreover, the ideas of the enlightenment and romantic thinkers were more than passing fads but rather were movements that had engaged in struggle since the times of the ancient Greeks and continue to the present day.

We see then, the romantics argued the world is far more complicated than what we have indicated to this point in this text. Therefore, in this last chapter we undertake a major departure. Up until now we have concentrated on the motion of relatively simple systems. Newton's laws of motion were sufficient for such systems. In this chapter we consider the physics of many particle systems that will require new principles to be understood.

References.

Issues in Science and Religion, Ian G. Barbour (Harper, 1966). See especially chapter 3.
The Project Physics Course, Rutherford, Holton, and Watson (Holt, Rhinehart and Winston, 1970).

A. What Are Temperature, Heat, and Internal Energy?

In this chapter we continue with the central theme of this book—the idea that motion is the foundation of all of classical physics. Up to this point we have examined many kinds of motion: ancient Greek views of motion, free fall, projectiles, circular motion, vibrations, wave motion, motion of a mass under the force of universal gravitation, constants of motion, the motion of charged particles in electric and magnetic fields, and the acceleration of charges as the means of producing electromagnetic radiation. The new orientation of this chapter is to attempt to understand the random or complex motion of particles that make up a system that contains many particles.

Although the adjective "random" has been used, from a Newtonian perspective there is no such thing. Once the initial conditions are given for a collection of particles and the forces acting on and between the particles are known then the system evolves in time in a completely deterministic fashion. In view of modern developments in chaos theory we know how slight changes in the initial conditions can bring amount major changes in behavior. Perhaps instead of using the word "random," a better choice might be "complicated." In any event, it is hard to predict the behavior of systems made of many particles except in certain special situations.

The many-particle system we will fixate on is that of a gas inside a cylinder that is fitted with a piston. The reason for the importance of this system is historical. The gas-cylinder system was of central importance during the industrial revolution of the nineteenth century. During this period, the newly invented steam engine became as important then as the computer is today. In addition, in the twentieth century the development of the gasoline and diesel engines provide reason for the importance of the gas-cylinder system to fundamental physics.

This leads us to the question, what forms of energy are present in a gas? If the cylinder is moving as a whole then the gas will have translational kinetic energy. But translational energy is not the focus of this chapter. Rather, we are interested in the random motion of the atoms. Random kinetic energy is one of the primary ingredients of what is called the internal energy of a system. In addition, the atoms generally interact with each other—a form of internal potential energy. Therefore, the **internal energy** of a many-particle system, such as a gas, is defined as the random internal kinetic energy plus the internal potential energy of interaction between the particles of the system.

Internal Energy

$$E_{int} \equiv K_{random} + V_{int} \tag{1}$$

Another basic concept of many-particle physics is that of temperature. The point of view adopted here is to define **temperature** as a property of a system that is measured by an ordinary thermometer. This definition is an example of what philosophers of science call an **operational definition**, by which they mean defining a quantity by the precise steps that are needed to measure the quantity. It was only later in the development of statistical physics that temperature became understood on a more microscopic level as a measure of the random kinetic energy of atoms.

Recall there are three temperature scales that are in use: Fahrenheit, Celsius, and Kelvin (or Absolute). Of course, Fahrenheit is familiar since it is the scale used in everyday life in the US. Water boils at 212° F and freezes at 32° F, which means there are (212–32 =) 180 degrees between these two points. In medical fields it is common to use the Celsius scale defined by 100° C for boiling water, 0° C for freezing water, and 100° between these points. Often one must convert a temperature in Fahrenheit to the equivalent temperature in Celsius or vice versa using the formula (derived in Example one below),

$$°F = 9/5° \, C + 32. \tag{2}$$

Example One.—*Origin of Equation (2).*

Show where equation (2) comes from.

Solution.

Consider the graph below where we have plotted °F versus °C using the two points (32° F = 0° C and 212° F = 100° C) and assuming a linear relationship.

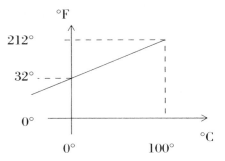

The equation for a straight line is $y = mx + b$, where b is the y-intercept and m is the slope of the line. The y-intercept in the graph is 32° and the slope is found by using the two points,

$$m = \text{rise/run} = (212° - 32°)/(100° - 0°) = 1.8 = 9/5.$$

Making the substitutions in the formula for the straight line, $y = mx + b$,

$$y \rightarrow \text{°F} \quad x \rightarrow \text{°C} \quad b \rightarrow 32° \quad m \rightarrow 9/5 \text{ gives,}$$

$$\text{°F} = 9/5 \text{ °C} + 32°.$$

To take a numerical case, this equation gives the amusing result, –40° C equals –40°F.

There is a third temperature scale, the Kelvin or Absolute scale, and it is the most important scale for work in **thermodynamics**, which is the study of heat. Before the advent of quantum mechanics in the twentieth century, people believed at absolute zero all atomic motion ceases. In classical physics we can continue to say at zero Kelvin all motion ceases. The Celsius and Absolute scales are related by

$$\text{K} = \text{°C} + 273. \tag{3}$$

(For an interesting short review of the history of temperature scales see, *The Mechanical Universe: Introduction to Mechanics and Heat*, Richard P. Olenick, Tom M. Apostol, and David L. Goodstein (Cambridge UP, 1985), pp. 299–300.)

So, there we have it, two basic concepts of thermodynamics are internal energy and temperature and the latter may be stated using one of the three temperature scales.

Example Two.—*The "Woodstock of Physics."*

In 1987 the first high-temperature *superconductors* were discovered. These ceramic-like compounds, abbreviated '123' by physicists, have the property that below a certain temperature their electrical resistance vanishes. The temperature where the resistance vanishes is called the transition temperature, T_c. Above T_c the materials behave like ordinary electrical conductors or semiconductors while below T_c the materials are superconducting. The value of T_c for 123 is around 110 K, and so 123 is called a high-T_c compound. Before 1987 the highest transition temperature known was about 25 K.

(a) Determine the value of 123's T_c (110 K) in Celsius and Fahrenheit.

(b) Given the results in (a), why is 123 called a high-T_c?

Solution.

(a) By equation (3), $\text{K} = \text{°C} + 273,$

which gives $\text{°C} = \text{K} - 273 = 110 - 273 = \underline{-163° \text{ C}},$

and by equation (2) we find $\text{°F} = 9/5 \text{ °C} + 32 = 1.8(-163) + 32 = \underline{-261° \text{ F}}.$

(b) Clearly, –261° F is not literally a "high temperature" but compared to previous transition temperatures it certainly is. Moreover, 110 K is considerably above the temperature of liquid nitrogen (77 K). This means placing 123 in liquid nitrogen will make it superconducting. Before the high-T_c's were discovered superconductors could only be created by placing materials in liquid helium, which is at 4.2 K. Liquid nitrogen is much less expensive than liquid helium, and this increases the likelihood of using superconductors in applications. However, progress in the applications of superconductivity has been much slower than people anticipated when the high-T_c's were first discovered. Superconductivity remains a continuing area of physics research. (The March 1988 meeting of the American Physical Society in New York City was heavily attended and was where the first reports of the high-T_c discovery were made; thus the name the "Woodstock of Physics.")

Another basic thermodynamic concept is heat, denoted Q. To give some indication of how the meaning of words change with time, consider the definition of heat given in the original version of the *Encyclopaedia Britannica* from 1769:

> **Heat**, in the animal economy, known by the several names of natural heat, vital heat, innate heat, and animal heat, is commonly supposed to be that generated by the attrition of the parts of the blood, occasioned by its circulatory motion, especially in the arteries.

To define heat as the term is used today it is necessary to consider two systems, for example, two containers of gas denoted system A and system B. Each system will have an amount of internal energy and will be at a certain temperature, T_A and T_B. Suppose the two systems are placed in contact. When this is done it is found the system with the higher temperature cools while the system at the lower temperature warms up. Eventually, the two systems reach a common final temperature called the equilibrium temperature. This phenomenon is understood by observing that the internal energy of the originally hotter system is lowered while the internal energy of the originally cooler system is raised. Therefore, there has been a net transfer of internal energy from the hot body to the cold body. The transfer of internal energy due to a temperature difference is called **heat**.

Accordingly, heat is not the temperature or the internal energy of a system but an energy transfer process. Perhaps an analogy is in order. Consider a lake. At any given moment the lake contains a certain amount of water. Think of the water as analogous to the internal energy of a system. If a storm arises, the amount of water in the lake will increase due to the rain. Rain is the transfer of water from the clouds to the lake and plays a role that is analogous to heat in the case of thermodynamics. This parable is summarized in Figure 1.

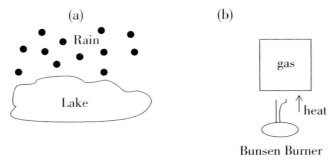

FIG. 1. (A) RAIN FALLS ADDING WATER TO A LAKE
(B) IN ANALOGY, HEAT ADDS ENERGY TO A GAS.

B. The Ideal Gas-Piston System.

Armed with the three new concepts of internal energy, temperature and heat, we are ready to model thermodynamic systems. Historically, thermodynamics was developed primarily during the 1800s and was instrumental to the understanding and development of many of the devices invented or perfected during the industrial revolution, such as the steam engine. Scientists turned their attention to the engine and asked, exactly what is basic to the operation of such devices? Their conclusion was, the essentials are, a cylinder, a working substance (e.g. a gas), and a piston to perform work.

A gas may be described by certain variables such as, the number of moles of gas, n, the volume of the container, V, the pressure of the gas, P, and finally the temperature, T. Let us consider each of these parameters in turn since each is fundamental to a thermodynamic system. The number of moles of a gas of N atoms is defined by,

$$n \equiv N/N_A. \tag{4}$$

The quantity N_A is called **Avogadro's number** and has the value 6.02×10^{23}. Avogadro's number is for scientists what a dozen is to bakers. For example, if we have 1 mole of atoms we have 6.02×10^{23} atoms. The next parameter, volume, needs no explanation. The **pressure**, P, of a gas is the force the gas exerts on a wall of its container divided by the area of the wall, A.

Pressure
$$P \equiv F/A. \tag{5}$$

Notice the units for pressure are Newtons per square meter. However, there are a multitude of pressure units in common use. One person might express pressure in atmospheres, another in mm of mercury, and yet another in Pascals ($= 1$ N/m^2), etc. But the MKS pressure unit is N/m^2 (same as Pascals). For example, 1 atm $= 1.01 \times 10^5$ Pascals. Lastly, in thermodynamics we always express temperature in absolute or Kelvin units. Since most of the thermodynamic equations have to express temperature in Kelvin it is best to only use Kelvin to be safe.

With this background we may now define an ideal gas as a gas that obeys the ideal gas law which relates the above parameters according to this experimentally based equation,

Ideal Gas Law
$$PV = nRT. \tag{6}$$

CAUTION: The temperature in (6) MUST be expressed in Kelvin!

In equation (6), the universal gas constant, R (in MKS units) has the value,

$$R = 8.314 \text{ J/K.}$$

The ideal gas is the simplest kind of gas and moreover, it is the simplest of all physical systems. Real gases obey the ideal gas law provided the density and pressure of the gas is low. On the microscopic level, the atoms of an ideal gas elastically collide with each other and the walls of the container.

Example Three.—*Julius Caesar.*

When Julius Caesar expired, his last breath had a volume of about 500.0 cc, a pressure of 1.0 atm and a temperature of 27.0 °C. Determine the number of moles in his last breath assuming the gas to be ideal.

Solution.

Rearranging the ideal gas law of equation (6),

$$n = PV/RT.$$

The most common mistake in applying this equation is not putting quantities in the proper units. The one atm of pressure must be in N/m², hence $P = 1.01 \times 10^5$ N/m². The volume must be in m³ and recalling 1 m = 100 cm, we have

$$V = 500 \text{ cm}^3 \times (1 \text{ m}/100 \text{ cm})^3 = 500 \times 10^{-6} \text{ m}^3 = 5 \times 10^{-4} \text{ m}^3.$$

The temperature **must** be in Kelvin, $T = 27 + 273 = 300\ K$, and so it goes,

$$n = PV/RT = 1.01 \times 10^5 \times 5 \times 10^{-4} /(8.314 \times 300) = \underline{0.02 \text{ moles}}.$$

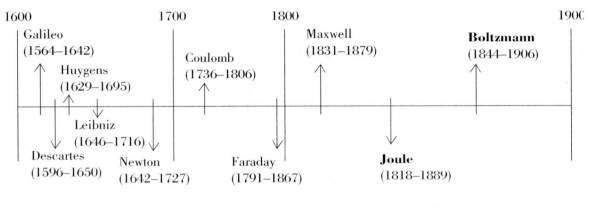

| 1600 | | 1700 | | 1800 | | 190C |

Galileo (1564–1642)

Huygens (1629–1695)

Coulomb (1736–1806)

Maxwell (1831–1879)

Boltzmann (1844–1906)

Leibniz (1646–1716)

Descartes (1596–1650)

Newton (1642–1727)

Faraday (1791–1867)

Joule (1818–1889)

←——— Age of Enlightenment ———✕——— Romantic Age ———→

Courtesy of Corbis.

C. James Joule (1818 – 1889).

Admittedly, James Joule is not a household name—most have never heard of him before. Here we give a brief synopsis of his life but before introducing Mr. Joule, let us summarily sketch a short rendition of the history of the development of the concept of heat and energy. By the late 1700s it was fashionable to model various physical quantities via an analogy with water. Both charge and heat were modeled as fluids. The heat fluid was called caloric. In this model, when a hot body came in contact with a cooler body, caloric would leave the hot object causing it to cool and enter the cooler body raising its temperature. The heat fluid was thought to be colorless, transparent, weightless, and indestructible. The latter word is one of the earliest inklings in the long process of the development of energy conservation. Our current principle of energy conservation and views on heat and entropy were so different from the older Newtonian physics that most of the developers of thermodynamics came from outside the field of physics. For example, the chemist Lavoisier uncovered one of the first known conservation laws (that of mass), Carnot was an engineer who thought deeply about the physics of the steam engine—the primary instrument of the Industrial Revolution, and Mayer's contribution to energy was made even though his original training was in medicine. To this list of non-physicists we can add an American soldier and Tory, Count Rumford (Benjamin Thompson), who was inspired to investigate heat as a result of his ruminations while witnessing the boring of a cannon. Count Rumford's observations are part of a long, tortuous process whereby the fluid model of heat was eventually to be replaced by the modern mechanical model. The mechanical and atomistic Newtonian model of nature is once again the winner against variant models! This takes us to the life and work of Mr. Joule.

James Joule was a brewer and is yet another case where the advancement of heat and energy was made by a non-physicist. First, a little about his personal background. Joule came from a relatively wealthy family who owned a brewery in Manchester, England. He had little formal schooling and never graduated from a university. At an early age, Joule and his brother, received a couple of years of private tutoring, primarily in mathematics, from the famous chemist John Dalton and this experience was to have long lasting influence on his development. He was quite simply an amateur scientist whose work was conducted in parallel with his usual functions at the brewery. Personally, he was of medium height and of average appearance and dress. But he was an independent thinker and excelled in his skill as a careful and creative experimentalist. The theoretical aspects of his work were left primarily to his friend and collaborator, the physicist William Thomson, who is better known as Lord Kelvin. James was married at the age of twenty-nine to Amelia Grimes who was thirty-three at the time. Amelia died unexpectedly seven years later and this left Joule distraught and withdrawn for a number of years. The couple had two children, a boy and a girl. Joule was politically conservative. On a side note, Joule gravely feared traveling by train but had no problem with boats. He was also not a great speaker.

In a series of experiments in the 1840s Joule was able to determine what is now called the mechanical equivalent of heat constant, J. These momentous experiments were initiated in the year 1843 but were largely ignored by the scientific community. However, by 1847 the experimental results finally made an impression on Stokes and Thomson, both well known scientists. Joules' most famous version of his experiments involved the dropping of weights that were attached to paddle wheels as illustrated in Figure 2. The mechanical energy from dropping the weights is converted into heating up the water by the paddle wheels. From the rise in temperature of the water Joule determined how many calories of heat would be needed for the same temperature rise. Then he set the number of calories equal to the mechanical work arriving at his value for J,

$$J = 4.184 \text{ Joules/calorie.}$$

In honor of James Joule, the unit for energy is the Joule.

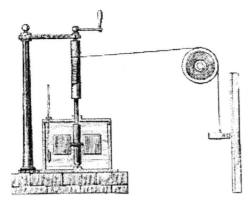

FIG. 2. MECHANICAL EQUIVALENT OF
HEAT APPARATUS OF JOULE. THE
FALLING WEIGHT TURNS THE HANDLE
CAUSING THE PADDLE WHEELS TO
DO WORK ON THE WATER. THIS
WORK INCREASES THE TEMPERATURE
OF THE WATER AS IF ONE HAD
HEATED THE WATER.

It was not until the 1850s that William Thomson (Kelvin) stated our modern definition of energy as the ability to do work. The concept of energy took decades to emerge and involved the work of numerous scientists, many of whom were not trained physicists.

References.

Great Physicists, William H. Cropper (Oxford UP, 2001).

Physics, the Human Adventure by Gerald Holton and Stephen Brush (Rutgers University Press, 2001).

D. First Law of Thermodynamics.

In thermodynamics a system is said to exist in a thermodynamic state when certain thermodynamic variables are not changing. The thermodynamic variables have already been introduced: temperature, pressure, volume and quantity of matter (e.g. number of moles). Systems can change state via various thermodynamic processes. The heart of thermodynamics concerns how these state changes are brought about. There are four fundamental laws of thermodynamics. In this text we will concentrate only on laws one and two since the "zeroth" and third law are not as basic.

The first law of thermodynamics is a special case of a principle we have already seen—the principle of energy conservation. In thermodynamics, the internal energy of a system, E_{int}, may change in two ways—by the system doing work, W, or by heating the system, Q. We adopt the convention where Q is taken as positive if one heats a system and is negative if heat leaves the system. The work, W, is taken as positive if the system does work on the environment and negative if work is done on the system. For a gas-cylinder system, the piston does the work. The first law is a relationship between internal energy change ΔE_{int}, Q, and W, where the latter two describe energy transfers to or out of the system.

First Law of Thermodynamics
$$\Delta E_{int} = Q - W \tag{7}$$

Notice equation (7) shows that if one heats a system ($Q > 0$) and does work on the system (W < 0) then the system's internal energy will increase by $Q + |W|$. For an isolated system, both Q and W will be zero by definition and in that case the internal energy will not change (conservation of energy), $\Delta E_{int} = 0$.

Example Four.—*Compressing a bicycle pump.*

The piston of a bicycle pump is pushed in so that 10 J of work is done on the enclosed air. At the same time the pump is thermally insulated so that no heat enters or leaves the pump. Find the change in internal energy of the air.

Solution.

Using $Q = 0$ and $W = -10$ J (since work is done on the air not by the air) in equation (7) gives

$$E_{int} = Q - W = 0 - -10 = \underline{+10\ J}.$$

Example Five.—*Specific heat.*

How much heat is required to raise the temperature of ten grams of water from 5° C to 75° C?

Solution.

Recall from elementary chemistry the **specific heat**, c, of a mass m of a substance is related to its increase in temperature, ΔT, that is brought about by an injection of heat, Q.

$$Q \equiv mc\Delta T. \tag{8}$$

The specific heat of water is* $c = 4,180$ J/kg-C, and inserting the numbers gives

$$Q = 0.010\ (4180)(75 - 5) = \underline{2,926\ J}.$$

Example Six.—*Thermal expansion and internal energy change.*

A ten meter long steel rod of mass 2.00 kg is heated with 10,000 J. Find (a) the rise in temperature of the rod and (b) the change in length of the rod.

Solution.

(a) We find in tables* the value for the specific heat of steel, 450 J/kg-C, and rearranging the expression in the previous example for specific heat we obtain,

$$\Delta T = Q/mc = 10,000/(2)(450) = \underline{11.1\ C°}.$$

(b) The thermal expansion ΔL of a rod of initial length L due to heating obeys the law of **linear thermal expansion**,

$$\Delta L = \alpha L\ \Delta T, \tag{9}$$

where α is called the thermal expansion coefficient of the material making up the rod. A table* gives for steel $\alpha = 12 \times 10^{-6}$ C°⁻¹. Inserting the numbers given and the answer to (a) we obtain,

$$\Delta L = (12 \times 10^{-6})\ 10(11.1) = \underline{0.00133\ m\ or\ 1.33\ mm}.$$

* *Physics, A General Introduction*, Alan Van Heuvelen (Little, Brown, 1982).

Courtesy of Corbis.

E. Ludwig Boltzmann (1844–1906).

"When the truth gets buried deep beneath a thousand years of sleep, time demands a turnaround and once again the truth is found."
—George Harrison (the Beatle) wrote this as a verse for the song by Donavan called "Hurdy Gurdy Man." Apparently, the verse wasn't included in the final recorded version of the song.

Ludwig Boltzmann sprang from a wealthy Viennese family. His father was a Protestant and his mother a Roman Catholic. Boltzmann's father died when Ludwig was only fifteen years old. By all accounts Boltzmann was an excellent student with especially high aptitude in mathematics and the sciences. He was short and stout with a great sense of humor and an informal manner. His eyesight was poor. At a young age he began taking piano lessons and was to become an excellent pianist with a strong attraction to the works of Beethoven and Mozart. He studied physics and mathematics at the University of Vienna, graduating at the age of twenty-two with a degree similar to the Master of Science, although the Viennese title of his degree was Doctor of Philosophy. During his time at the university Ludwig collaborated with his professor, Dr. Stefan, on thermodynamics research. The pair developed what is now called the Stefan-Boltzmann law of heat radiation that relates the absolute temperature of an object to the rate of radiative energy the object releases.

In 1868 Boltzmann became an assistant professor at the age of twenty-four. He was an excellent lecturer exhibiting great enthusiasm, organization and clarity of presentation without the use of lecture notes. Much of his academic career took place at the University of Graz and the University of Vienna. His research involved the thermal theory of the molecular dynamics of gases which also made use of the mathematics of probability and statistics. He arrived at a rather complicated result now called the Boltzmann H-theorem. Boltzmann especially distinguished himself by working on the concept of entropy and relating it to the properties of atoms and molecules. As an indication of his accomplishments in physics the emperor, Franz-Josef, offered Ludwig a rank among the nobility but Boltzmann declined the offer. He came from the upper middle class and preferred to remain middle class.

Ludwig married Henrietta von Ailgentler. The couple had two sons and three daughters. Henrietta was a school teacher who was ten years younger than Boltzmann when they were married. Boltzmann enjoyed walking in the woods, ice-skating, swimming and music. Outside of physics, he was particularly fond of the literature of the German romantic poet, Friedrich Schiller.

During the latter part of the nineteenth century and into the early twentieth century there was a movement in physics to reject the belief in atoms and molecules. A champion of this movement was one of Boltzmann's colleagues and critics, Ernst Mach. Ludwig was especially sensitive to the prevailing skepticism regarding atoms since so much of his research assumed their existence. Boltzmann committed suicide. A number of factors contributed to his suicide among which we site: professional criticism, a nervous breakdown, failing health due to a stroke and manic depression. In the end, however, Boltzmann's work was vindicated because in 1905 work by Einstein on the Brownian movement of gas particles put to rest the earlier skepticism about atomic theory. This work confirmed many of Boltzmann's ideas but too late to help Ludwig fend off his critics. Boltzmann's tombstone has his famous definition of entropy, Equation (11) below, prominently displayed. In the end his physics was correct and quite literally he had the last word on the subject.

"Deeper meaning resides in the fairy tales told to me in my childhood than in any truth that is taught in life." —Friedrich von Schiller

References.

Great Physicists, William H. Cropper (Oxford UP, 2001).
Remarkable Physicists, Ioan James (Cambridge UP, 2004).

F. Entropy.

The first law of thermodynamics is about internal energy and is a statement of the law of conservation of energy that includes the possibility of heating a system. The second law is about the entropy of a system. We are not going to pursue all of the detailed mathematics of entropy but will rather focus more on a qualitative understanding of this term. The entropy of a system is a property of the system that is distinct from the internal energy. Recall, the internal energy is the sum of the random kinetic energies of the atoms plus the internal potential energies associated with the forces the atoms exert on each other. The word entropy is the Greek word for transformation and it is used in two senses: there is a thermodynamic expression for entropy and a statistical definition of entropy. It has been shown the two ideas are not contradictory.

In thermodynamics the ***entropy*** change of a system occurs during a thermodynamic process such as heating a system. In particular, following Rudolf Clausius, entropy is defined by the expression,

$$\text{\textit{Thermodynamic Entropy}}$$
$$\Delta S \equiv Q/T. \text{ (rev)} \tag{10}$$

CAUTION: The temperature in (10) MUST be expressed in Kelvin!

The (rev) above is shorthand for reversible and therefore the equation applies only to reversible processes. Thermodynamic processes are either reversible or irreversible. In general, a good approximation is to say a ***reversible process*** is one that occurs very slowly. For example, the melting of ice is reversible since removing heat from liquid water at zero Celsius causes freezing to occur but adding heat to ice at zero Celsius will cause melting. The process easily goes both ways. An example of an irreversible process is sliding a block across a rough horizontal surface. The initial kinetic energy of the block is entirely lost to heating the surface and block. The process never spontaneously goes the other way, i.e. the stationary block never absorbs heat in the amount equaling its initial kinetic energy and then flies across the table.

Example Seven.—*Heating water again and finding the entropy change.*

Return to example five and estimate the increase in entropy of the water.

Solution.

From example five we found it took 2,926 J of heat to raise the temperature of the ten grams of water from 5 to 75°C. During this process the water's temperature obviously was not constant and therefore, equation (10) is not strictly valid for this process (the exact way of solving this problem involves integral calculus). However, we will use (10) to approximate the rise in entropy by letting the T represent the average temperature over the interval (in Kelvin!) and this gives $(5 + 75)/2 = 40°$ C or $273 + 40 = 313$ K. We find,

$$\Delta S \approx 2{,}926 \text{ J}/313 \text{ K} = \underline{9.35 \text{ J/K}}.$$

The units for entropy are J/K.

Another common definition for ***entropy*** is the statistical definition where the entropy of a system is a measure of how disordered the system is. Admittedly this is a rather vague statement. We place things on a more firm footing by considering Figure 3.

In Figure 3(a) is illustrated a system composed of twelve chairs (represented by the symbol •) in a room that are each allowed to reside within various identical small boxes represented by the symbol □. Following Boltzmann, we use Ω to indicate the degree of disorder of the system so that for a highly disordered system Ω is large. In (a) the chairs form an orderly array so that Ω_a is *small* but clearly the situation in (b) is more disordered than that in (a) and the disorder is even larger in (c). Therefore,

$$\Omega_c > \Omega_b > \Omega_a.$$

Boltzmann introduced the term entropy to represent how disordered a system is by defining the entropy of a system, S, to be proportional to the degree of disorder, Ω,

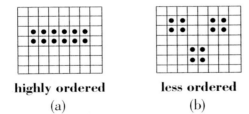

highly ordered   **less ordered**
(a)   (b)

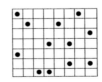

highly disordered
(c)

Fig. 3. The statistical definition of entropy is illustrated using chairs in a classroom. In (a) the chairs are highly ordered, in (b) less ordered and in (c) highly disordered.

Statistical Entropy

$$S \equiv k_B \ln \Omega \tag{11}$$

The proportionality constant in equation (11), $k_B = 1.38 \times 10^{-23}$J/K, is one of nature's fundamental constants and is called the Boltzmann constant. The degree of disorder, Ω, is found from the number of "microstates" for a given "macrostate," which is illustrated in Example 8 below. If Ω is large, S is large too.

For the system in Figure 3 we have,

$$S_c > S_b > S_a.$$

The following example will be used to more precisely define micro- and macrostate.

Example Eight.—*Entropy and four coins.*

Determine the entropy for the states of four coins.

Solution.

It is easy to fill in the following table and use Equation (11) to find the entropy.

Macrostates	Microstates	Ω	Prob.	$S/k_B = \ln\Omega$
1. 0 heads	TTTT	1	1/16	0
2. 1 head	HTTT, THTT, TTHT, TTTH	4	4/16	1.39
3. 2 heads	HHTT, HTHT, HTTH, THHT, THTH, TTHH	6	6/16	1.79
4. 3 heads	HHHT, HHTH, HTHH, THHH	4	4/16	1.39
5. 4 heads	HHHH	1	1/16	0

Assuming each of the microstates above (there are $1 + 4 + 6 + 4 + 1 = 16$ total microstates) have equal probability then macrostate three is the most probable (6/16) while the first and last have the least probability (1/16). *The most probable has the highest entropy.*

Example Nine.—*Heat conduction and entropy.*

A rod has a length L with cross-sectional area A. Suppose the ends of the rod are held at fixed temperatures such that there is a difference in temperature from one end to the other end of the rod, ΔT. There will exist in the rod a thermal current, $Q/\Delta t$ (in Watts), that represents the flow of energy down the rod from the hot to the cold end. This situation is modeled by the ***law of heat conduction,***

$$Q/\Delta t = k A \, \Delta T/L, \tag{12}$$

where k is called the thermal conductivity of the material out of which the rod is composed.

Suppose a steel rod of length ten meters and cross-sectional area 1 cm² has one end fixed at zero Celsius by a vat of cold water and the other at 100° C by a vat of hot water. The thermal conductivity of steel* is 50.2 Watts/mC. During a time interval of 60.0 s by how much does the entropy of the waters change? Note: $1 \text{ cm}^2 \times (1 \text{ m}/100 \text{ cm})^2 = 10^{-4} \text{ m}^2$.

*Physics, A General Introduction, Alan Van Heuvelen (Little, Brown, 1982).

Solution.

The amount of heat that leaves the hot water is $Q = [kA\Delta T/L]\,\Delta t$, or

$$Q = [50.2(10^{-4})100/10]\,60 = 3.012 \text{ J}.$$

Using this in equation (10) for both the hot and cold water gives,

$$\Delta S = \Delta S_{hot} + \Delta S_{cold} = -3.012/(100 + 273) + 3.012/(0 + 273) = \underline{+0.003 \text{ J/K}}.$$

The hot water's entropy declined but that of the cold water increased. The entropy change for the whole system was positive, which is not a coincidence but a consequence of the second law of thermodynamics (see below). After all, we know heat flows from hot to cold spontaneously.

G. Second Law of Thermodynamics and the End of It All.

The second law of thermodynamics is a statement about the entropy of a system.

Second Law of Thermodynamics

The entropy, S, of a closed system only increases with time, or in symbols,

$$\Delta S > 0. \tag{13}$$

Historically, the second law had important implications about how efficiently such devices as steam engines could operate. Nineteenth century scientists envisioned idealized engines that might conceivably convert heat entirely into work. But under further scrutiny the scientists concluded that such perfectly efficient engines would violate the second law. It was shown that all manner of perpetual motion machines violate equation (13). No matter how hard we try, some heat is lost to the environment in every real machine. Even so, much of the motivation for the development of thermodynamics dealt with such practical issues as making steam engines operate more efficiently.

But here we will consider the second law more from a statistical rather than thermodynamic perspective. Therefore, let us try to understand why the statement in equation (13) makes sense by returning to the example in Figure (3) involving the chairs in a room. Imagine the room in question is an elementary school classroom and at noon everyday of school a photographer enters the room and takes a photograph. In all, say we have 180 pictures of the room. In general, would you find more pictures that look like Figure 3(a) or 3(c)? Of course, the answer is there would be far more photos resembling 3(c) because of the nature of small children. But why is this so? A moment's thought leads us to conclude:

Disorder occurs more often because there are more ways of being disordered than ways of being ordered.

This means disorder is more probable and therefore the natural tendency is for the disorder and entropy of an isolated system to increase as time goes by. I had to attach the adjective "isolated" because in the above example of the chairs we had to assume the janitor did not come into the room every evening and change the configuration from 3(c) back to (a).

The above thoughts are in accordance with the statistical understanding of entropy and disorder. As we have seen, there is also the older concept of entropy that defines entropy in terms of the heat injected into a system. Since heat is the most disordered form of energy, the statistical and thermodynamics definitions are not contradictory. More precisely, adding heat increases disorder and increases entropy.

The second law of thermodynamics and the concept of entropy lead us to the belief that events have a natural direction of flow. That is, for an isolated system, events unfold so as to increase entropy and disorder. One consequence of this fact is an increase in the amount of random energy in isolated systems. We know that energy is continually being converted to one form from another but the total energy of isolated systems is conserved. The second law, which pertains to isolated systems, implies nature prefers energy changes that increase the amount of random energy. For example, energy flows from a hot body to a cold body but this process does not go the other way for an isolated system. In view of these considerations, during the latter half of the nineteenth century it was suggested the second law is nature's arrow for time. Taking this to the extreme, some suggested since the entropy of the universe continually increases, eventually the universe will die from a "heat death." At the end of the nineteenth century the idea of a universal heat death appeared in popular literature (e.g. H. G. Well's book, *The Time Machine*). Going even further out on the limb of speculation, some suggested the law of entropy increase may be applied to human history in general, and therefore things are continually getting more and more corrupt. Here is a case where the physics seems to support the Hebrew linear view of history over the Greek cyclical views. However, it is not obvious that physics has anything to say about human history since physics deals primarily with matter in motion, and humans may be a different story altogether.

Nowadays, the second law is viewed as statistical in nature, and therefore, it is possible, although highly improbable, to violate it. For example, consider Maxwell's demon.

Maxwell invented the demon in 1871 in order to show how it is, in principle, possible to violate the second law of thermodynamics by having a system with initially uniform temperature to spontaneously (via the demon) develop high and low temperature regions. Perhaps it is best to let the master explain this himself [where we are quoting from Maxwell's book, *Theory of Heat* (Longmans, Green and Company, London, 1871), p. 308]:

> One of the best established facts in thermodynamics is that is is impossible in a system enclosed in an envelope which permits neither change of volume nor passage of heat, and which both the temperature and the pressure are everywhere the same, to produce any inequality of temperature or of pressure without the expenditure of work. This is the second law of thermodynamics, and it is undoubtedly true so long as we can deal with bodies only in mass and have no power of perceiving or handling the separate molecules of which they are

FIG. 3.   MAXWELL'S DEMON
Reprinted from *American Journal of Physics 23,*
no. 7, October 1955, by permission of American
Institute of Physics.

made up. But if we conceive a being whose faculties are so sharpened that he can follow every molecule in its course, such a being, whose attributes are still as essentially finite as our own, would be able to do what is at present impossible to us. For we have seen that the molecules in a vessel full of air at uniform temperature are moving with velocities by no means uniform though the mean velocity of any great number of them, arbitrarily selected, is almost exactly uniform. Now let us suppose that such a vessel is divided into two portions A and B, by a division in which there is a small hole, and that a being, who can see the individual molecules, opens and closes this hole, so as to allow only the swifter molecules to pass from A to B, and only the slower ones to pass from B to A. He will thus, without expenditure of work, raise the temperature of B and lower that of A, in contradiction to the second law of thermodynamics.

Therefore the demon, Fig. 1, was supposed to effect in a very short time what would probably take a very long time if left to the ordinary laws of chance. However, it was soon recognized that the task set the demon was difficult, indeed paradoxical, and such well-known writers as Brillouin and Weiner have discussed theoretical objections to the theoretical ability of the demon to perform his assigned duties.

Let us be clear about what Maxwell is saying. His hypothetical demon would allow heat to flow between two regions that started out with the same temperature. The demon does this by allowing faster molecules to go into one chamber and slower molecules into the other chamber. But the two-chamber system may still be considered isolated since the demon does no work or causes no heating of the system. Therefore, by allowing one side to get warmer and the other colder such a demon violates the second law. And yet, the demon does not violate the first law of thermodynamics.

One can imagine many hypothetical processes that violate the second but not the first law of thermodynamics. To site just one case, consider dropping an egg onto a hard floor— it splatters. Without violating the first law, all of the pieces of egg could absorb energy from the floor to reform and jump back onto the table top. This does not occur because it violates the second law since by reforming this reduces the entropy of the egg.

H. Two Mysteries.

Most people think of physics as a subject where everything is certain and completely understood. It's all black or white. However, even in the field of *classical* physics there are some deep mysteries. Two examples of such mysteries are the "reversal paradox" and the "recurrence paradox." Both involve the second law of thermodynamics and the apparent conflict between the second law and classical mechanics. We leave the reader of this textbook with a short account of these two perplexing paradoxes, keeping in mind that a paradox does not necessarily mean a contradiction but only an *apparent* contradiction. At one time these paradoxes led physicists to doubt some of the work of Boltzmann.

The *reversal* paradox became a contentious item of discussion in the late 1800s. It arises for the following reason. The laws of classical mechanics work whether time moves forward or backward. What this means is, by looking at a classical physical system and applying classical laws, a system could evolve in time or the same train of events could occur in the opposite order. The laws of classical physics would work no matter the ordering of the events. For instance, one could make a movie of a classical system and the laws of physics would be obeyed whether the movie were played forward or backward. This means the classical laws of physics do not have a preferred order, that is, time does not have an arrow. Lord Kelvin stated, ". . . if the motion of every particle of matter in the universe were precisely reversed at any instant, the course of nature would be simply reversed for ever after." However, this seems to contradict what we have said based on the second law of thermodynamics—time does have an arrow for an isolated system, namely the events are ordered in a way that the entropy of the system always increases. It is beyond the level of this book to prove in detail that in fact the reversal paradox does not contradict classical mechanics. In short, the contradiction is avoided by a careful statement of the second law. Suffice it to say, the reason the reversal paradox does not contradict classical mechanics is due to the statistical nature of the second law. Physicists no longer view the second law of thermodynamics as an absolute law. Entropy of isolated systems can decrease but the chances of this occurring are extremely improbable.

The second paradox we examine is more difficult to refute. The *recurrence* paradox also surfaced in the late 1800's. During that period the French mathematical physicist Poincare proved a theorem that had wide ramifications. Loosely stated, Poincare proved on the basis of classical mechanics any finite system will, given enough time, return to almost any initial state of the system. The time for the system to return to the initial state is called a Poincare period and the cycle is called a Poincare cycle. This theorem suggests that if the universe is nothing but a finite collection of particles obeying classical laws of motion then the same events will occur over and over again. So, for example, if the molecules of the universe ever came back to exactly the same state they had at some previous time then thereafter history would be repeated. Each state of the universe will repeat over and over forever. However, such occurrences would refute the heat death that is implied by the second law of thermodynamics.

Once again, a paradox arises due to the apparent contradiction between Poincare's theorem that results from classical mechanics and the ramifications of the second law of thermodynamics. The law of entropy increase suggests a linear view of events and the presence of times' arrow. The recurrence paradox continues to trouble physicists today, although we now know classical mechanics is not the final word.

The above ideas from physics may be extended to history. For example, some have argued that history is cyclical rather than linear. The ancient Hebrew and Christian view of history was predominately linear, meaning history has a purpose or goal and therefore, had a beginning (creation) and will have an end (judgment). On the other side, a cyclical view of history is in agreement with ancient Greek conceptions of the nature of history (and in line with the thoughts of most other world civilizations). Once more, perfect motion for the Greeks was circular not linear.

Such ideas of cyclicality also have appeared in literature. Consider the 1822 poem, *Hellas*, by the romantic poet Percy B. Shelley.

> The World's great age begins anew,
> The golden years return.
> The earth doth like a snake renew
> His winter weeds outworn . . .

> Another Athens shall arise
> And to remoter time bequeath,
> like sunset to the skies,
> The splendor of its prime . . .

We also find an attraction for recurrence in the works of the highly influential German philosopher, Nietzsche. The eternal recurrence appears in Nietzsche's book, *Thus Spoke Zarathustra* and, in addition, his book the *Gay Science*, where he wrote,

> This life as you now live it and have lived it, you will have to live once more and innumerable times more . . .

> The eternal hourglass of existence is turned over and over, and you with it, a dust grain of dust.

Closer to our time, historical cyclicality and linearity was the subject of the fascinating book, *The Myth of the Eternal Return* by Mircea Eliade. Clearly physics both influences and is influenced by the wider culture.

In conclusion, we ask the question, can physics shed light on areas of thought outside of physics? Each person must answer this question for herself but whatever stance one takes, remember it can be dangerous to extrapolate from physics to other areas of life. After all, the above paradoxes arise from within the world of classical physics and therefore, may not hold when one advances to modern physics. Even if the paradoxes may be refuted by modern physics, one must always keep in mind that physics is open-ended, and what is held to be true today may be overturned tomorrow. Remember, it took centuries to overturn the erroneous Aristotelian mechanics.

"Those are my principles, and if you don't like them . . . well, I have others."— Groucho Marx

References.

The Project Physics Course, Rutherford, Holton, and Watson (Holt, Rhinehart and Winston, 1970).
Statistical Mechanics, Kerson Huang (Wiley, 1963).
The Myth of the Eternal Return, Mircea Eliade (Princeton University Press, 1954).
The Portable Nietzsche, Ed. W. Kaufman (Penguin, 1954).

Summary.

Complex many particle systems are described using new terms such as temperature, heat, internal energy and entropy. The three common temperature scales are Celsius, Fahrenheit, and Kelvin (absolute). Ideal gases are especially simple systems that have been used to develop thermodynamics. The first law of thermodynamics is a conservation of energy expression involving heat, work and the internal energy of a system. Entropy may be expressed in the language of thermodynamics or as a statistical quantity. The second law of thermodynamics states that the entropy of an isolated system always (almost certainly!) grows. Two nineteenth-century physicists' lives are summarized, James Joule and Ludwig Boltzmann. The chapter and book ends with the reversal and the recurrence paradoxes each of which seem to lead to a contradiction between classical mechanics and the second law of thermodynamics.

QUESTIONS.

1. Show how the ideal gas law implies Boyle's Law, Charles' Law, and Gay-Lussac's Law as special cases. Consult the internet or a chemistry text for the statement of these three laws.

2. An apple drops from a desk (ignore friction) and lands on a soft cushion. What happened to the energy of the apple?

3. Explain the significance of Joule's mechanical equivalent of heat experiment.

4. Look up in the library or on the internet information about theories of heat that preceded the mechanical model of heat presented in this chapter. In particular, study the caloric and phlogiston models and write a short summary of these outmoded models.

5. Much of the mechanical model of heat we studied in this chapter well suits the atomic model of matter. Look up in the library or on the internet information about the theory of atoms. In particular, study the Roman atomist Lucretius and the Greek atomist Democritus and write a short summary of these individuals' opinions.

6. Find out why the ancient Greeks had difficulty in believing in the possibility of a vacuum.

7. A teaspoon of water and a lake have the same temperature. Do the two have the same internal energy?

8. You can use running hot water to loosen a lid of a bottle. What is the physics behind this?

9. Our text presented the conservation of energy and the concept of heat as partly due to James Joule in the mid-nineteenth century. However, many other individuals also contributed significantly to the development of these concepts. Using the library or internet, read about the work in this area by the German physician, Julius Robert Mayer and the German physicist and physician, Hermann von Helmholtz.

10. This chapter presented the first and second laws of thermodynamics. Look up the zeroth and third laws of thermodynamics.

11. Exactly what is taking place (at the atomic level) when heat flows along a rod from the hot end to the cold end?

12. Our text presented the kinetic theory of gases and the second law of thermodynamics with the concept of entropy as primarily due to Ludwig Boltzmann and James Clerk Maxwell during the latter half of the nineteenth century. However, many other individuals also contributed significantly to the development of these concepts. Using the library or internet, read about the work in this area by German scientist Rudolph Clausius, English physicist William Thomson (Lord Kelvin), and the early nineteenth century French engineer Sadi Carnot.

13. Circle the most disordered:

    (a) an unbroken egg; an egg that fell onto a hard floor

    (b) a cylinder with a gas concentrated in one corner; a cylinder with a gas dispersed

    (c) a new and unopened deck of playing cards; playing cards scattered onto a table

    (d) your room at the beginning of the semester versus near the end

14. A man opens a bottle of cologne in your lecture hall. Use the second law of thermodynamics to make an argument for why soon everyone in the room can smell the cologne.

15. A liquid freezes going from more disorder to less disorder. Does this violate the second law of thermodynamics? Explain.

16. This question concerns a thermodynamic process called a ***free expansion.*** A thermally insulated container is divided in half by a movable partition. In the left chamber is a gas while the right chamber is a vacuum. The partition is removed and the gas fills the entire container. Is the first law of thermodynamics violated? Is the second law of thermodynamics violated? What happened to the entropy of the system?

17. System A has three times the internal energy than system B. Which way will heat flow if the two systems are placed in thermal contact?

18. Consider the following scenario. A lake has heat flow spontaneously from the right half of a lake to the left half. The right half becomes cold while the left half hot. Does this process obey the first law of thermodynamics? the second law of thermodynamics? Explain.

19. Consider the following scenario. A rock falls from rest onto a pile of soft mud. Neglect air friction. Consider the reverse process. The rock in the soft mud absorbs the same energy from the mud (the mud gets cooler) and leaps back up to its original height. Does this reversed process obey the first law of thermodynamics? the second law of thermodynamics? Explain.

20. Why does a perpetual motion machine violate the second law of thermodynamics? (Hint: Look up other statements of the second law, in particular, statements involving heat engines.)

21. How is the theory of evolution compatible with the second law of thermodynamics? (See *Physics Matters*, James Trefil and Robert M. Hazen (Wiley, 2004) p. 283.)

PROBLEMS.

1. The dark side of the moon has a temperature of $-173°$ C. Convert this temperature to Fahrenheit and Kelvin.

2. On a hot day in Florida the temperature reaches 105° F while on a cold day in Green Bay the temperature was −30° F. Convert these temperatures into Celsius and Kelvin.

3. The center of the earth has a temperature of roughly 10,000° F. Convert this to Kelvin and Celsius.

4. Find the temperature of absolute zero in Celsius and Fahrenheit.

5. A 60.0 kg woman wears spiked high-heels. The total area of the two spikes is 10^{-5} m². Assuming all of her weight is carried by the two spikes, what pressure is exerted on the floor?

6. Each tire of a 1,500.0 kg car has a contact area of 0.015 m² with the ground. Find the pressure by one of the tires on the road.

7. The pressure of an ideal gas triples while the temperature is fixed. What is the ratio of the new volume to the original volume of the gas?

8. The volume of an ideal gas doubles while the pressure remains fixed. What is the ratio of the new temperature of the gas to the original temperature?

9. An *isothermal* expansion of an ideal gas is a process in which the volume increases but the temperature is fixed. What happens to the pressure of the gas if the volume doubles?

10. An *isobaric* expansion of an ideal gas is a process in which the volume increases but the pressure is fixed. What happens to the temperature of the gas if the volume doubles?

11. A balloon contains 16.0 grams of Helium gas (one mole of He has a mass of 4.0 grams). The volume of the gas is 0.10 m³ and the temperature is 30.0° C. Find the number of moles and the pressure of the gas.

12. A person's middle ear at sea level is at atmospheric pressure and has a volume of about 0.5 cm³. Assuming constant moles and temperature for the gas inside the ear, what will the volume be at an altitude of 2,000 m above sea level where the pressure is 0.75 atm?

13. A basketball has a radius of 0.10 m and is immersed in the atmosphere at 1 atm pressure. (a) Find the volume of the ball. (b) Below the water of a pool the pressure is 2.0 atm. Find the new volume and radius of the ball. Assume the temperature of the ball does not change.

14. At the top of Mt. Everest the pressure is 0.31 atm and the temperature is $-30.0°$ C. Find the number of moles of gas molecules there in every cubic meter.

15. A bottle of soda has an air bubble at the top. The air has a pressure of 1.2 atm and temperature of 27° C. Determine the temperature needed to raise the pressure to 1.5 atm (this pressure will cause the top to pop off.)

16. One cubic m of an ideal gas is at room temperature (23° C) and atmospheric pressure (1 atm). How many moles of gas are present?

17. What is the change in internal energy of a system when 15.0 J of work is done on the system while 5.0 J of heat are taken out of the system?

18. During a certain process 15.0 J of heat goes into a system while the system does 10.0 J of work. Find the internal energy change.

19. In an isothermal process an ideal gas changes state with the temperature and the internal energy of the gas constant. What must be true of the heat absorbed and the work done by the gas for such a process?

20. In an adiabatic process an ideal gas is insulated so that no heat enters or leaves the gas. What must be true of the change in internal energy of the gas if the gas does positive work while expanding?

21. A lead bullet of mass 5.00 grams travels with a speed of 250.0 m/s and strikes a block of wood. Assume 50% of the bullet's initial kinetic energy becomes heat during the collision and determine the rise in temperature of the bullet. (The specific heat of lead is 130.0 J/kgC.)

22. Many years ago a crater was formed in Arizona due to a falling meteor. The meteor had a mass that has been estimated to be 5×10^8 kg and an initial speed just before impacting the earth of 10,000.0 m/s. The specific heat of the meteor is 900 J/kgC. (a) Find the initial kinetic energy of the meteor and (b) assuming 15% of that energy was converted to heat at impact, by how much did the temperature of the meteor rise?

23. A steel beam has a length equaling the height of the Sears Tower in Chicago, 475 m. How much longer is the beam in the summer when the temperature is 35° C than in the winter when the temperature is −15° C? (The thermal expansion coefficient for steel is $\alpha = 12 \times 10^{-6}$ C$^{\circ-1}$.)

24. A steel beam has a length equaling that of the Golden Gate Bridge in San Francisco, 4000 ft. How much longer is the beam when its temperature increases from 30° F in the winter to 85° F in the summer? (The thermal expansion coefficient for steel is $\alpha = 12 \times 10^{-6}$ C$^{\circ-1}$.)

25. A wall of a mud hut is 50.0 cm thick with an area of 25.0 m². The thermal conductivity of the wall is 0.5 watt/mC°. Assume the temperature inside the hut is 16° C and the outside temperature is −10.0° C (it is winter). Find (a) the rate of energy loss through the wall due to heat conduction and (b) the amount of energy loss through the wall in one day.

26. A polar bear is covered with fur that is about 1.5 cm thick and has a thermal conductivity of 0.075 watt/mC. The total area of the bear's body that is covered by the fur is 0.30 m². If the skin of the bear is at 35° C and the bear lies in snow that has a temperature of −5° C then what is the rate of heat loss due to conduction for the bear?

27. A 4.0 kg block slides across a rough horizontal table starting with an initial speed of 10.0 m/s. The table and block maintain a constant temperature of 22.0° C. The block is stopped by the friction. (a) Determine the initial kinetic energy of the block. (b) Assuming all of the block's kinetic energy heats the block + table, find the rise in entropy of the table + block for this process (approximate the process as reversible). (c) Are your results consistent with the second law of thermodynamics?

28. A 2.0 kg block slides across a rough horizontal table starting with an initial speed of 6.0 m/s. The table and block maintain a constant temperature of 24.0° C. The block is stopped by the friction. (a) Determine the initial kinetic energy of the block. (b) Assuming all of the block's kinetic energy heats the block + table, find the rise in entropy of the table + block for this process (approximate the process as reversible). (c) Are your results consistent with the second law of thermodynamics?

29. Clausius was a nineteenth-century scientist who developed the following statement of the second law of thermodynamics: "Heat will not of its own accord pass from a cooler body to a hotter one." To understand how this is related to the statement of the second law given in our text, consider a cold system that has a fixed temperature of T_C and a hot system at a fixed temperature of T_H. Assume an amount of heat Q leaves the cold system and goes into the hot system. In terms of Q, T_C and T_H, what is the change in entropy of (a) the cold system, (b) the hot system, and (c) the universe? (d) Are your results consistent with the second law of thermodynamics? Explain.

30. Repeat problem 29 with the following values: T_C is $0°$ C, T_H is $24°$ C and Q is 10.0 J.

31. The total number of microstates for three dice is $6^3 = 216$. What is the probability of throwing a sum equal to 7?

32. The total number of microstates for three dice is $6^3 = 216$. What is the probability of throwing a sum equal to 5?

33. Consider a system of five coins. For this system make a table similar to that made in example eight for four coins.

34. Two dice are rolled. Let the sum of the numbers appearing on the dice represent the macrostate of the dice and for each macrostate list the possible microstates (e.g. 2: —1 + 1 snake eyes, 3: —1 + 2 or 2 + 1, etc.). Make a table similar to the table in example eight with the columns labeled macrostate, microstates, Ω, probability, and entropy. What macrostate has the greatest probability of occurrence and largest entropy?

Hints and answers to problems.

1) –279° F, 100 K   2) 314 K, 239 K   3) 5538 C, 5811 K   4) –273 K, –459 F   5) 6 × 10⁷ N/m²   6) 250,000 N/m²   7) 1/3   8) 2   9) 1/2   10) 2   11) 4 moles, 100,766 N/m²   12) 2/3 × 10⁻⁶ m³   13) Hint: take a cube root 0.00419 m³ 0.00209 m³, 0.079 m   14) 15.5 moles/m³   15) 375 K or 102 C   16) 41 moles   17) $W = -15 \, J$ and $Q = -5 \, J$, 10 J   18) $Q = 15 \, J$, $W = 10 \, J$, 5 J   19) $Q = W$ 20) less than zero   21) 120 C   22) 2.5 × 10¹⁶ J, 8330 C   23) 0.285 n 24) 0.451 m 25) 650 W, 5.62 × 10⁷ J   26) 60 W   27) 200 J, 0.678 J/K   28) 36 J, 0.121 J/K > 0, yes   29) $-Q/T_C$, Q/T_H, $Q(1/T_H - T_C) < 0$, no   30) –0.0366 J/K, 0.0337 J/K, –0.00293 J/K, $\Delta S < 0$, no   31) $P = 15/216 = 6.94 \%$ 32) $P = 6/216 = 2.78\%$ 33) 32 total microstates :0, 1, 2 . . . , 5 heads   34) 36 microstates, max probability is $P(\text{sum is 7}) = 17\%$

GLOSSARY.

Acceleration   velocity change divided by a very small time interval or slope of the tangent line to the velocity versus time graph.

Alternating Current   a current made of moving charges that reverse their direction of motion in the circuit and for which the size of the current varies in time usually in a sinusoidal manner.

Ammeter   a device used to measure current.

Angular Acceleration   change in angular velocity divided by a small time interval.

Angular Displacement   change in angular position.

Angular Momentum   a particle moving in a circle has angular momentum given by the product of its momentum times the radius of the circle or equivalently, the product of its moment of inertia (rotational mass) times its angular velocity.

Angular Position   the angle an object makes relative to a reference line.

Angular Velocity   angular displacement divided by a small time interval.

Authority   truth that is based on expert witnesses.

Average Acceleration   velocity change divided by the time interval or slope of a line segment connecting two points on a velocity versus time graph.

Average Velocity   displacement divided by the time interval or slope of a line segment connecting two points on a position versus time graph.

Battery   electric device with two terminals where a potential difference (voltage difference) is maintained between the terminals. A battery therefore is also a source of electrical energy.

Celestial Realm   the heavens above the earth.

Centripetal Acceleration   acceleration of a particle undergoing uniform circular motion. It points toward the center of the circle.

Charge   one of the few fundamental properties of a particle. Particles are either positively or negatively charged. Others include mass.

Closed Circuit   a complete circuit such that current can be present.

Completely Inelastic Collision   a collision in which the momentum of the (isolated) system is conserved but not the kinetic energy and when the two bodies collide and subsequently stick together after the collision.

Conductor   a material that allows charges to move inside it.

Conversion Factor   an equality expressed in two different units, e.g. 1 ft = 12 in.

Cosmology study of the large scale structure of the universe.

Cross or Vector Product a way of multiplying vectors that yields another vector that has certain properties. The product vector has a direction given by the right-hand screw rule. The product magnitude is the product of the magnitude of the two original vectors times the sin of the angle between the original vectors.

Current the amount of charge that moves past a point in a conductor divided by the time interval for such movement.

Deductive Reasoning reasoning from general principles to specific cases.

Diffraction the fanning out of light that has passed through an opening.

Dipole two point charges (Positive and Negative) near each other or two magnetic poles (North and South) which are always near each other.

Direct Current a current composed of charges that move in only one direction around the circuit.

Dispersion occurs when the speed of a wave depends on its wavelength. For example, the index of refraction of a medium depends on wavelength if the medium is dispersive.

Displacement change in position or difference in two positions.

Displacement Current a quantity that has units of current that is related to the rate of change of electric flux or a time-varying electric field.

Dynamics the branch of mechanics that seeks to unravel the causes of acceleration, that is, force.

Elastic Collision a collision between two objects that form an isolated system and for which both the momentum and kinetic energy of the system are conserved (constant).

Electric Field electric force on a test charge divided by the charge of the test charge.

Electric Potential also called Voltage. This is loosely like pressure in that if the voltage is different between two points of space then a charge will experience work as it moves between these points. The Voltage difference is the work divided by the charge.

Electrostatics the field of electricity dealing with stationary charges.

Elysian Fields in Greek mythology, the place where exceptionally good humans spent eternity.

Energy the ability to do work. There many different kinds of energy.

Entropy in statistical physics entropy is a measure of the disorder of a system. In thermodynamics, entropy is found by measuring how much heat is reversibly added to a system and dividing that by the absolute temperature of the system.

Epistemology the subfield of philosophy concerned with the question, how do we know something is true.

Ether   the fifth element and which all celestial objects are made of.

Falsifiable   the notion that it must be possible, in principle, to prove a theory wrong for the theory to be scientific.

Fermi Problem   a problem solving method that only seeks an approximate solution and uses only common knowledge in its reasoning.

Force   a push or pull. Examples include gravitational, electrical and magnetic forces in addition to normal, tension, spring forces, and that old "devil," friction. Forces cause accelerations.

Frequency   the number of vibrations per second of a vibrating body or of a wave.

Fuse   a safety device placed in a circuit so that if the current becomes too large the device creates an open circuit, thereby making the current vanish.

Geocentric   model that places the Earth at the center of the universe.

Gravitational Field   gravitational force on a test mass divided by the mass of the test mass.

Hades   abode of the dead humans in Greek mythology.

Heat   the transfer of energy due solely to a temperature difference.

Heliocentric   places the Sun at the center of the universe.

Ideal Gas   a collection of particles that elastically collide with each other and the walls of the container.

Impulse   is the product of a force that acts over a time interval times the time interval. Impulses cause momentum changes.

Index of Refraction   a property of a medium that is the ratio of the speed of light in vacuum to the speed of light in the medium, and therefore is always greater (or equal to) one.

Induced Voltage   a voltage that arises around the perimeter of a surface when the magnetic flux passing through that surface depends on time (Faraday's Law).

Inductive Reasoning   reasoning from specific cases to the general case.

Initial Position   position when the time is zero.

Initial Velocity   velocity when the time is zero.

Insulator   a material in which charges do not move inside or on it.

Interference   the combining of two waves that arrive at the same point from different directions. The two wave functions add together and is called interference.

Internal Energy   the sum of the random kinetic energy of the atoms of a system and the internal potential energies between the atoms due to their interaction with each other.

Kinematics   the branch of mechanics that simply describes motion without trying to understand the causes.

Kinetic Energy   motion energy, that is product of 1/2 mass of a particle times the square of the particle's speed.

Law of Inertia   a particle moves with constant velocity unless a net force acts on it.

Law of Parsimony   the viewpoint that all things being equal, choose the simplest theory among competing theories.

Lines of Force   a graphical means of describing a region in which a field is present. The denser the lines the larger the field and the lines point in the direction of the field.

Magnetic Field   a magnetic field is an alteration of the space surrounding an electric current and is evident when another moving charge experiences a force when it is near the current. A compass needle also experiences a force when it is brought near the current.

Magnetic Flux   any field can penetrate through a surface and the flux of the field is the product of the surface area times the component of the field perpendicular to the surface. Therefore, the greater the number of lines of force of the field that pass through the surface the larger the flux.

Mass   a measure of the amount of material present in a system or the amount of inertia present.

Mechanics   the study of motion.

Microstates and Macrostates   concepts in statistical physics that denote the state of a system. A given macrostate generally has many associated microstates.

Moment of Inertia   a property of a body that rotates about an axis of rotation. The property depends on the axis, the mass and how the mass is distributed about the axis. This is also known as rotational mass.

Momentum   the product of the mass of a particle times the velocity of the particle. The more momentum a particle has, the harder it is to stop the particle.

Monopole   a single point charge (positive or negative) or a single magnetic pole (North or South).

Motional Emf   an induced voltage that arises when a closed circuit passes into a region where there exists a magnetic field.

Natural Motion   movement of an object toward its natural place.

Natural Place   the place an object seeks to return to based on the composition of the object.

Net Force   the sum of all the force vectors that are acting on a system.

Open Circuit   a break in a circuit such that current can no longer be present.

Operational Definition   a term made popular by the logical positivists school of philosophers of science. A physical quantity is only defined when detailed steps are given as to how to measure that quantity.

Parallel Circuit   a set of circuit elements are placed parallel to each other so that generally a different current passes through each element. Each element has the same voltage across them, though.

Period of Motion   time for a circling particle to complete one full circle or time for a vibrating object to complete one full vibration.

Polarization   if the electric field vectors in a light beam all lie in the same plane then we say the light is (plane) polarized.

Position   the distance from the origin to the location of a particle.

Potential Energy   energy of position, that is, the energy stored in a system due to a force doing work on the system without increasing the kinetic energy of the system. There are many kinds of potential energies, the most important for this book is gravitational and electrical potential energies.

Power   the amount of work done during a small time interval divided by the time interval.

Prime Mover   being outside the outer shell of stars who keeps the heavens rotating.

Real Image   an image that would appear on a screen or for which the rays are converging toward the image.

Recurrence paradox   the idea that since any classical physical system will eventually return to nearly any given initial state therefore, this seems to contradict the second law of thermodynamics.

Reflection   this occurs when a wave moving in one medium, encounters a second medium, and bounces back into the original medium.

Reversal Paradox   the idea that since the laws of physics operate equally well going forward or backward (i.e. they are reversible) therefore, the second law of thermodynamics seems to contradict the reversable laws of physics.

Scalar   a quantity that is described by giving only its magnitude, e.g. mass.

Scientific Notation   a short hand way of representing numbers by using powers of ten.

Scientism   the belief that the best route to truth is via the scientific method.

Series Circuit   a set of circuit elements are placed end to end so that generally a different voltage difference is across each element. The same current is in each element, though.

Shades   term used for dead humans in Greek mythology.

Specific Heat   one of the most fundamental thermal properties of a material which relates how much heat is required to raise the temperature of a certain mass of the material.

Speed   absolute value of velocity and therefore, always positive.

Standing Wave   a wave pattern on a string that does not move down the string but only up and down vertically.

Tarturus   in Greek mythology, the above of evil persons in the afterlife.

Temperature   in thermodynamics that property of a system that is measured by a thermometer. In statistical physics, temperature is proportional to the random kinetic energy of the atoms of a system.

Terminal Speed   the constant speed of fall present when an object's weight is balanced by air friction.

Terrestrial Realm   the part of the universe consisting of the earth and under the earth.

Tesla   the MKS unit for magnetic field.

Thermal Expansion   the expansion of most systems upon heating.

Thermodynamics   the theory of heat, work, internal energy and entropy of physical systems. This book covers the first and second law of thermodynamics.

Time   the reading on a stopwatch.

Time Interval   a change in time or the difference in two times.

Torque   the turning ability of a force. A torques cause angular accelerations.

Traveling Wave   a wave pulse that moves down a string.

Vector   a quantity that is described by giving both its magnitude and direction, e.g. velocity.

Velocity   displacement divided by a very small time interval or slope of tangent line to the position versus time graph.

Violent Motion   forced motion.

Virtual Image   an image that would not appear on a screen or one for which the rays appear to diverge from the image.

Voltmeter   a device used to measure the voltage between two points.

Wave Function   for a string wave, this function describes the displacement of the string from its equilibrium position.

Wave Speed   the speed that a wave pulse travels down a string.

Wavelength   the distance in space corresponding to one complete vibration of a wave.

Weight   the force on a mass due to the gravitational attraction of the earth.

Work   the work done by a constant force during a displacement is the displacement times the component of the force that is parallel to the displacement.

INDEX.

A

Acceleration, 41, 113
Adding and subtracting vectors, 61–65
Alternating current (AC), 237
Ammeters, 240
Angle of reflection, 180
Angle of refraction, 180
Angular acceleration, 113
Angular displacement, 113
Angular momentum, 114–15
Angular position, 113
Angular velocity, 113
Anti-nodes, 179
Aristotle's categories of motion, 27–30
Authority, 2
Average acceleration, 41
Average velocity, 39

B

Battery, 235, 240–41

C

Celestial realm, 25–26
Centripetal acceleration, 71
Charge, 204–20
Closed circuit, 236
Completely inelastic collision, 141–42
Conductors, 206
Conservation of energy, 148
Conservation of momentum, 140–43
Conversion factors, 8–9
Cosmology, 24
Coulomb's law, 207–208
Cross or vector product, 261
Current, 233–36

D

Deductive reasoning, 3–4
Diffraction, 184–85
Dipole, 258–59

Direct current (DC), 236–40
Dispersion, 185
Displacement, 38
Displacement current, 296
Dot product, 143–44

E

Elastic collision, 150
Electric field, 209–11
Electric flux, 294
Electric potential (voltage), 211–18
Electric potential energy, 211–18
Electromagnetic induction, 284–87
Electrostatics, 206
Elysian fields, 25
Energy, 143–51
Entropy, 327–30
Epistemology, 2
Ether, 26
External forces, 141

F

Falsifiable, 6
Faraday's law, 284–85
Fermi problem, 11
First law of thermodynamics, 324–25
Force, 84–89
Free fall, 45–47
Frequency, 174, 176
Friction, 88
Fuse, 237

G

Galileo, 34–36
Geocentric model, 25
Gravitational field, 110–12, 116–17
Gravitational potential energy, 147

H

Hades, 25
Harmonics, 179

Heat, 320
Heat conduction, 329–30
Heliocentric model, 25

I

Ideal gas, 320–22
Impulse, 137–40
Index of refraction, 182
Induced voltage, 284–87
Inductive reasoning, 3–4
Initial position, 38
Initial velocity, 39
Insulators, 204
Interference, 178, 184–85
Internal energy, 318
Irreversible process, 328

K

Kepler's laws of planetary motion, 115–16
Kinetic energy, 145–47

L

Law of inertia, 3–4
Law of parsimony, 4–5
Law of reflection, 180–81
Law of refraction, 181–84
Linear thermal expansion, 325
Lines of force, 209–10

M

Magnetic field, 258–60
Magnetic flux, 281–84, 295
Magnetic force law, 262
Mass, 85
Maxwell's equations, 293–97
Moment of inertia, 113–14
Momentum, 137–42
Monopole, 258
Motional emf, 286–87

N

Natural motion, 28
Natural place, 28
Net force, 62
Newton's three laws of motion, 84–87

Nodes, 179
Normal force, 88–89

O

Oersted's law, 258
Ohm's law, 240–43
Open circuit, 236
Operational definition, 318

P

Parallel circuit, 237–40
Period of motion, 71, 116, 174
Period of the wave, 176–77
Period of vibration, 174
Polarization, 185
Position, 37
Potential energy, 211–18
Power, 151
Prime mover, 26
Principle of superposition, 208

R

Real image, 181
Recurrence paradox, 333–34
Reductionism, 3
Reflection, 180–81
Refraction, 181–84
Reversal paradox, 333
Reversible process, 327–28
Right-handed screw rule #1, 259–62
Right-handed screw rule #2, 262

S

Scalar, 61
Scalar product, 143–44
Scientific notation, 8
Scientism, 3
Second law of thermodynamics, 330–32
Series circuit, 237–40
Shades, 25
Short circuit, 236–37
Significant figures, 9
Specific heat, 325

Speed, 39
Standing wave, 179–80
Superconductor, 319–20
Superposition principle, 177–79

T

Tartarus, 25
Temperature, 318
Temperature scales, 318–19
Tension, 88
Terrestrial realm, 25
Tesla, 262
Test charge, 209
Thermal expansion, 325
Thermodynamics, 319, 324–25, 330–32
Time, 37
Time interval, 37–38
Torque, 112–16, 267
Traveling wave, 176–78

U

Unit conversions, 8–9

V

Vector, 61–65, 261
Velocity, 39
Violent motion, 28
Virtual image, 181
Voltmeters, 240

W

Wave function, 176–77
Wavelength, 176–79
Wave speed, 177
Weight, 88
Work, 143